D0914783

DICKENS AND THACKERAY STUDIED IN THREE NOVELS

DICKENS & THACKERAY
STUDIED IN
THREE NOVELS

BY THE

HON. ALBERT S. G. CANNING

Author of

"HISTORY IN SCOTT'S NOVELS," "SHAKESPEARE STUDIED IN EIGHT PLAYS," "BRITISH WRITERS ON CLASSIC LANDS," "SCOTT STUDIED IN EIGHT NOVELS," ETC., ETC.

KENNIKAT PRESS, INC./PORT WASHINGTON, N. Y.

Originally published in 1911
Reissued in 1967 by Kenniat Press

Library of Congress Catalog Card No: 67-27583

Manufactured in the United States of America

"The proper study of mankind is man
Created half to rise and half to fall,
Great lord of all things, yet a prey to all,
Sole judge of truth in endless error hurled,
The glory, jest, and riddle of the world."

POPE'S *Essay on Man.*

"Whoever thinks a faultless piece to see,
Thinks what ne'er was, nor is, nor e'er shall be,
In every work regard the writer's end
Since none can compass more than they intend,
And if the means be just, the conduct true,
Applause in spite of trivial faults is due."

POPE'S *Essay on Criticism.*

Contents

PART I

DICKENS

PART II

THACKERAY'S "VANITY FAIR"

Prefatory Note

THE studies on "Pickwick" and "Nicholas Nickleby" are here republished, revised and enlarged. The one on "Vanity Fair" is entirely new. This work is not intended so much for those well acquainted with Dickens and Thackeray, as for general readers, to whom I hope it may be useful.

A. S. G. CANNING.

PART I

DICKENS

DICKENS & THACKERAY STUDIED IN THREE NOVELS

DICKENS

INTRODUCTION

DURING the life of Sir Walter Scott no writer of fiction equalled him in popular favour throughout Great Britain, nor were the works of any other novelist so extensively read. The able and instructive works of his great literary predecessors, Addison, Fielding, Richardson, and Dr. Johnson, were known to comparatively few.

The number of Englishmen who were in the habit of reading was probably not a sixth part of what it now is. A shopkeeper or a farmer who found any pleasure in literature was a rarity. In these circumstances the sale of the *Spectator* must be considered as indicating a popularity quite as great as that of the most successful works of Sir Walter Scott and Mr. Dickens in our own time.[1]

Macaulay's admiration for Addison, however, seems rather excessive in the following passage in the same essay :

If we wish to find anything more vivid than Addison's best portraits, we must go either to Shakespeare or Cervantes.

---

[1] Lord Macaulay's "Essay on Addison."

Yet an educated, enlightened posterity, both in England and abroad, will probably consider the characters drawn by Scott and Dickens as fully equal in truth to nature to those of Shakespeare, and superior to any that either Addison or Cervantes attempted. For surely their two chief characters, Don Quixote and Sir Roger de Coverley—the first an evident caricature, though both so admirable in their way—can neither of them be considered as natural or as interesting as many characters described by Scott and Dickens. Yet all these illustrious writers had contributed in their different ways to elevate and improve the literary taste of England, and, of course, render it more fastidious. Scott's works, however, attracted the public mind to very different subjects from those treated of by former writers. The "Historical Novel," if not actually invented by him, he yet accomplished with a success and popularity before unknown. The characters, events, manners, and customs of former ages he described with a truth and power which made his works almost equally interesting and instructive to all intelligent minds, even among the comparatively uneducated. After his death, though he had many imitators, none approached, far less equalled, him in genius or popularity. Yet his great mind owed little to any literary predecessors, nor did his grand example inspire any literary successors He appeared and disappeared, at first perhaps even more wondered at than admired, and was somewhat slowly, though steadily, appreciated by the educated world.

A few years after Scott's death, while his numerous imitators all comparatively failed to attract public attention, a young London writer appeared, who, though unlike Scott in many respects, became his virtual successor in influencing the literary taste of England in fiction. This was Mr. Charles Dickens, justly described by his biographer as the most popular novelist England ever produced.[1] If Walter Scott owed little or nothing to preceding writers, the same may surely be said of Dickens. He from the first struck out an entirely new line for himself, and, owing to his original genius, might, from his style of writing, have never consulted another man's book. Neither the records of historians, the inventions of novelists, nor the ideas of poets, apparently furnished him with any assistance. Dryden's opinion of Shakespeare in this respect well describes the perfect originality of Mr. Dickens :

> When he describes anything, you more than see it, you feel it too. Those who accuse him to have wanted learning give him the greater commendation ; he was naturally learned ; he needed not the spectacles of books to read Nature ; he looked inwards and found her there.

Thus, at a time of English history when education was more general and esteemed than ever before, Charles Dickens, of undistinguished origin, was imperfectly educated, even by his own admission. In Forster's "Life of Dickens," vol. i., alluding to his neglected youth, Dickens expressly calls himself

> a not-over-particularly-cared-for boy ;

yet without influential friends, fortune, or external aid of any kind, he raised his name and reputation among

[1] Forster's "Life of Dickens."

the richest, wisest, and most learned of his countrymen, and rapidly forced them to acknowledge him as the greatest living writer of fiction in England. In this respect the friendless and triumphant young writer deserves the praise Shakespeare bestows on Cardinal Wolsey :

> For being not propped by ancestry, neither allied
> To eminent assistants; but spider-like
> Out of his self-drawing web—
> The force of his own merit makes his way.
> A gift that Heaven gives.—*Henry VIII.*

Instead of describing, like Addison, Fielding, and Richardson, country gentry or London men of fashion, or attempting to write the historical romances and legends of Sir Walter Scott, without alluding to the classic writers of antiquity, with which Dr. Johnson's learned pages abound—without, indeed, saying much about either famous men or famous incidents of his own or of any other age—Dickens chiefly tried to attract the interest by describing the characters, habits, and language of the middle and lower, often the very lowest, classes in modern London. Out of such apparently unpromising materials, unaided and unfriended, the amazing genius of Dickens constructed a long succession of sketches, tales, and novels which finally attracted more attention and obtained more readers than any works of fiction had ever done before in England. The historian Alison says[1] that during the first half of this century romances and novels chiefly described high life, but that this tendency changed, and new writers appeared, who

[1] "History of Europe from Fall of Napoleon," vol. i.

discarded all attempts at patrician-painting, and confined themselves to describing the manners, ideas, habits, &c., of middle and low life in England. Among these Dickens certainly occupied the first place, and, indeed, no other writer has approached nor even much resembled him. His descriptions of character are generally English throughout; he never attempted describing either Scottish or Irish people, which had caused some persons to rather hastily declare that he could not have done so. But this can never be known, for where there has been no attempt, it is both absurd and unfair to assume failure.

In his first work, "Sketches by Boz," Dickens confines himself chiefly to London and its suburbs, with which he was thoroughly acquainted. In these original and most amusing papers, he never introduces any aristocratic families, nor does he mention farmers or labourers. He describes chiefly lodging-house keepers, shopkeepers, petty tradesmen, &c., whose social peculiarities, vanity, and paltry ambition he ridicules freely, though without the least bitterness; so that these sketches were as much liked among the class they describe as by any other, owing to their mingled truth, wit, and thorough good-nature. Yet amid even these most amusing and comic descriptions, there occur some melancholy thoughts which were evidently the dawn of those

remarkable powers for the pathetic [1]

which his later works developed in all their wonderful intensity. Amid all the merriment roused by the

[1] Alison.

"Tuggses at Ramsgate," "Horatio Sparkins," &c., his "Thoughts about People" showed that Dickens, even when young, with all his keen sense and enjoyment of the ludicrous, possessed a serious mind and a most sympathetic spirit. Yet in this, his first publication, he dwells little on grave subjects, but chiefly tries to amuse and cheer, and probably few, if any, books in the English language ever caused so much laughter before.

His descriptions of London on a winter's night and summer's morning are the first proofs of the intense interest he took in its description. "The streets of London, to be beheld in the very height of their glory, should be seen on a dark, dull, murky winter's night, when there is just enough damp gently stealing down to make the pavement greasy, without cleansing it of any of its impurities, and when the heavy, long mist which hangs over every object makes the gas lamps look brighter, and the brilliantly lighted shops more splendid, from the contrast they present to the darkness around." In all his works he may be said never to keep long out of London. His thoughts always return to it; he seems always to have something new to say about it, and certainly no other novelist, before or since his time, has shown the same knowledge of it. Walter Scott lays only two of his admirable novels in London,[1] in which he introduces his readers to the Courts of James I. and Charles II. Both these kings he describes, with their courtiers and ministers, together with some desperate robbers, bravos, and reckless adherents of a frivolous and voluptuous

[1] "Nigel" and "Peveril of the Peak."

Court; while the heroes and heroines are amiable and accomplished young people, either belonging to the aristocracy or aspiring to become so. But in Dickens's first London sketches the sayings and doings of the London middle classes are alone described, and chiefly in a comic manner, while a few remarks on the pawnshops, drinking-houses, and jails of the metropolis are occasionally introduced with singular effect, rendering the light and gay chapters around them all the brighter and themselves more effective and striking from the force of the contrast. Thus both these great novelists have, in turn, written the truth about the state of London, past and present.

During the lapse of centuries, the changes in its social and political condition had been great indeed. In the times which Scott describes, London was comparatively small and poor, agitated and endangered by political and religious dissensions of extraordinary violence. The conduct and example of the Court then exercised vast influence over the nation at large. The Sovereign, nobility, landed gentry, and clergy shared the government of the country among them, and chiefly guided public opinion, while the middle and lower classes were comparatively uneducated and powerless. In the times which Dickens describes, England was enjoying a long domestic peace; while the middle and lower classes were far more numerous, far better educated, and far more influential. No political or religious dissensions of much consequence threatened the public peace. The Sovereign's power was more limited than ever before by parliamentary restraint, and, though generally approved and respected, no longer tyrannised or had the power to tyrannise over, or even to direct the views and opinions of, the nation. Life and property were also comparatively secure; both Jews and Christians of all denominations, relieved from persecution and penalties, mingled together, especially in London, on terms of friendship, and showed a common respect for the established laws.

The Jews are not now excluded from political power. They possess it, and as long as they are allowed to accumulate large fortunes they must possess it.[1]

Yet, notwithstanding these vast improvements in the social state of London, an immense amount of suffering still existed among its poorer inhabitants. The treatment of prisoners in jails, especially in debtors' prisons; the neglect and cruelty endured by pauper children in London workhouses, and the terrible temptations to robbery which so rich a city offered to its poorer inhabitants—these were now the chief curses of London's teeming population, and apparently replaced the religious and political persecutions of former times in causing crime and misery in the capital of a Christian and civilised land. To draw attention to these evils, to mitigate and if possible remove them, were the first objects to which young Mr. Dickens devoted his talents, amid the comic descriptions suggested by his lively fancy and brilliant wit. Perhaps no one has succeeded better, or discovered a more effectual plan of drawing popular attention to public abuses, evils, and wrongs, than Dickens has done by mingling terrible descriptions

[1] Macaulay's Essay on the "Civil Disabilities of the Jews."

of London misery and crime with the most amusing sketches of London life.

Many people who would have avoided a grave, solemn treatise on this subject, studied it attentively in pages where such painful instruction was blended with so much exquisite wit and amusement. The result was that the more educated and wealthier classes throughout England acquired a knowledge of their poorer neighbours—their wants and actual conditions—of which many were previously almost as ignorant as foreigners. While describing and keenly sympathising with the sufferings of the poor and unfortunate, he never causes among them the least ill-feeling against the wealthy and prosperous, which a man of his talent might certainly have done, if he had wished, with dangerous effect. But he knew the real interest, as well as the peculiarities of his countrymen, with almost equal correctness. He firmly and steadily appealed to the good feelings and common sense of *all* classes, and thus elicited a general sympathy for and interest in the unfortunate, without either arousing the fears or endangering the safety of the prosperous and wealthy. He knew the calm justice of the English character sufficiently to be convinced that the public mind of the country only required enlightenment about the wants and sufferings of its poorest inhabitants to grant the requisite attention and consequent relief. His object was evidently never to induce the most wronged and suffering to desire revolution or even encourage discontent, but to induce the common intelligence of the country, in all its different classes alike, to redress real grievances and alleviate undeniable sufferings.

For these purposes he employs the most eloquent language and accomplishes the most graphic and powerful descriptions of life and character ever attempted by any novelist. Accordingly his works, from their very first appearance, were sought for, read, and mentally devoured by the British public, with an eager delight never surpassed, if equalled, in the history of fictitious literature. It is probable that the times when Dickens wrote were highly favourable for inquiry into every sort of social abuse, suffering, or mismanagement. The spread of general education throughout England, the perfect freedom of the Press, the increase of newspapers, the thoughtful calm of domestic peace, and the comparative absence of religious and political animosities—all these national advantages favoured the efforts of the energetic young author by securing both an impartial and a general attention to the views expressed in his writings.[1]

Dickens, without exciting or even mentioning

[1] As the first Lord Lytton, the eminent contemporary and personal friend of Dickens, thoughtfully observed: "What I see in England, comparing this century with the last, is the advancement of numbers, the more general culture of intellect, the milder constructions of Law, the greater tenderness to suffering and erring humanity, the more decent respect to domestic sanctities, the more intellectual not unreasoning acquiescence in religious truths" (*Caxtoniana*). It is a gratifying fact that these two great English novelists of the nineteenth century, both men of such keen insight into human character, agree as to the moral and intellectual improvement of the age; for Dickens, at the close of his "Pictures from Italy," expresses the same opinion as Lord Lytton: "That the Wheel of Time is rolling for an end, and the world is in all great essentials better, gentler, more forbearing, and more hopeful as it rolls."

religious or political animosities, without arousing the suspicions of the loyal or the hopes of the disaffected among the British people, yet earnestly and enthusiastically drew universal attention to scenes of social suffering and injustice which, though existing all around his readers, and especially in London, struck many of them with actual astonishment.

Doubtless many lectures, sermons, speeches and treatises had previously described the state of London and the many miseries of its poorer inhabitants, but probably the repulsive nature of the subject had discouraged many in its proper study and examination. Some worthy but misjudging people would have indignantly censured the public apathy or indifference, encouraged revolutionary ideas, and irritated the ignorant multitude by furious denunciations of the heartlessness of the wealthier classes towards them.

Dickens from the first took another and a surer way to effect his purpose, and thus showed a knowledge of English character which seems to have been born with him—to have come from intuition ; for he had no personal experience of the public to rely on, no literary friends to advise him how to lay hold of it, influence it, or attract it. To do this has always been, indeed, the grand and worthy ambition of able statesmen and intelligent practical divines ; but many of the most gifted and excellent men, with every worldly advantage of wealth, rank, and education, have signally failed not only to influence, but even to attract, public attention. Yet this unknown young author, from the very beginning of his literary labours, succeeded first in attracting public notice, and afterwards general assent and admiration. He carefully blends the comic and sad sketches together with that remarkable skill in gratifying the general taste which always distinguished him. When his readers are sated with laughter at his wit, he introduces pages of suffering and sorrow which, described with all the vividness of truth, interest even the most obdurate or unimaginative, while they fairly melt the hearts of the sympathetic. Like Shakespeare and Scott, Dickens wrote for all denominations of educated men, neither offending nor gratifying religious prejudices. He first charms readers by his wit, fun, and humour, giving them real pleasure of the most wholesome kind, and then, before the most captious critic can call him frivolous, he describes scenes of woe and melancholy which, founded on truth, enhanced, not exaggerated, by the force of his genius, impress all thoughtful minds with irresistible power.

How Dickens, when so young at the outset of his career, knew the English public taste so accurately is the more surprising, as he certainly owed nothing to the advice or assistance of any one. He, as it were, attracted and charmed the public at once, took their attention by storm, and, by the practical magic of his pen, set thousands of people thinking, many for the first time, upon subjects about which clergymen had preached, speakers had declaimed, and statesmen had legislated, amid comparative indifference on the part of the public. In the first Sketches, which so well reveal the dawn of his genius, Dickens describes neither beauty, bravery, love, war, nor wisdom. There is nothing romantic in them; no sentimental scenes to interest novel-readers; no exposure of religious error to interest controversialists; and no political allusions to attract, rouse, or gratify party feelings. All such matters, usually the chief subjects of fictitious literature, are utterly, perhaps purposely, omitted. It is the streets of London as they are that he describes, with the real condition of their inhabitants, enlivened constantly by the wittiest sketches of amusing characters placed in ridiculous situations—all possible and many probable.

It might be hard to say among what class of readers Dickens's works were most popular, as from their first appearance they were universally read, enjoyed, and approved. They offended no one, while their extraordinary interest and peculiar style atoned for their occasionally painful and commonplace subjects, even in the minds of most fastidious or sentimental readers. While the gay and lively were moved to constant laughter by their wit and merriment, the most grave and thoughtful found in them ample subjects for deep and serious reflection. Thus the general public were effectually captivated, not by the brief power of sensational attraction, but by the combined sense and brilliancy of a young author able to amuse and enlighten at the same time, and whose success in doing both was unprecedented in English literature, even in his first sketches of London life and character. They came, indeed, upon the public quite by surprise, being utterly unlike any previous publication. Scott's admirable novels chiefly described Scotland, or former periods of English history; he never describes, and seldom mentions, modern London. Fielding's works chiefly described the country, its squires, clergymen, and farmers. Dr. Johnson wrote exclusively for the educated classes; and though well acquainted with London life, and a most observant, humane man, he seldom, even in his recorded conversations, mentions the lowest classes of the London population.

The popular novelists before Dickens usually preferred inventing and describing people of rank, beauty, or talent, often more to please the fancy than improve the reason, or increase the knowledge of their readers. The sermons, lectures, and writings of benevolent clergymen often doubtless implored relief for the poor and unfortunate in the true spirit of charity; but to make them subjects of *interest* as well as attention to the thoughtless, frivolous, and worldly was indeed to place the poor in a position before the public seldom before effected, or perhaps attempted, by either the most charitable or democratic. Yet this result even the first works of Dickens achieved to a most surprising extent. Throughout England, and in London especially, readers of all classes began, many for the first time, to take real and lively interest in the sayings and doings of the poorest of the London population. The frivolous and sensation-loving reader, as well as the thoughtful and compassionate, were alike attracted to a subject hitherto thought either painful or repulsive, by the singular charm and interest of Dickens's writings.

Few people, if any, would have believed it possible that descriptive pictures of low life among coarse, ridiculous, vulgar, or miserable people could actually be made most interesting to the fastidious, frivolous, and romantic, as well as to the charitable or reflecting.

Yet Dickens's original genius enlisted them all alike in his vast array of admiring readers, and a greater literary triumph in a philosophical sense has, perhaps, never been achieved. Thus sentimental novels, describing fashionable life, rank, wealth, and beauty, comparatively yielded in attraction and demand, even among fashionable people, to Dickens's intensely interesting sketches of the lowest among the London population, and to such an extent, indeed, that even their peculiar expressions, slang talk, and vulgarity lost much of their repulsiveness in public estimation. Perhaps in this respect the change in public opinion was, for a time at least, carried rather too far. Instead of the former exaggerated and fastidious aversion to vulgar language and slang expressions on the part of the better educated, they now were thought rather witty and amusing by many people—more indeed from Dickens's exquisite judgment and skill in their use and adaptation, than from much real wit or humour in the strange jargon itself.

The literary success of the "Sketches by Boz" was, perhaps, as complete and satisfactory as the author could have wished, and far more so than either he or his most sanguine friends could have anticipated. Dickens's literary triumph in this first work was a decisive proof of the healthy English taste for a work of real merit, in which amusement and information were so skilfully blended that few indeed could finish its perusal without mingled feelings of sincere admiration for its author, both as a writer and as a philanthropist. This extraordinary young man, without influential friends or connections, carelessly or imperfectly educated, and possessing no social advantage, by the unaided power of his brilliant genius and keen judgment won general esteem by his first book in the critical world of English literary society. Few books in the English language were ever so laughed over before, while his more pathetic works were to follow. This first proof of Dickens's genius was published while he was still very young, with the world of reality opening around him, and before he could have personally experienced many of its sorrows and trials which so surely accompany the advance of life.

Accordingly, his two first books—the "Sketches" and "Pickwick Papers"—are both the earliest and most comic of all his works. Chapter after chapter in each abounds in varied fun and wit, while only a few in either reveal his great powers for pathetic description. His very name became almost synonymous with fun, wit, and merriment, while his future works were destined to be chequered and varied by very different emotions. His first appearance in the literary world was that of comic brilliancy itself, diffusing laughter and enjoyment everywhere, and of a kind equally original, wholesome, and permanent. He wrote the "Sketches" under the assumed name of "Boz," which roused public curiosity greatly to discover who the unknown yet popular author could be whose book was so eagerly sought for, and as much admired as it was read. No distinguished name, family influence, school fame, or college reputation for rising talent introduced the young author to the British public, or in any way bespoke its favourable expectation. The singular *alias* of Boz concealed for some time a name hitherto unknown, yet destined to attain deserved celebrity, till it was finally abandoned and public curiosity gratified, when some witty, expressive lines appeared :—

> Who the dickens Boz could be
> Puzzled many a learned elf,
> Till Time unveiled the mystery,
> And Boz appeared as Dickens' self.

THE "PICKWICK PAPERS"

CHAPTER I

THE "PICKWICK PAPERS"

SOON after the "Sketches" were published the "Pickwick Papers" appeared in monthly numbers. The immense success of this work not only maintained, but largely increased, the literary fame Dickens had already acquired. This work became a universal favourite, and was certainly a most original one. Mr. Pickwick, a worthy, rather elderly, single gentleman, lives among a circle of intimate friends, all of them either in London or its neighbourhood. He is himself an agreeable, and probably a rare instance of courage, benevolence, and almost childish simplicity combined. Such a character was likely indeed in London to be imposed on, cheated, and victimised by designing people of all sorts; but nothing of his early history is told. He is introduced when rather past the prime of life, having a large fortune, and apparently in no particular profession. He constantly utters and performs the most benevolent sentiments and duties, being a real philanthropist, without either plausible cant or a sanctimonious bearing. His faithful, shrewd, witty servant, Samuel Weller, is perhaps the most amusing and original character in the whole book. His quaint sayings and shrewd remarks, though mostly in slang phrases, were read with general delight, and probably the slang language of the London streets was never so much known and studied before by readers of education till this book appeared.

Throughout the whole story Mr. Pickwick and Sam are strongly attached, and eminently suited to each other. They are alike upright and kind-hearted, but the confiding and generous simplicity of the master is admirably appreciated and rewarded by the shrewd, invincible fidelity of the servant. Mr. Pickwick's friends, Messrs. Winkle, Tupman, and Snodgrass, are three sentimental, rather silly, yet very amusing Londoners. Old Mr. Wardle is, perhaps, rather a feeble picture of a small country squire. He seems rather more like a retired Londoner living in the country than a country gentleman; while his mother, sister, and daughters all slightly resemble certain characters in the "Sketches," for they are more like London people or suburbans than country gentry. Mr. Jingle, the fashionable swindler, and his servant, Job Trotter, faithful to him, but roguish towards everybody else, are drawn with remarkable skill, force, and consistency, the mingled craft, wit, and trickery in the former, and of fidelity and cunning in the latter, are described as if from Dickens's personal knowledge, but no hint is given of their being drawn from life. Jingle, despite his cunning, falsehood, and impudence, is not without some better feelings, and the same may be said of Job Trotter, his servant, always faithful to him, so that readers are more amused than angry with them both, even during their brief success in knavery. The swindler, Mr. Jingle, succeeds in setting poor old Miss Rachael against her true lover, Tupman, and elopes with her himself. The runaways are hotly pursued, and at length found by her brother, old Wardle, indignant at her folly, and by the manly, almost kind Mr. Pickwick, accompanied by his practical and sensible lawyer, little Mr. Perker. He detects Jingle's real character immediately and makes the following treaty with him:

"Now, sir," said the little man as he carefully closed the door, "we are both men of the world, and *we* know well enough that our friends here are not—eh?"

Mr. Jingle's face gradually relaxed, and something distantly resembling a wink quivered for an instant in his left eye.

Perker vainly offers first fifty, then seventy and eighty pounds if Jingle gives up Miss Rachael, and at last asks him:

"Well, my dear sir, well, just tell me what will do?"

"Expensive affair," said Mr. Jingle, "money out of pocket—posting nine pounds, licence three—that's twelve—compensation a hundred—a hundred and twelve—breach of honour and loss of the lady——"

"Yes, my dear sir, yes," said the little man with a knowing look, "never mind the last two items."

Jingle's elopement with Miss Rachael Wardle, having supplanted the sentimental Tupman in her favour, and his mercenary surrender of her for a small sum of money, is such a thoroughly amusing transaction, that readers cannot dislike the swindler as much as he deserves, owing to the amusement derived from his unceasing fun and raillery. The previous interchange of ill-natured remarks, though certainly unkind, between Miss Rachael Wardle and her two nieces is extremely amusing, and as naturally related as if the author had actually himself heard it. Miss Rachael is evidently afraid lest the soft-hearted and soft-headed Mr. Tupman may marry one of them instead of herself, though there is no sign of either of these lively young ladies caring the least for this elderly, sentimental gentleman. Accordingly she tries to point out all the defects which she either knows or invents to Mr. Tupman :

"Do you think my dear nieces pretty?" whispered their affectionate aunt.

"I should if their aunt wasn't here." . . .

"Oh, you naughty man! But if their complexions were a *little* better, don't you think they would be nice-looking girls—at least by candle-light?"

"Yes, I think they would," said Mr. Tupman, with an air of indifference.

But not yet sure of this indifference, the aunt persists in her searching examination :

"Oh, you quiz!—I know what you were going to say."

"What?" inquired Mr. Tupman, who had not precisely made up his mind to say anything at all.

Miss Rachael proceeds to attribute ideas and opinions to him :

"You were going to say that Isabella stoops—I know you were—you men are such observers. Well, so she does . . . and certainly if there is one thing more than another that makes a girl look ugly it is stooping. I often tell her that when she get a little older, she'll be quite frightful. Well, you *are* a quiz!"

Mr. Tupman had no objection to earning the reputation at so cheap a rate, so he looked very knowing and smiled mysteriously.

"What a sarcastic smile," said the admiring Rachael; "I declare I'm quite afraid of you."

"Afraid of me!"

"Oh, you can't disguise anything from me—I know what that smile means very well."

"What?" said Mr. Tupman, who had not the slightest notion himself.

"You mean," said the amiable aunt, sinking her voice still lower—"You mean that you don't think Isabella's stooping is as bad as Emily's boldness. Well, she *is* bold. You cannot think how wretched it makes me sometimes—I'm sure I cry about it for hours together. . I wish I could think it was only manner. I hope it may be.". . .

"I'm sure aunt's talking about us," whispered Miss Emily Wardle to her sister, "I'm quite certain of it—she looks so malicious."

"Is she?" replied Isabella. "Hem! aunt, dear!"

"Yes, my dear love!"

"I'm so afraid you'll catch cold, aunt. I have a silk handkerchief to tie round your dear old head—you really should take care of yourself—consider your age!" [1]

The first chapters of "Pickwick" are all droll and lively; wit, fun, and merriment in every page till the chapter describing the clown's death. This vivid description confirms the previous impression, derived from the "Sketches," of Dickens's great powers for pathetic delineation, his object in this sad chapter being to draw attention to the real state, hardships, and sufferings of those unfortunate people whose lives are devoted to amusing the public, and who literally live upon the applause which their efforts arouse, yet whose real condition is so secluded from public sight that they are too often little benefited by public charity. The readers of "Pickwick," in the midst of laughter, pause at such a sad chapter as this, which makes all the more impression by appearing so suddenly and unexpectedly amid so much merriment, wit, and cheerfulness. It was, doubtless, all the

[1] Chap. iv.

more effective on this account, the author's object being to draw general attention to the state of poor actors and artists, who are often so strangely admired and despised, alternately, by thoughtless people, but who have latterly been much more the subjects of awakened and benevolent attention. Yet Dickens does not dwell longer than he thinks necessary for his excellent purpose on this sad subject, but again diverts his readers through many chapters with a succession of humorous scenes.

The account of the contested election, though most amusing and laughable, may be thought rather exaggerated; but the party at Mrs. Leo Hunter's, a lady who collects all the clever, or rather, pretentious, people she can about her, is described with great care and an evident purpose. Young as Dickens was when he wrote this description, he had probably seen enough of the world to know how often affected, vain, and silly people get the reputation of being clever themselves, and of patronising talent in others. Mrs. Leo, though perhaps a good-natured, well-meaning person, is also a compound of vanity and pretension. She has herself written a ridiculous little poem, called the "Expiring Frog," and she delights to assemble people round her who possess little more talent than herself, and to hear and exchange flattery with her guests. The whole scene at her house is an admirable caricature of folly, vanity, and affectation, all three weaknesses being keenly exposed, though with perfect good-nature. To most intellectual people, in London especially, there can hardly be a greater pleasure, or more useful one, than to visit the houses of persons who introduce people capable of mutually appreciating worth and talent. At such places Dickens was probably often a guest; but Mrs. Leo Hunter's entertainment is the degrading caricature of this sort of hospitality, where a set of conceited fops and impostors are invited to flatter each other and their hostess, and be flattered by her in a competition of general conceit and vanity. Mr. Pickwick, a modest, upright man, is quite out of place at such a party; but his constant courtesy and good-nature make him a favourite everywhere, and often a victim to the caprices and cunning of others.

As the story proceeds, Dickens resolves to entangle his worthy hero with London lawyers of the most roguish kind, from whose cunning and trickery so many have suffered. To expose such people, Dickens, instead of making long denunciations of legal craft or mismanagement, which, however true, would have attracted comparatively slight notice, rouses public attention at once by involving his poor hero in an absurd trial for breach of promise of marriage with his passionate, vulgar landlady, Mrs. Bardell, a widow. Worthy Mr. Pickwick when engaging Sam Weller explains to Mrs. Bardell, when her little son is away, that he has engaged a new inmate for her house—in his own kind, easy way of talking. Mrs. B. mistakes his meaning altogether, thinking and hoping that Pickwick is making love to her, of which he has not the least idea. He asks his landlady:

"Do you think it's a much greater expense to keep two people than to keep one?"

"La, Mr. Pickwick," said Mrs. Bardell, colouring up to the very border of her cap, as she fancied she observed a species of matrimonial twinkle in the eyes of her lodger; "La, Mr. Pickwick, what a question!"

. . . "Well," said Mr. Pickwick, "what do you think?"

"Oh, Mr. Pickwick," said Mrs. Bardell, trembling with agitation, "you're very kind, sir."

"It'll save you a good deal of trouble, won't it?" said Mr. Pickwick.

"Oh, I never thought anything of the trouble, sir," replied Mrs. Bardell, "and of course I should take more trouble to please you then, than ever; but it is so kind of you, Mr. Pickwick, to have so much consideration for my loneliness."

"Ah, to be sure," said Mr. Pickwick; "I never thought of that. . . ."

"I'm sure I ought to be a very happy woman," said Mrs. Bardell.

"And your little boy," said Mr. Pickwick.

"Bless his heart," interposed Mrs. Bardell with a maternal sob.

"He too will have a companion," resumed Mr. Pickwick—"a lively one who'll teach him, I'll be bound, more tricks in a week than he would ever learn in a year." And Mr. Pickwick smiled placidly.

"Oh, you dear——" said Mrs. Bardell. Mr. Pickwick started.

"Oh, you kind, good, playful dear," said Mrs. Bardell; and without more ado, she rose from her chair, and flung her arms round Mr. Pickwick's neck, with a mixture of tears and a chorus of sobs.

"Bless my soul!" cried the astonished Mr. Pickwick. "Mrs. Bardell, my good woman—dear me, what a situation—pray consider—Mrs. Bardell, don't—if anybody should come——"

"Oh, let them come," exclaimed Mrs. Bardell frantically; "I'll never leave you—dear, kind, good soul," and with these words Mrs. Bardell clung the tighter.

At this embarrassing moment Mr. Pickwick's three bachelor friends, Messrs. Tupman, Snodgrass, and Winkle, all enter the room, and all are inclined to believe that their old friend, despite of his denials, has been making love to his landlady. All Mrs. Bardell's friends take her side also, and this ridiculous, yet unfortunate, scene for Mr. Pickwick greatly aids in causing an action for breach of promise against him.

While readers are thoroughly amused with this trial, Dickens contrives to deal the most effective and damaging blows at legal artifice and rascality embodied in Mrs. Bardell's lawyers, Messrs Dodson and Fogg, whose names are ever since associated with legal knavery wherever the English language is spoken. These men take up Mrs. Bardell's ridiculous case apparently on speculation that Mr. Pickwick should certainly pay their costs, and they secure themselves from loss by inducing their duped and ignorant client to sign a document making herself liable for their expenses if Mr. Pickwick should either win the case or prefer imprisonment to paying money. A more rascally transaction was seldom undertaken by any rogues, either within or outside the legal profession; but the whole affair is described with such wit, spirit, and fun that readers are forced to laugh heartily before studying the matter seriously.

In real life, sincere pity for Mr. Pickwick and indignation against his persecutors would have been generally aroused; but in the hands of such a writer as Dickens the whole trial, with all its attendant proceedings, becomes a first-rate comedy, amusing and delighting every one from beginning to end. Yet even during the course of this trial there are allusions to, and anecdotes of, the business doings of Messrs. Dodson and Fogg, among which the disgraceful case of Ramsay (chap. xx.) is the most striking, which, if fully detailed and dwelt upon, would indeed have checked all mirth in the readers of "Pickwick," and excited the profoundest disgust and indignation. But by such means the attention of only a few reflecting persons would have been aroused; the reading public, especially in fiction, require amusement and laughter as well as deep interest. Dickens evidently knew this well from the first, and, by constantly making his readers laugh by dwelling on the comic side of the disgraceful Pickwick trial, he manages to expose and condemn Messrs. Dodson and Fogg more effectively than either he or any one else could have done by the most solemn or vehement censure and denunciation. Thus by mixing fun, wit, and cutting sarcasm together, he literally obtained universal attention. It was the public *generally* to whom he appealed, not to the compassionate or philosophic alone; and he succeeded almost beyond belief, for probably no fictitious work in English ever found so many readers, while the famous trial for breach of promise was thought a comic masterpiece, even in a long work of such continued and varied wit and fun. Yet, with all his merriment, Dickens occasionally in this book reveals those great powers of describing the tragic and terrible, the first dawn of which appeared in the "Sketches."

In "Pickwick" the most striking proof of his pathetic power is, perhaps, shown in the "Madman's MSS." This chapter occurs, as it were, by accident, having no connection with the story whatever. It is introduced like a dark shadow, to exhibit in all the brighter colouring the general brilliancy, wit, and sparkle around it. As far as it goes, though it is very short, a finer specimen of pathetic description has seldom been written. It is the narrated confession of a dangerous madman, sometimes aware of his condition, with some noble feelings, far above the meanness and cunning of those who surround him, and of whom he is in some respects the victim. His language and ideas express a remorseful, sensitive spirit, excited and wounded to a dangerous extent; incapable, indeed, of the true penitence of a rational mind, yet evidently retaining some noble thoughts which vainly contend with the awful infliction of insanity, which finally renders him a guiltless, irresponsible victim of other people's designs. Whether such singular instances are rare or even possible can, perhaps, hardly be known except to medical men of practical experience. This case is apparently a complete invention, no note or reference being given about its derivation.

This remarkable and specially mournful, interesting chapter may recall to some readers a chapter in Miss Braddon's admirable novel "Lady Audley's Secret." It is where the insane Lady Audley herself owns that she is a madwoman, describing the state of her disordered mind with singularly careful accuracy. Dickens may have written more wisely than Miss Braddon in this remarkable instance. He appends to his madman's confused and excited personal confession an explanation of the man's real state of mind written by another hand. Dickens's mode of thus viewing or describing insanity apparently agrees with Shakespeare's idea, when Hamlet assures his mother he is not mad as she supposes, in language which few, if any, but Shakespeare could command:

> "It is not madness that I have uttered;
> Bring me to the test, and I the matter will
> Re-word which madness would gambol from."
>
> *Hamlet*, Act iii.

After this remarkable chapter, the story proceeds as before, without further allusion to it; probably it was only introduced to show the varied powers of the writer, perhaps for a mental change, after a long course of comic sketches, and to render them all the more agreeable to himself and his readers. Indeed, all through "Pickwick" and the "Sketches" this inclination to pathetic description seems contending in the author's mind with that keen sense of the ludicrous, brilliant wit and lively fancy which chiefly characterised his first two works, and made him thought a first-rate comic writer, whose powers for the pathetic were only slightly indicated. The famous trial in "Pickwick" is a strong proof how deep a sense of legal injustice and knavery was striving in Dickens's mind with all his natural wit, drollery, and power of exciting laughter. He wisely resolved, however, to make this transaction highly amusing and diverting to all readers, to excite their laughter and merriment, and thus leave a thoroughly cheerful impression on their minds, and at the same time to expose and condemn the state of the law which sanctioned the rascally conduct of the attorneys Messrs. Dodson and Fogg. It is this judicious mixture of the ludicrous and amusing with the serious and instructive which makes this trial, and, indeed, the whole book, so generally acceptable to all classes of readers.

At this trial a Serjeant Buzfuz appears for Mrs. Bardell. His vehement absurdities are indeed too much for poor innocent Mr. Pickwick to endure with temper or patience, but they succeed completely with certainly a very stupid jury. He thus addresses them:

"The plaintiff, gentlemen, is a widow; yes, gentlemen, a widow. . . . Mrs. Bardell's opinions of the opposite sex were derived from a long contemplation of the inestimable qualities of her lost husband. . . . 'Mr. Bardell,' said the widow, 'was once a single gentleman himself; *to* single gentlemen I look for protection, for assistance, for comfort, and for consolation—*in* single gentlemen I shall see something to remind me of what Mr. Bardell was, when he first won my young and untried affections; to a single gentleman therefore shall my lodgings be let.' Actuated by this beautiful and touching impulse . . . the lonely and desolate widow dried her tears, furnished her first floor, caught her innocent boy to her maternal bosom, and put the bill up in her parlour window Did it remain there long? No. The serpent was on the watch, the train was laid, the mine was preparing. . . . Before the bill had been in the window three days—three days, gentlemen—a Being erect upon two legs, and bearing all the outward semblance of a man and not of a monster, knocked at the door of Mrs. Bardell's house. . . . This man was Pickwick—Pickwick, the defendant.

"Of this man Pickwick I will say little; the subject presents but few attractions; and I, gentlemen, am not the man nor are you, gentlemen, the men to delight in the contemplation of revolting heartlessness, and of systematic villainy. . . . My client's hopes and prospects are ruined and it is no figure of speech to say that her occupation is gone indeed. The bill is down, but there is no tenant. . . . All is gloom and silence in the house, even the voice of the child is hushed, his infant sports are disregarded when his mother weeps. . . . But Pickwick, gentlemen, Pickwick rears his head, with unblushing effrontery, and gazes without a sigh on the ruin he has made. Damages, gentlemen—heavy damages is the only punishment with which you can visit him, the only recompense you can award to my client. And, for those damages, she now appeals to an enlightened, a high-minded, a right-feeling, a conscientious, a dispassionate, a sympathising, a contemplative jury of her civilised countrymen."[1]

While laughter and enjoyment are excited and maintained throughout, true and valuable information is, likewise, given to readers of the strange abuses with which the English law was at this time disgraced

[1] Chap. viii.

—of the shameful cunning, deceit, and trickery which often prevailed under its sanction, and of the real danger to the public welfare of allowing such practices to continue with legal impunity.[1] But the British people, though informed and enlightened about legal roguery and mismanagement, were never made revolutionary or seditious by Dickens's writings. They were, indeed, all the more induced to examine and amend the state of the law, but not even the lowest or most ignorant section of them were rendered the least inclined to wreak vengeance, or even feel irritation, against any particular person or class of persons. It was his judicious use of great talents, guided by clear judgment, which enabled Dickens to enlist, as it were, the mind of England on his side, to share his sentiments and views to their fullest extent. The most enthusiastic demagogue, eloquent politician, or sincere clergyman, might have declaimed for years about the iniquity of English lawyers, the defective state of the law, the mismanagement of prisons, and the sufferings of deceived clients, and yet not have produced as much effect on the public mind as Dickens accomplished by his descriptions in "Pickwick" alone. Dickens's talents as an actor are well known, and in his public reading of the Pickwick trial they were strongly indicated. The way in which, by sudden changes of his voice and expression, the fretful little judge, the pompous Serjeant Buzfuz, the nervous Mr. Winkle, the offended Mrs. Cluppins, and the witty Sam Weller, all started into life, will not easily be forgotten

[1] Upon this subject Mr. Dickens, when quite young, received valuable information from his eminent legal friend, Mr. Serjeant Talfourd (see Forster's "Life of Dickens").

by the present writer, who was fortunate enough to hear these readings. Dickens, unassisted and alone, thus brought the whole trial scene before the senses of the audience. He had a most remarkable way of changing his expression of face before introducing any new character. For instance, the little judge looked stern, Winkle trembled, Mrs. Cluppins looked indignant, and Sam winked, before any of them spoke. Dickens's public readings were, indeed, a great intellectual triumph for any man to achieve. In the midst of the gay London season he read the Pickwick trial in St. James's Hall, which was crammed to overflowing, and many people were turned away from the doors. He had no assistance, there was neither music nor speech-making; alone he stood and read to a delighted audience at such a place and in such a season, and all he read was his own composition. Yet no angry mob, no rioters calling for vengeance on law and lawyers, or turning their ignorant rage against individuals, were ever aroused by the power and truth of this great writer's description. It was not to such he appealed, except by giving them harmless amusement. It was the good sense and calm judgment of the respectable and reflecting members of the community that he addressed, and succeeded in convincing for the best of purposes.

After the Bardell trial, poor Mr. Pickwick, refusing to pay the costs and damages incurred, is, consequently, removed to the Fleet Prison. In his preface to a late edition of this work Dickens states what must be truly gratifying to all humane readers:

> I have found it curious and interesting looking over the sheets of this reprint to mark what important social improvements have taken

place about us almost imperceptibly, even since they were originally written. . . . Legal reforms have pared the claws of Messrs. Dodson and Fogg . . . the laws relating to imprisonment for debt are altered, and the Fleet Prison is pulled down !

Except the trial scene, the most impressive chapters are xl. and xli., describing the dreadful state of this prison, as it doubtless existed when Dickens wrote; its wretched rules and regulations, and the neglected, sad condition of its luckless inmates. Old and young, cheats, swindlers, and innocent, unhappy debtors, were here confined and huddled together, apparently quite excluded from the outer world, and seldom visited by either magistrate or clergyman. No mention is made of either interesting themselves about a place the miserable state of which so specially required their attention. To prevent some fastidious or nervous readers from avoiding these chapters in disgust or horror, Mr. Dickens introduces some amusing and comparatively harmless rogues like Smangle, Mivins, &c.; but the death of the old Chancery prisoner, neglected and half-starved, tells its own tale of misery and strange injustice. Yet his case is too painful to dwell upon. Dickens presents it suddenly, describes it in a few powerful lines, and leaves it to make its proper impression on the minds of all thoughtful readers. The account of this man's death is as brief as it is affecting (chap. xliii.). The reflecting must study it, the most thoughtless can hardly avoid its perusal, while its effect will probably be much the same on all readers of common sense and ordinary humanity.

That such a case was not uncommon even at this time (1832–33) in London seems certain; and how such abuses of all right, law, and justice could exist in London, the heart of civilisation, where Christianity was preached and generally professed, it is difficult indeed to explain. But it is very remarkable that the attractive pen of a novelist drew more practical attention to the state of London prisons than either the speeches or writings of legislators and clergymen, whose special duty was surely to examine and bring to light such matters. These debtors' prisons were, apparently, worse managed, and their wretched inmates more thoroughly neglected, than were the political prisons and prisoners of former times, whose fate was indeed usually cruel and often unjust, but whose sufferings were, perhaps, equalled by those of luckless debtors, who were usually more unfortunate than criminal. These "prison chapters" in "Pickwick," therefore, may well cause thoughtful readers to wonder what excuse a civilised Government and community could offer for such extraordinary neglect, especially during a time of domestic peace, with ample leisure to examine and improve the condition of all existing institutions. Were the Sovereign, the Parliament, and the clergy satisfied with, or in unaccountable ignorance of, such things? The latter is most probable, and seems confirmed by the earnest and indignant attention which Dickens's revelations aroused.

The excellent Mr. Pickwick's own conduct in this dreadful jail, both in word and deed, rather resembles that of the worthy Vicar of Wakefield when in a similar situation. Dickens was evidently more anxious to interest his readers for the unhappy prisoners in general; while Goldsmith aroused interest chiefly, if not solely, for the poor Vicar himself, and he leaves the prisoners, to whom Dr. Primrose preaches so eloquently, comparatively undescribed. During his residence in the Fleet Prison Mr. Pickwick suddenly meets his old acquaintances, Jingle and Job Trotter—the former no longer the gay, witty, dashing swindler, captivating Miss Rachael Wardle in place of Mr. Tupman superseded ; but now half-starved, half-clad, and reduced to the last extremity. Mr. Pickwick, who had not only been ridiculed but duped and deceived by this man, now sees him in humbled dejection, suffering alike in body and mind. Even when describing his deplorable state, Dickens's wit and comic genius never forsake him. When the kind Mr. Pickwick asks Jingle to speak to him in private, the poor broken-down Jingle, in describing prison limits, answers in his usual odd, hasty style, once rather witty, but now no longer cheerful :

"Certainly . . . can't step far—no danger of over-walking yourself here. Spike Park—grounds pretty—romantic, but not extensive—open for public inspection—family always in town—housekeeper desperately careful—very."

"You have forgotten your coat," said Mr. Pickwick.

"Eh ?" said Jingle. "Spout—dear relation—Uncle Tom—couldn't help it—must eat, you know. Wants of nature—and all that."

"What do you mean ?"

"Gone, my dear sir—last coat—can't help it. Lived on a pair of boots—whole fortnight. Silk umbrella—ivory handle—week—fact—honour—ask Job—knows it."

"Lived for three weeks upon a pair of boots and a silk umbrella with an ivory handle !" exclaimed Mr. Pickwick.

"True," said Jingle, nodding his head. "Pawnbroker's shop—duplicates here—small sums—mere nothing—all rascals."

"Oh !" said Mr. Pickwick, much relieved by this explanation ; "I understand you—you have pawned your wardrobe."

"Everything—Job's too—all shirts gone—never mind—saves washing. Nothing soon—lie in bed—starve—die. Inquest—little bone-house—poor prisoner—common necessaries—hush it up—gentlemen of the jury—warden's tradesmen—keep it snug—natural death—coroner's order—workhouse funeral—serve him right—all over—drop the curtain."

Jingle delivered this singular summary of his prospects in life with his accustomed volubility and with various twitches of the countenance to counterfeit smiles. Mr. Pickwick easily perceived that his recklessness was assumed.

His charity towards Jingle, though described in few words, is perhaps in a moral sense the finest passage, for its length, in the whole book.

"Come here," said Mr. Pickwick, trying to look stern, with four large tears running down his waistcoat. "Take that, sir." Take what? In the ordinary acceptation of such language it should have been a blow. As the world runs it should have been a sound, hearty cuff, for Mr. Pickwick had been deceived, duped, and wronged by the destitute outcast who was now wholly in his power. Must we tell the truth? It was something from Mr. Pickwick's waistcoat pocket, which chinked as it was given into Jingle's hand, and the giving which somehow or other imparted a sparkle to the eye and a swelling to the heart of our excellent old friend as he hurried away." [1]

The account of both Jingle and the old Chancery prisoner actually suffering from starvation and pawning their clothes for food, is almost too dreadful for belief. But that such was the state of some imprisoned debtors in London seems evident, even from the preface to "Pickwick." Although Jingle and others are described as starving, and pawning their clothes from hunger, it is not stated by Dickens, either in the story or in the accompanying notes, that any deaths from actual starvation ever occurred in the

[1] Chap. xiv.

Fleet Prison; but it is to be feared such cases may have occurred, though they are not positively avowed.

That such abuses existed in the London public institutions when "Pickwick" was written is really astonishing. These statements came upon the majority of the public apparently by surprise. These horrors were then found to exist in the metropolis—inhabited by so many intelligent, well-educated people, who lived close to where such sufferings occurred, which they might have easily remedied, but of which they seemed to be in unaccountable ignorance. The whole character and career of the prisoner Jingle are very striking. He is seldom introduced, yet he is one of the most remarkable personages in the story. Although an arrant rogue and swindler, he retains some good qualities, besides being witty and amusing. He and his servant Job are both liberated by the generous Mr. Pickwick, and leave England with many promises of amendment, while their benefactor remains himself in self-imposed confinement, for, though a rich man, he steadily refuses to pay the absurd penalty laid upon him, preferring the alternative of a long imprisonment. He would probably have carried out this resolution, and thus disappointed the rapacity of Messrs. Dodson and Fogg, had not these worthies previously secured themselves from all possible loss by inducing their dupe, Mrs. Bardell, to become liable for their expenses in case of Mr. Pickwick's continued firmness in refusing to pay their costs.

As a fair contrast to these odious knaves, Dickens introduces a worthy, sharp lawyer in Mr. Pickwick's adviser, Mr. Perker, who, after Mrs. Bardell's arrest by Dodson and Fogg, has a long interview with his stout-hearted old client. After a long explanation and entreaty, he induces Mr. Pickwick, out of pity for his imprisoned opponent and still more for his faithful servant Sam, who insists on sharing his master's captivity, to actually pay the costs to Messrs. Dodson and Fogg, conditionally on his and her release, and also upon her solemnly declaring that the whole charge for breach of promise of marriage was utterly false. Upon these terms Mr. Pickwick, Sam Weller, and Mrs. Bardell are alike liberated from the dismal Fleet Prison. When Mr. Pickwick is paying Messrs. Dodson and Fogg, who call upon him, their costs, he loses his temper and despite the efforts of his cool, sensible little lawyer, Mr. Perker, tells these knaves his opinion of them, which, after being paid, amuses them highly:

"Do you know that I have been the victim of your plots and conspiracies? Do you know that I am the man whom you have been imprisoning and robbing? Do you know that you were the attorneys for the plaintiff in Bardell and Pickwick?" . . .

"Yes, sir," replied Dodson, "we do know it."

"Of course we know it, sir," rejoined Fogg, slapping his pocket—perhaps by accident. . . .

"You are," continued Mr. Pickwick, "you are a well-matched pair of mean, rascally, pettifogging robbers." . . .

"There," said Perker, in a most conciliatory tone. "My dear sirs, he has said all he has to say; now pray go. Lowten (to the clerk), *is* that door open?"

Mr. Lowten, with a distant giggle, replied in the affirmative.

"There, there—good morning—good morning—now pray, my dear sirs—Mr. Lowten, open the door. . . . Why don't you attend?"

"If there's law in England, sir," said Dodson, looking towards Mr. Pickwick and putting on his hat, "you shall smart for this."

"You are a couple of mean——"

"Remember, sir, you pay dearly for this," said Fogg.

"—Rascally, pettifogging robbers!" continued Mr. Pickwick, taking not the least notice of the threats that were addressed to him.

"Robbers!" cried Mr. Pickwick, running to the stair-head, as the two attorneys descended.

"Robbers!" shouted Mr. Pickwick, breaking from Lowten and Perker, and thrusting his head out of the staircase window.

When Mr. Pickwick drew in his head again, his countenance was smiling and placid, and he declared that he had now removed a great weight from his mind and that he felt perfectly comfortable and happy.[1]

After this scene the story is all wit, fun, and merriment again; the interesting and worthy characters enjoy themselves in peace, and are thoroughly happy in their different ways.

Sam Weller, in intelligence, is a decided improvement on his worthy but rather intemperate old father, who is terribly annoyed for some time by his second wife's being duped by a knavish, drunken Dissenting minister—the Rev. Mr. Stiggins. This man is only slightly sketched, and not in a way that could offend any religious denomination, while Dickens avoids saying to which he nominally belongs. Mr. Pickwick lives to see all his numerous friends happy and comfortable around him; and Sam, though married to a suitable housemaid, resolves never to leave him if he can help it. In this truly comic story there are no actual heroes or heroines; for Winkle and Snodgrass are both too ridiculous and even cowardly, though not unamiable, to deserve that name, while their brides, the Misses Wardle, are seldom mentioned, and are neither very interesting nor apparently intended to be so. Mr. Pickwick and Sam Weller

[1] Chap. xxv.

are the real heroes, and Mrs. Bardell certainly not the heroine, though she aspires by every legal means to hold that position; while Sam's bride, Mary, takes no part in the story. Sam writes a valentine to her in the presence of his worthy old father, a former coachman. It is indeed a most amusing composition and quite worthy of the genuine wit of Charles Dickens:

Sam dipped his pen into the ink to be ready for any corrections and began with a very theatrical air . . . "'Lovely creetur.'"

"'Taint in poetry, is it?" interposed his father.

"No, no," replied Sam.

"Wery glad to hear it," said Mr. Weller. "Poetry's unnat'ral . . . never let yourself down to talk poetry, my boy. Begin agin, Sammy." . . .

"'I feel myself ashamed and completely circumscribed in addressin' of you, for you *are* a nice girl and nothin' but it.'"

"That's a wery pretty sentiment," said the elder Mr. Weller, removing the pipe to make way for the remark.

"Yes, I think it is rayther good," observed Sam, highly flattered.

"Wot I like in that 'ere style of writin'," said the elder Mr. Weller, "is that there ain't no callin' names in it—no Wenuses nor nothin' o' that kind. Wot's the good of calling a young 'ooman a Wenus or a angel, Sammy? . . . You might jist as well call her a griffin, or a unicorn, or a king's arms at once, which is wery well known to be a collection of fabulous animals," added Mr. Weller. . . . "Drive on, Sammy."

Sam compiled with the request. . . .

"'Afore I saw you, I thought all women were alike.'"

"So they are," observed Mr. Weller parenthetically.

"'But now,' continued Sam, 'now I find what a reg'lar soft-headed, inkred'lous turnip I must ha' been. . . . So I take the privilege of the day, Mary, my dear—as the gen'l'm'n in difficulties did, ven he walked out on a Sunday—to tell you that the first and only time I see you, your likeness was took on my heart in much quicker time and brighter colours than ever a likeness was took by the profeel machine (wich p'raps you may have heerd on, Mary, my dear) altho' it *does* finish a portrait, and put the frame and glass on complete with a hook at the end to hang it up by and all in two minutes and a quarter.' "

"I am afeerd that werges on the poetical, Sammy," said Mr. Weller dubiously.

"No it don't," replied Sam, reading on very quickly, to avoid contesting the point:

"'Except of me, Mary my dear, as your walentine and think over what I have said. My dear Mary, I will now conclude.' That's all," said Sam.

"That's rayther a sudden pull-up, ain't it, Sammy?" inquired Mr. Weller.

"Not a bit on it," said Sam; "she'll vish there was more and that's the great art o' letter-writing." [1]

The whole book is the reverse of sentimental; it is intensely comic in the best sense of that word, varied by a few brief but most powerfully written pathetic passages, which, however, do not affect or involve the leading characters.[2] Perhaps no work of fiction in English has ever diffused so much mirth and enjoyment among all classes as this most original and thoroughly standard work. Its popularity was literally enormous, and, though appreciated on the Continent and in America, was specially suited to the English taste. It probably found more readers in London, proportionately, than anywhere else—the scene being chiefly laid in the metropolis, and most of the chief characters derived from London life and experience.

A very amusing dispute is described between rival

[1] Vol. ii. chap. v.

[2] "The plan of 'Pickwick' was simply to amuse. It was to string together whimsical sketches of the pencil by entertaining sketches of the pen. But genius is a master as well as a servant, and when the laughter and fun were at their highest, something grave made its appearance" (Forster's "Life of Dickens," vol. i.).

newspaper editors, Messrs. Pott and Slurk, contending for popularity in a country district. Mr. Slurk alights at an hotel in a place which he believed was a great admirer of his political views, but finds the landlord does not even know him:

> "Do you know me?" he demanded.
> "I have not that pleasure, sir," replied the landlord.
> "My name is Slurk," said the gentleman.
> The landlord slightly inclined his head.
> "Slurk, sir," repeated the gentleman haughtily. "Do you know me now, man?"
> The landlord scratched his head, looked at the ceiling and at the stranger, and smiled feebly.
> "Do you know me, man?" inquired the stranger angrily.
> The landlord made a strong effort and at length replied, "Well, sir, I do *not* know you."
> "Great heavens!" said the stranger, dashing his clenched fist upon the table. "And this is popularity! . . . This, this is gratitude for years of labour and study in behalf of the masses. I alight wet and weary; no enthusiastic crowds press forward to greet their champion, the church bells are silent, the very name elicits no responsive feeling in their torpid bosoms. It is enough," said the agitated Mr. Slurk, pacing to and fro, "to curdle the ink in one's pen and induce one to abandon their cause for ever." [1]

In reviewing the whole story of "Pickwick" there may appear some likeness between its brave, kind-hearted, and simple-minded hero and the poor knight, Don Quixote, of Cervantes,[2] whom Dickens mentions in his preface to "Oliver Twist." There seems to be certainly some strong points of resemblance between them. Thus Dr. Johnson writes that

> Cervantes had so much kindness for Don Quixote that where-

---

[1] Chap. xxiii.

[2] "Sam Weller and Mr. Pickwick are the Sancho and Don Quixote of Londoners" (Forster's "Life of Dickens," vol. i.).

ever he is or whatever he does, he is made by matchless dexterity commonly ridiculous but never contemptible.[1]

In like manner the excellent, trustful, unsuspicious Mr. Pickwick often says and does fanciful, eccentric, if not foolish things, but never incurs the blame or the contempt of the reader. In this respect the kindly old London gentleman and the generous, noble-hearted Spanish knight are certainly like each other. Both are elderly, single men of benevolent character and great simplicity, carried almost to a childish extent in each case ; and they are alike attended by a faithful servant, and surrounded by friends and relatives who do not resemble them, and perhaps hardly understand them thoroughly. But the objects of their two creators, Dickens and Cervantes, were very different, which, of course, determine the conduct and fate of both characters. Don Quixote dies from mingled mental disappointment and bodily exhaustion, having discovered and confessed that the world of reality was very different from that of his imagination, and he earnestly endeavours to atone for all the extravagance of his enthusiastic fancy to the last moment of consciousness. Mr. Pickwick, despite his numerous misfortunes and vexations, in false imprisonment and shameless robbery, is kind and benevolent to the last. His bitter experience of rascals and rascality, falsehood and ingratitude, never sours his temper nor hardens his heart towards others, which is often the most dangerous, if not the inevitable, result of such experience. The story in this respect leaves him, as it finds him, beaming with kindness, affection, and

[1] "Life of Butler" (Lives of the Poets).

generosity to all who enjoy his friendship or even acquaintance. The last passage describing him is very touching; and probably most readers who have experienced the trials and sorrows of the world will agree with Dickens in his brief yet philosophic reflection:

> Let us leave our old friend in one of those moments of unmixed happiness of which, if we seek them, there are ever some to cheer our transitory existence here. There are dark shadows on the earth, but its lights are stronger in the contrast. Some men, like bats or owls, have better eyes for the darkness than for the light; we who have no such optical powers are better pleased to take our last parting look at the visionary companions of many solitary hours, when the brief sunshine of the world is blazing full upon them.

He thus leaves the excellent and pleasing creation of his fancy amid his best friends in health and happiness—just, indeed, as all appreciating readers would wish to leave him; and thus ends a work which, for mingled fun, wit, and excellent morality combined, has, perhaps, hardly an equal in English fictitious literature.

“NICHOLAS NICKLEBY”

CHAPTER II

"NICHOLAS NICKLEBY"

IN the words of Mr. Forster, after the publication of "Pickwick,"

> young Mr. Nicholas Nickleby stepped into his shoes;[1]

for the two books were about the same size, and published in the same form ot illustrated monthly numbers. This story, however, was written much more on the plan of a regular novel than either "Pickwick" or "Oliver Twist." The young hero, Nicholas, is a pleasing, interesting, consistent character, and his sister Kate perhaps more so. Though Nicholas is indeed well worthy of the reader's liking and sympathy during his many painful experiences, he has been apparently found fault with by some people, as Dickens thus concludes his preface to a late edition about his young hero:

> If Nicholas be not always found to be blameless or agreeable, he is not always intended to appear so. He is a young man of an impetuous temper and of little or no experience, and I saw no reason why such a hero should be lifted out of nature.

The adventures of this brother and sister and their experiences, chiefly when apart from each

[1] "Life of Dickens," vol. i. chap. ix.

other, compose the greater part of the work. They are in poor circumstances, having lost their father, who had ruined himself by speculation, and they come, with their widowed mother, to London from the country to seek professions.

Mrs. Nickleby is one of the most amusing characters Dickens has in this novel described—kind-hearted but silly and fanciful to a most absurd degree. She and her children first apply for assistance to their brother-in-law and uncle, Mr. Ralph Nickleby, a hard-hearted, wealthy old moneylender, who becomes the chief villain of the story. He recommends for his niece Kate a situation in a milliner's and dressmaking establishment, when poor Mrs. Nickleby, anxious to agree with him, and nearly always mistaken in what she says, exclaims in a few sentences which for their length well express her wrong-headed, silly way of talking and thinking.

"What your uncle says is very true, Kate, my dear. I recollect when your poor papa and I came to town after we were married, that a young lady brought me home a chip cottage bonnet with white and green trimming, and green persian lining, in her own carriage, which drove up to the door full gallop—at least I am not quite certain whether it was her own carriage or a hackney-chariot, but I remember very well, that the horse dropped down dead as he was turning round, and that your poor papa said he hadn't had any corn for a fortnight."

This anecdote, so strikingly illustrative of the opulence of milliners, was not received with any great demonstration of feeling, inasmuch as Kate held down her head while it was relating, and Ralph manifested very intelligible symptoms of extreme impatience.

From their first meeting Ralph conceives a strange if not unaccountable dislike to Nicholas, and this feeling deepens into the most intense hatred. Nicholas, though most amiable and respectful, is also irritated by his uncle's unexpected harshness towards his mother and sister; so that there is little attempt on either side to conciliate. Ralph, however, procures for Nicholas a miserable situation as usher in a Yorkshire school, kept by a Mr. Squeers; and thither the young man goes, delighted at having anything to do, and leaving his mother and sister in London, under the doubtful guardianship of Ralph, whom he dislikes, but tries to think the best of.

Before starting for Yorkshire, Nicholas makes acquaintance with Newman Noggs, now his uncle's clerk, and a "reduced" gentleman. This man is one of the most original and remarkable characters in the book, though seldom mentioned. He is a consistent friend to Nicholas and his sister Kate, and, though harshly treated by Ralph, is always faithful to, though suspicious of, his odious employer. During Nicholas's journey to Yorkshire he hears two anecdotes, comic and tragic, from some fellow-travellers. The first one, called the "Five Sisters of York," though prettily told, leaves a sad impression on the reader, and is not a first-rate specimen of Dickens's pathetic style. It is an old legend, which, though related with taste and feeling, might perhaps have been rendered more effective even by inferior authors. The comic tale of the German "Baron of Grogzwig," though rather amusing, is a faint specimen of Dickens's power for the humorous, as the "Five Sisters" is a somewhat weak one of his tragic powers. But the arrival of Nicholas at Dotheboys Hall, the account of that school, its master, mistress, and crowd of wretched pupils are described with Dickens's greatest skill. He is here quite in his element, and this part of the story made an immense impression upon the English reading public, which has seldom been surpassed.

Squeers, his wife, son, and daughter, are as odious a family as can well be imagined in every respect, and, though slightly different from each other, a great likeness pervades the whole group. It is surprising, however, that Squeers should be represented as being so ignorant and vulgar, as well as brutal and cunning. He would probably have been more successful in imposing on the public, and quite as bad a man yet, with more education and with more plausible manners. He is merely a low, coarse, ignorant rogue, cruel and vindictive, though rather amusing. His first introduction, when waiting at the booking-office in London to take Nicholas with him to his Yorkshire school, reveals his character clearly enough; two unlucky little boy-pupils are also with him, waiting to be taken to the odious school appropriately termed Dotheboys Hall. One of the lads sneezes:

"Halloa, sir," growled the schoolmaster, "what's that, sir?"

"Nothing, please, sir," replied the little boy.

"Nothing, sir!" exclaimed Mr. Squeers.

"Please, sir, I sneezed," rejoined the boy. . . .

"Oh, sneezed, did you?" retorted Mr. Squeers. "Then what did you say 'nothing' for, sir?"

In default of a better answer to this question, the little boy screwed a couple of knuckles into each of his eyes and began to cry, wherefore Mr. Squeers knocked him off the trunk with a blow on one side of his face and knocked him on again with a blow on the other.

"Wait till I get you down into Yorkshire, my young gentleman," said Mr. Squeers, "and I'll give you the rest. Will you hold that noise, sir?"

Then when a stranger is about to enter the office Mr. Squeers changes his tone and manner remarkably.

" Put your handkerchief in your pocket, you little scoundrel, or I'll murder you when the gentleman goes."

The stranger enters and the schoolmaster immediately becomes kind, gentle, and benevolent, exclaiming :

" My dear child . . . all people have their trials. This early trial of yours that is fit to make your little heart burst and your very eyes to come out of your head with crying, what is it ? Nothing ; less than nothing. You are leaving your friends, but you will have a father in me, my dear, and a mother in Mrs. Squeers. At the delightful village of Dotheboys, near Greta Bridge in Yorkshire, where youths are boarded, clothed, booked, washed, furnished with pocket money, provided with all necessaries."

His wife seems, if possible, worse than himself, though seldom mentioned ; yet even in the little said of her seems about the worst and most atrocious of all Dickens's female characters, for there are dark hints of some wretched pupils having died from her and her husband's united cruelty. They keep their hapless pupils in most complete subjection ; beat, starve, and ill-use them in every possible way. They seem to have absolute power over them all, and to be never visited by any one, and therefore under no superintendence whatever. The following account of the Dotheboys Hall pupils made, doubtless, a strong impression on most readers, and is certainly not to be easily forgotten :

" Pale and haggard faces, lank and bony figures, children with the countenance of old men, deformities with iron upon their limbs, boys of stunted growth, and others whose long, meagre legs would hardly bear their stooping bodies, all crowded on the view together.

With every kindly sympathy and affection blasted in its birth, with every young and healthy feeling flogged and starved down, with every revengeful passion that can fester in swollen hearts, eating its evil way to the core in silence, what an incipient hell was breeding there!" [1]

Here, again, readers may reasonably wonder, as in the prison and workhouse scenes of "Pickwick" and "Oliver," where were the clergymen of the parish, or the nearest magistrates. How could this wretched place and horrible system have long existed without the knowledge of either? That such schools were actually in Yorkshire when this book was written seems certain, but it is to be feared that clergy and magistrates could not have been entirely ignorant of such horrors in their neighbourhood.[2] Yet in this story Dickens never mentions the clergyman of the parish in which Dotheboys was situated; no careless or cruel magistrates and doctors in league with Squeers are introduced either. The school is and has evidently been for many years as completely neglected as if in some deserted island, instead of in one of the chief English counties. In real life other people beside the schoolmaster's family would have been fearfully to blame in such a case; for magistrates, clergymen, and doctors were all long established, and sufficiently numerous throughout Yorkshire as in the rest of England; and their utter neglect of duty, and wilful ignorance of such long-continued barbarity to

[1] Chap. viii.

[2] "The debtors' prisons described in 'Pickwick,' the parochial management denounced in 'Oliver,' and the Yorkshire schools exposed in 'Nickleby' were all actual existences, which now have no similar existence than in the forms he (Dickens) thus gave to them" (Forster's "Life of Dickens," vol. i. chap. viii.).

helpless children, deserved nearly as much blame as the cruelty of a schoolmaster. Dickens writes in a preface to a late edition of this work :

> Of the monstrous neglect of education in England and the disregard of it by the State as a means of forming good or bad citizens and miserable or happy men, this class of schools long afforded a notable example. Although any man who had proved his unfitness for any other occupation in life was free without examination or qualification to open a school anywhere ; although preparation for the function he undertook was required for the surgeon who assisted to bring a boy into the world, or might one day assist perhaps to send him out of it—in the chemist, the attorney, the butcher, the baker, the candlestick maker—the whole round of crafts and trades, the schoolmaster excepted ; and although schoolmasters as a race were the blockheads and impostors that might naturally be expected to arise in such a state of things and to flourish in it ; these Yorkshire schoolmasters were the lowest and most rotten rung in the whole ladder. . . . I make mention of the race as of the Yorkshire schoolmasters in the past tense. Though it has not yet finally disappeared, it is dwindling daily.

But Dickens neither blames nor indeed mentions anybody but the Squeers family in connection with the management of Dotheboys Hall.

The chief and most interesting young victim among the wretched pupils is the youth nicknamed Smike, whose reason has been affected by ill-usage, though retaining sense enough to be most grateful for any kindness, and he attaches himself to Nicholas from the first. He is employed as a mere drudge by the Squeerses ; all pretence of teaching him has been given up for some time, and he is, in fact, the slave of the establishment, having neither friend nor relation. Amid all these scenes of gloom and suffering, the incident of Miss Squeers falling in love with Nicholas, who does not return it, is an amusing relief ;

and a very comic tea-party ensues, composed of Nicholas, Miss Squeers, her friend Miss Price, a pleasant contrast to herself, and her lover John Browdie, a rough, good-natured Yorkshire yeoman. The old Squeerses are comfortably and prudently excluded from this little flirting party, which, however, ends in a most amusing lovers' quarrel, though it is least so to poor Nicholas, who, unable to conceal his thorough aversion to the whole house of Squeers, immediately forfeits his newly-acquired place in Miss Squeers's good graces. He and Smike now suffer together from every sort of oppression and torment, though, of course, in different ways; when the latter attempts flight, but is caught, brought back, and instantly condemned to a fearful flogging by the enraged Squeers.

Then comes the most exciting scene, perhaps, in the whole book. The reader is shocked, horrified, and exasperated to the last degree by the fearful threats and cruelty of Squeers and his wife; the miserable Smike, perfectly helpless, is about to be flogged within an inch of his life at least, when Nicholas, rushing to the rescue, beats the villain Squeers in a way which gladdens and relieves the reader's heart. For the first time in the story Squeers's cruelty is stopped and punished, and Nicholas, with Smike, leaves Dotheboys Hall for ever. They meet worthy John Browdie on their way, and tell him the news; but though he is glad to hear it, and well aware of the state of the school, he does nothing, and contemplates doing nothing, to assist the hapless boys left in Squeers's power. Strange to say, Nicholas also, brave, intelligent, full of sense and feeling as he is, carries Smike off with him to London to seek their fortunes together, but takes no step to relieve the miserable crowd of sufferers left behind them. It appears singular that neither he nor the comparatively stupid though kindly John Browdie ever think of informing the neighbouring clergy or magistrates, and asking them to use their eyes, by visiting this wretched school, and judging for themselves, as well as by report, of its horrible condition; but such an idea apparently never occurs to either Nickleby or Browdie.

Had Squeers been some child-eating ogre in an enchanted castle, or a savage chief in a remote country, he could hardly have been more independent of all civilised control or supervision. Nicholas and Smike are, indeed, thankful to leave the neighbourhood, and are congratulated on their escape by honest John Browdie; but the Squeerses are left in almost despotic power over their wretched little kingdom of suffering children, virtually monarchs of all they survey, and apparently responsible to nobody. During a long period in this very interesting and bustling story, Dotheboys Hall is not mentioned; for Nicholas and Smike are fully occupied in pushing their fortunes in London and elsewhere; while Squeers, with his savage temper probably not improved by his well-deserved thrashing, is left in absolute, undisturbed control, and, probably, carries out his scholastic system more fully than ever, to relieve his wounded feelings of mind and body. A foreigner reading this story might almost imagine there were neither magistrates nor clergy in Yorkshire or its neighbourhood, for many people with such evidence as Nicholas possessed would have strongly, and it is to be hoped not vainly, appealed to both. But Dickens never mentions either clergy or magistrates in this story, and to all appearance Dotheboys Hall had never been visited by any of them. Dickens apparently does not accuse either of these classes of knowing about the existence of such schools without remonstrance, but writes as if he himself had just discovered them and drew public attention to them at the same time, otherwise his just mind and powerful pen would probably not have spared either wilful neglect or connivance. He thus excited no popular indignation whatever against clergy or magistrates, both to some extent responsible for the continuance of such abuses if within their knowledge, but writes like a traveller hastening to apprise his fellow-countrymen about his discoveries, of which they had little, if any, previous idea. This plan, however, succeeded perfectly, and a few tyrannical, and probably guilty, schoolmasters were furious at their system being exposed. In the preface to "Nickleby," Dickens states that more than one Yorkshire schoolmaster laid claim to being the original of Mr. Squeers; that one consulted a lawyer about bringing an action against the author of Dotheboys Hall, and that another meditated a journey to London for the sake of committing

an assault and battery upon his traducer.

Dickens expresses natural and wholesome satisfaction at these involuntary tributes of respect to his genius and motives, which are, indeed, worthy of equal admiration throughout this entire story.

Many wretched schools were now attended to, and the thoughts of the public were eagerly directed to a subject about which the previous general ignorance seems unaccountable. But though Dickens, by this story, directed general attention and interest to neglected schools, there ensued no public expression of angry surprise; no violent indignation meetings were assembled on the subject. Some eloquent demagogues would have excited ignorant crowds to fury by declaiming in pathetic words and furious invectives about the miseries and wrongs which Dickens, by the peaceful, silent, yet most effective medium of an admirable tale, proclaimed to the British public. The practical result was, it is to be hoped and believed, as satisfactory as the author could have expected, or, perhaps, wished. The names of Squeers and Dotheboys Hall were soon spread through every English town and district; indignation and astonishment were equally aroused, and general inquiries were made about schools and their management, without a single riot or the least risk of any popular disturbance. With that remarkable knowledge of the English character which Dickens evidently possessed, even before he could have had much experience of it, he guessed the best plan for accomplishing his design. He appealed to the feelings, and enlightened the minds of the public by a delightful book, suited to the taste of most and to the sense of all; and, without calling a single public meeting or arousing popular indignation by any other means than his written revelations, quietly awaited the marvellous success which he deserved and obtained.

Although the description of Dotheboys Hall takes

up a very short part of this long story, it perhaps engrosses attention more than any other. Poor Nicholas and Smike, however, probably try to forget it; and by the help of Newman Noggs the former gets some employment, while his sister Kate has also her own trials and troubles, among which her life at the Mantalinis' dressmaking establishment is described in the most amusing way. These Mantalinis have thus Italianised their real English name of Muntle owing to the popularity of foreign taste and style in dress, which Dickens mentions very sarcastically. The first introduction of the Mantalinis, the absurd, conceited, rather cunning spendthrift, and the vain, silly wife, explains their characters at once; and Miss Nickleby, when calling at their house, overhears their private conversation in the next room to where she was waiting:

"If you will be odiously, demnebly, out*ri*geously jealous, my soul," said Mr. Mantalini, "you will be very miserable."

"I *am* miserable," returned Madame Mantalini, evidently pouting.

"Then you are an ungrateful, unworthy, demd unthankful little fairy," said Mr. Mantalini.

"I am not," returned Madame with a sob. . . . "You were flirting with her during the whole night," said Madame Mantalini, . . . "and I say once more that you ought not to waltz with anybody but your own wife, and I will not bear it, Mantalini, if I take poison first. . . ."

"She will not take poison and have horrid pains, will she?" said Mr. Mantalini, "because she had a demd fine husband, who might have married two countesses and a dowager."

"Two countesses," interposed Madame; "you told me one before."

"Two!" cried Mantalini. "Two demd fine women. . . ."

"And why didn't you?" asked Madame playfully.

"Why didn't I?" replied her husband. "Had I not seen at a

morning concert, the demdest little fascinator in all the world, and while that little fascinator is my wife, may not all the countesses and dowagers in England be——"

Mr. Mantalini did not finish the sentence, but gave Madame Mantalini a very loud kiss, which Madame returned. . . .

"And what about the cash, my existence's jewel?" said Mantalini. "How much have we in hand?" . . .

"You can't want any more just now," said Madame coaxingly.

"My life and soul," returned her husband, "there is a horse for sale at Scrubbs's. . . going, my senses' joy for nothing. . . . A hundred guineas down will buy him; mane and crest and legs and tail, all of the demdest beauty. I will ride him in the park before the very chariots of the rejected countesses. The demd old dowager will faint with grief and rage, the other two will say, 'He is married, he has made away with himself, it is a demd thing, it is all up!' They will hate each other demnebly and wish you dead and buried. Ha! ha! Demmit!"

Madame Mantalini's prudence, if she had any, was not proof against these triumphal pictures. After a little jingling of keys, she observed that she would see what her desk contained." [1]

Kate is sadly teased, worried, and overworked by the affected Madame Mantalini and the spiteful Miss Knag, her assistant, who is jealous of her beauty, which is unfortunately admired by the customers; yet still she suffers no hardships like what her brother has experienced. It happens that a young lady with her elderly future spouse calls at Madame Mantalini's, when the lady, seeing Miss Knag watching her curiously, exclaims petulantly to Madame Mantalini:

"Of all things in the world, . . . I hate being waited upon by frights or elderly persons. Let me always see that young creature, I beg, whenever I come. . . ."

"She *is* universally admired," replied Madame Mantalini. "Miss Knag, send up Miss Nickleby. You needn't return."

When these customers have gone, poor Kate

[1] Chap. xvii.

returns downstairs, where she finds and experiences a curious scene:

In place of Miss Knag being stationed in her accustomed seat, preserving all the dignity and greatness of Madame Mantalini's establishment, that worthy soul was reposing on a large box, bathed in tears, while three or four of the young ladies in close attendance upon her, together with the presence of hartshorn, vinegar, and other restoratives, would have borne ample testimony, even without the derangement of the head-dress and front row of curls, to her having fainted desperately.

"Bless me!" said Kate. "What is the matter?"

"Matter," cried Miss Knag, suddenly coming all at once bolt upright, to the great consternation of the assembled maidens. "Matter! Fie upon you, you nasty creature. . . . Here she is," continued Miss Knag getting off the box . . . "here she is, everybody is talking about her—the belle, ladies—the beauty, the—oh, you bold-faced thing!"

At this crisis Miss Knag was unable to repress a virtuous shudder: . . . after which Miss Knag laughed, and after that cried.

"For fifteen years," exclaimed Miss Knag, sobbing in a most affecting manner, "for fifteen years have I been the credit and ornament of this room and the one upstairs. Thank God," said Miss Knag, stamping first her right foot and then her left with remarkable energy, "I have never in all that time, till now, been exposed to the arts, the vile arts, of a creature who disgraces us all with her proceedings, and makes proper people blush for themselves." [1]

But Kate's greatest trial comes when her uncle Ralph invites her to meet his gay, profligate acquaintances, Lord Frederick Verisopht and Sir Mulberry Hawk, at his house, with no other lady there. These guests are two of Ralph's business acquaintances, Verisopht being a silly, rich young dupe of the old usurer; and his companion, Sir Mulberry, a fierce bully and duellist, who, already ruined himself, now

[1] Chap. xviii.

lives upon young Verisopht, whom, in alliance with Ralph, the moneylender, he is robbing effectually. Ralph, by this introduction, probably hopes that Verisopht may marry his niece; but it is clear he cares little if he marries or makes her his mistress, provided by her attraction he can retain and strengthen his hold on the rich young victim.

Previous to this abominable transaction, Nicholas and Smike leave London, joining a travelling party of actors in the provinces, and both rather like their new way of life. This theatrical company, managed by a Mr. and Mrs. Crummles, are most amusingly described. Mr. Crummles's praises of his professional pony to Nicholas, while driving towards the theatre in Portsmouth, are intensely comical:

"Many and many is the circuit that pony has gone," said Mr. Crummles, . . . "he is quite one of us. His mother was on the stage . . . she ate apple-pie at a circus . . . fired pistols, and went to bed in a nightcap, and in short took low comedy entirely. His father was a dancer."

Nicholas asks if he was at all distinguished.

"Not very," said the manager. "He was rather a low sort of pony . . . When the mother died he took the port-wine business . . . Drinking port-wine with the clown, but he was greedy and one night bit off the bowl of the glass, and choked himself, so that his vulgarity was the death of him at last."

When they arrive at the theatre the manager's little daughter, whom the other actors, at least in his presence, call "The infant phenomenon," is acting a combat with a savage personated by a Mr. Folair. At the end of this rather long mock encounter:

The savage and the maiden danced violently together, and finally, the savage dropped down on one knee and the maiden stood on one leg upon his other knee, thus concluding the ballet, and leaving the spectators in a state of pleasing uncertainty whether she would ultimately marry the savage, or return to her friends. . . . "This, sir,' said Mr. Vincent Crummles bringing the maiden forward, "this is the infant phenomenon, Miss Ninetta Crummles."

While praising his daughter and saying she is only ten years old, the gentleman who had been acting the savage came up :

"Talent there, sir," said the savage nodding towards Miss Crummles." . . .

"Ah!" said the actor, "she is too good for country boards . . . she ought to be in one of the large houses in London . . . Did you ever see such a set-out as that?" whispered the actor, . . . as Crummles left them to speak to his wife . . .

"You don't mean the infant phenomenon?"

Nicholas believes, apparently, that the girl is so acknowledged by the theatrical company, but he is soon undeceived :—

"Infant humbug, sir," replied Mr. Folair. "There isn't a female child of common sharpness in a charity school, that couldn't do better than that. She may thank her stars she was born a manager's daughter. . . . Isn't it enough to make a man crusty to see that little sprawler put up in the best business every night and actually keeping money out of the house by being forced down people's throats, while other people are passed over? Isn't it extraordinary to see a man's confounded family conceit blinding him even to his own interest? Why I *know* of fifteen and sixpence that came to Southampton one night last month to see me dance the Highland Fling; and what's the consequence? I've never been put up since—never once—while the infant phenomenon has been grinning through artificial flowers at five people and a baby in the pit, and two boys in the gallery, every night." [1]

Yet it seems remarkable that Dickens, himself

[1] Chap. xxxiii.

such an excellent actor and so fond of promoting theatrical amusement, should describe these actors and their ways with such ridicule, though without any bitterness. His doing so, despite his own private tastes, rather recalls Walter Scott's good-humoured ridicule of antiquarian enthusiasm, though himself so fond of antiquarian research.[1] Dickens, while causing his readers to laugh heartily at the Crummleses and their company, yet makes most of them amusing and interesting to the public, who are sometimes inclined to view and treat actors with contempt or prejudice. Nicholas writes a play for his fellow-performers, and is asked anxiously by Mr. Folair and a Mr. Lenville, the last a tragedian, what parts he is assigning to them in his coming production:

> "What do you do for me?" asked Mr. Lenville. . . . "Anything in the gruff and grumble way?"
>
> "You turn your wife and child out of doors," said Nicholas, "and, in a fit of rage and jealousy, stab your eldest son in the library."
>
> "Do I though?" said Mr. Lenville. "That's very good business."
>
> "After which," said Nicholas, "you are troubled with remorse till the last act and then you make up your mind to destroy yourself. But just as you are raising the pistol to your head a clock strikes—ten."
>
> "I see," said Mr. Lenville; "very good."
>
> "You pause," said Nicholas, "you recollect to have heard a clock strike ten in your infancy. The pistol falls from your hand—you are overcome—you burst into tears and become a virtuous and exemplary character for ever afterwards."
>
> "Capital," said Mr. Lenville; "that's a sure card, a sure card. Get the curtain down with a touch of nature like that and it'll be a triumphant success."

[1] "The Antiquary," chap. xxxi.

"Is there anything for me?" inquired Mr. Folair anxiously.

"Let me see," said Nicholas, "you play the faithful and attached servant; you are turned out of doors with the wife and child."

"Always coupled with that infernal phenomenon," sighed Mr. Folair.[1]

Nicholas is suddenly recalled from theatrical emotions and excitements to those of real life. Newman Noggs, the steady friend of the young Nicklebys and the honest servant of the old one, apprises Nicholas of his sister's persecution by Sir Mulberry and Lord Verisopht, and he hurries to her rescue. Ralph's conduct to his niece seems rather contradictory, and hardly consistent with the utter hard heart and savage temper which he invariably displays in every other part of the story. He admits to himself that if it were not for Mrs. Nickleby and Nicholas, his house should be Kate's home.

In that one glimpse of a better nature, born as it was in selfish thoughts, the rich man felt himself friendless, childless, and alone.

These feelings seem hardly natural in a man like Ralph; if capable of such, he would probably not have hated Kate's brother from the first so bitterly without the least cause, real or imaginary. He makes no complaint against his nephew; he simply from the first dreads being burdened, annoyed, or in any way involved with poor relations. In short, there seems nothing in Ralph's conduct towards every one which does not manifest the same thoroughly hardened, unfeeling character, confirmed and intensified by old age. Moreover, at the very time when he thus relents towards Kate, he is actively encouraging the

[1] Chap. xxiv.

dangerous addresses to her of the two profligates, the bully and the dupe, Sir Mulberry and Lord Verisopht. It is difficult to understand exactly what Ralph's feelings towards Kate are at this juncture—the only part of the story, however, in which his hardened, consistent nature seems vacillating. While he mainly causes his niece's persecution by these men, he is described as angry with them all the time for doing precisely what he wished them to do. Dickens himhimself seems rather puzzled by the conduct he imputes to Ralph Nickleby in the following passage:

> It is one of those problems of human nature which may be noted down, but not solved—although Ralph felt no remorse at that moment towards the innocent, true-hearted girl, although his libertine clients had done precisely what he had expected, precisely what he had most wished, and precisely what would most tend to his advantage, still he hated them for doing it from the very bottom of his soul.[1]

Many mean and worthless people might thus hesitate between their better feelings and their interest, but Ralph never before or after this time appears capable of any hesitation between such influences. His conduct throughout is thoroughly consistent up to this time, when he certainly appears to feel emotions hardly compatible with his character. When Nicholas leaves the actors in the provinces, most of the company much regret his departure. They are described—the Crummleses and Snevelliccis—as pompous and affected people with some good qualities, and a very large allowance of envy and jealousy. In describing the nervous anxiety of country acting companies when visited by a London theatre manager,

[1] Chap. xxviii.

Dickens and Thackeray much resemble each other, and likely both these London writers described what they had frequently observed and witnessed. In this respect Thackeray's Bingley and company and Dickens's Crummles and company are much alike in similar exciting circumstances. Thackeray says of Mr. Dolphin, the London manager, witnessing a play in the country:

He had not been ten minutes in the theatre, before his august presence there was perceived by Bingley and the rest and they all began to act their best and try to engage his attention. . . . In vain the various actors tried to win the favour of the great stage Sultan. . . . Bingley yelled and Mrs. Bingley bellowed and the manager only took snuff out of his great gold box. It was only in the last scene,[1] when Rolla comes in staggering with the infant to Cora [acted by Miss Costigan], who rushes forward with a shriek and says, "O God, there's blood upon him," that the London manager clapped his hands, gave his secretary a slap on the shoulder and said, "By Jove, Billy, she'll do."[2]

Dickens thus describes Crummles and his company when likewise visited in their theatre at Portsmouth by a London manager:

Everybody happened to know that the London manager had come down specially to witness his or her own performance, and all were in a flutter of anxiety and expectation. . . . Once the London manager was seen to smile—he smiled at the comic countryman's pretending to catch a blue-bottle while Mrs. Crummles was making her greatest effort. "Very good, my fine fellow," said Mr. Crummles, shaking his fist at the comic countryman when he came off, "you leave this company next Saturday night." . . . At length the London manager was discovered to be asleep, and shortly after that he woke up and went away, whereupon all the company fell foul of the unhappy comic countryman, declaring that his buffoonery was the sole cause.[3]

---

[1] Sheridan's "Pizarro."

[2] "Pendennis," chap. xiv.

[3] Chap. xxx.

This theatrical company, however, is rather a favourable contrast to that described in "Gil Blas," though there is some resemblance between the two sketches. Very few authors of fiction have described this class; which is surprising, considering the interest with which their efforts and talents inspire the general public. But Dickens evidently enjoys their descriptions, and the lives of Nicholas and Smike among them are very pleasant and cheerful, and a happy change from the Yorkshire school.

Nicholas, on reaching London, has a violent scene with Sir Mulberry Hawk, whom he overhears ridiculing his sister in a public coffee-room. During this quarrel blows are exchanged, and Sir Mulberry is thrown from his gig, in which this midnight fracas occurs, and severely injured. Nicholas then rescues his sister from any further intercourse with their odious uncle, between whom and themselves there is now a complete and permanent breach, while poor Mrs. Nickleby, whose silliness is half-amusing, half-provoking, is nearly as much inclined to blame Nicholas as her brother-in-law. But the dawn of good fortune now shines upon the poor brother and sister, for two excellent new characters, the Brothers Cheeryble, rich London merchants, elderly men, and delightful contrasts to Ralph Nickleby, now employ Nicholas in their house of business, and, with their worthy clerk, Tim Linkinwater, become his firm friend and benefactors throughout. Dickens, with sincere pleasure, tells his readers that these brothers were drawn from real life at the time he was writing this book, though, of course, bearing different names.[1]

[1] They were Manchester merchants, according to Mr. Forster.

They appear in good time to support Nicholas and Smike; for the numerous villains in this story, among whom Ralph is the centre and the master mind, are all in London plotting against them in different ways. Sir Mulberry, incited by Ralph while recovering from his injuries, vows vengeance against Nicholas, and Mr. Squeers now reappears in London, eager to regain possession of Smike, who certainly was a very useful drudge at Dotheboys Hall. He is, indeed, actually caught, or rather kidnapped in London streets, and carried off by Squeers to his lodgings, preparatory to being conveyed to Yorkshire, and there undergoing a long arrear of flogging; but John Browdie rescues him, to the great relief of the reader. Ralph Nickleby and Squeers, however, now more united than ever by their common hatred to Nicholas, devise a plot with an old hypocrite named Snawley, pretending that Smike is the latter's son, and they accordingly claim him, but are successfully repelled by Nicholas, assisted by John Browdie.

During all this time Ralph continues to inflame Sir Mulberry Hawk's rage against Nicholas, and Sir Mulberry actually contrives, and partially divulges to Lord Verisopht, a plot to waylay and beat Nicholas savagely, somewhere in the streets of London. Sir Mulberry says he will not make his intended attack on Nicholas

> a case of murder; but it shall be something very near it, if whipcord cuts and bludgeons bruise.[1]

In this half-revealed plot he is actively aided by Ralph. This seems a strange idea for a fashionable

[1] Chap. l.

“man about town” like Sir Mulberry to contemplate. Unscrupulous and vindictive as he is, he would surely know English law and the usages of modern society too well to suppose he could either commit, or authorise others to commit, a dangerous assault in London, without the greatest risk to himself. In former times such assaults in London streets were common enough, in days when rich or fashionable profligates had ruffians in their pay, and when the imperfect state of the law rendered its defiance or evasion comparatively easy. For instance, in the reign of Charles II., the Duke of Buckingham, or other licentious courtiers, might have thus wreaked their secret vengeance on enemies whose lower rank precluded them from being challenged to a duel with rapiers or pistols. But during the nineteenth century, when the events in “Nickleby” are supposed to occur, such murderous outrages in London streets, authorised by men in Sir Mulberry's social position, were seldom, if ever, known. However, Sir Mulberry's sudden quarrel with his young dupe, Lord Verisopht, whom he shoots in a duel, drives him abroad for a time, while Nicholas has quite enemies enough to deal with in London, of whom Ralph is always the chief.

A suitable heroine for Nicholas is now rather mysteriously introduced—a certain Miss Madeline Bray, only child of a selfish and ruined invalid. Mr. Bray is completely in the power of an old moneylender named Arthur Gride, a friend and ally of Ralph's, whom he much resembles, though he is older and both more amorous and timid at the same time, for Ralph Nickleby seems equally incapable of either love or terror. Gride has an old, deaf, cunning housekeeper, Peg Sliderskew, who naturally enough disapproves of a handsome young mistress being put over her. She tries to warn her old miser of a master against his intended young bride:

"Take care you don't find good looks come expensive."

"But she can earn money herself, Peg," said Arthur Gride, . . . "she can draw, paint, work all manner of pretty things. . . . She'll be very cheap to dress and keep, Peg; don't you think she will?"

"If you don't let her make a fool of you, she may," returned Peg.

"A fool of *me!*" exclaimed Arthur. "Trust your old master not to be fooled by pretty faces, Peg; no, no, no—nor by ugly ones neither, Mrs. Sliderskew," he softly added by way of soliloquy.

"You're a-saying something you don't want me to hear," said Peg; "I know you are."

"Oh dear! the devil's in this woman," muttered Arthur; adding with an ugly leer, "I said I trusted everything to you, Peg, that was all."

"You do that, master, and all your cares are over," said Peg approvingly.

"*When* I do that, Peg Sliderskew," thought Arthur Gride, "they will be." [1]

Old Arthur, however, is now bent upon marrying Miss Bray; and she consents, to save her father, who is in Gride's debt, and therefore quite in his power. Nicholas is acquainted with Madeline's character and sad position through the Brothers Cheeryble, while old Arthur makes Ralph his confidant, and thus the uncle and nephew are again opposed in this matter as they have been all through the story. The sudden death of Mr. Bray occurs most opportunely, just before his daughter's marriage with his hateful old creditor. The disappointed suitor, on returning home, finds his old housekeeper has disappeared, taking with

[1] Chap. li.

her certain valuable articles, and among them an important paper which the knavish usurer had kept concealed, and by which Miss Bray is entitled to some property. This precious document Ralph sets Mr. Squeers to find; and that worthy soon discovers the housekeeper, Peg Sliderskew, and a very comic scene ensues between them, when they are themselves fortunately tracked and detected by Newman Noggs and a nephew of the Brothers Cheeryble. These two recover the precious paper, and thus Ralph, Squeers, and Arthur Gride, the three old villains of the story, are alike baffled and disconcerted. Squeers and Gride, previously almost tools in the hands of Ralph, a far bolder man than either, now begin to distrust and fall from him. Both Squeers and old Arthur are amusing rogues in their different ways, despite their common villainy; Ralph alone is grave, stern, and hard as flint itself—nothing, indeed, amusing in him, but everything to abhor and dread. When Ralph visits Squeers, after the latter's arrest, the latter is half tipsy, and all the more amusing; his mental confusion being intensely comic at this juncture. Squeers firmly refuses, however, to aid Ralph any more, and bewails the certain downfall of Dotheboys Hall, with half-drunk, pathetic solemnity:

> "My moral influence with them lads is a-tottering to its basis. The images of Mrs. Squeers, my daughter, and my son Wackford, all short of vittles, are perpetually before me; every other consideration melts away, and vanishes in front of these, and the only number in all arithmetic that I know of, as a husband and a father, is number one, under this here most fatal go."[1]

---

[1] Chap. lx.

Arthur Gride now disappears altogether, having lost his expected bride, his old housekeeper, and his papers at one blow. Mr. Squeers is imprisoned for being found in possession of the stolen document; while Ralph's other tool, Mr. Snawley, confesses he is not Smike's father, and deserts Ralph, like the others. The latter, while plotting more villainy, is now confronted with a former acquaintance of his, a man named Brooker, through whom the startling discovery is made that Smike, the unknown, ill-used youth, was Ralph's only son, long supposed to be dead. This revelation is made to Ralph Nickleby at night by both Newman Noggs and Brooker, before the Brothers Cheeryble. The effect of this communication, loss of money, defeat of his knavish schemes, and the complete triumph of Nicholas, drive even this hardened old usurer to virtual madness, and he commits suicide the next morning when alone in his own house. When he is gone all danger and difficulty disappear also. Nicholas is to be married to Miss Bray, and Kate to young Mr. Cheeryble, while Squeers is transported, and Dotheboys Hall school finally broken up, amid loud uproar among the liberated pupils.[1]

Newman Noggs, Miss La Creevy, and all the numerous good "oddities" in the book end well and happily, and thus the story, in which mirth and sadness, comedy and tragedy, are blended with remarkable skill and effect, is brought to a very satisfactory close. In reviewing "Nicholas Nickleby"

[1] "The discovery is made, Ralph is dead, the loves have all come right, and I have now only to break up Dotheboys and the book together" (Dickens's letter to Forster, "Life of Dickens," vol. i.).

throughout, this skilful mixture of sad and comic scenes makes it difficult to say if the book is cheerful or not till the happy end decides the question to the sympathetic reader's comfort and relief. While the good and bad characters are contending with about equal energy, perseverance, and even violence, there are a vast number of others who, though taking little part in the story, help to enliven it immensely, and have, indeed, combined to render it the general favourite it always was from the first. Among these comparatively unimportant personages, the Mantalinis, with their affectation, vanity, and quarrels, are perhaps the most orginal and amusing. Mr. Mantalini has six times successfully pretended to poison himself, thus frightening his silly wife into paying his many debts, on condition of his consenting to live. On the seventh poisoning occasion, however, Madame Mantalini, now nearly ruined, at last distrusts him, and Ralph Nickleby, who has often lent money to Mantalini, calls at his house, and finds him lying extended on the floor, his wife and Miss Knag and several milliner girls around him:

Mr. Mantalini's eyes were closed and his face was pale . . . and his teeth were clenched and he had a little bottle in his right hand and a little teaspoon in his left, and his hands, arms, legs and shoulders were all stiff and powerless. And yet Madame Mantalini was not weeping upon the body, but scolding violently upon her chair, and all this amid a clamour of tongues perfectly deafening.

. . . . .

" Mr. Nickleby," said Madame Mantalini, " by what chance you came here, I don't know."

Here a gurgling noise was heard to ejaculate—as part of the wanderings of a sick man—the words " Demnition sweetness ! " but nobody heeded them. [Madame Mantalini then declares that she will never trust her husband again with money.] . . . Quite unmoved by some most pathetic lamentations on the part of her husband that the apothecary had not mixed the prussic acid strong enough,

and adds that Miss Knag has now possession of the house and all the stock it contains. Madame Mantalini after this admission leaves the room, and the old-moneylender, Ralph, leaves the house, saying to himself in bitter sarcasm about the ruined Mantalini, by whose reckless folly he has considerably profited:

"... Half knave and half fool and detected in both characters —I think your day is over, sir."[1]

But a last glimpse of the unfortunate spendthrift Mantalini is given in chapter lxiv., when Nicholas and Kate, walking in a by-street, hear the following dialogue between a man and a woman, from a cellar they are passing:

"You nasty, idle, vicious, good-for-nothing brute," cried the woman, stamping on the ground, "why don't you turn the mangle?"

"So I am, my life and soul!" replied a man's voice, "I am always turning, I am perpetually turning, like a demd old horse in demnition mill. My life is one demd horrid grind!"

Kate now recognises the tone of Mr. Mantalini, while her brother, creeping down some steps,

looked into a small boarded cellar. There amidst clothes-baskets and clothes, stripped to his shirt-sleeves . . . there endeavouring to mollify the wrath of a buxom female, the proprietress of the concern, and grinding meanwhile as if for very life at the mangle, whose creaking noise, mingled with her shrill tones, appeared almost

[1] Chap. xliv.

to deafen him—there was the graceful, elegant, fascinating, and once dashing Mantalini. . . .

"You're never to be trusted," screamed the woman. "You were out all day yesterday and gallivanting somewhere. Isn't it strange that I paid two pounds fourteen for you, and took you out of prison, and let you live here like a gentleman, but must you go on like this; breaking my heart besides?"

"I will never break its heart, I will be a good boy and never do so any more; I will never be naughty again; I beg its little pardon," said Mr. Mantalini, dropping the handle of the mangle and folding his palms together. "It's all up with its handsome friend, he has gone to the demnition bow-wows. It will have pity? It will not scratch and claw but pet and comfort? Oh, demmit."

Very little affected, to judge from her action, by this tender appeal, the lady was on the point of returning some angry reply, when Nicholas, raising his voice, asked his way to Piccadilly. Mr. Mantalini turned round, caught sight of Kate, and without another word, leapt at one bound into a bed which stood behind the door and drew the counterpane over his face, kicking meanwhile convulsively.

"Demmit," he cried, in a suffocating voice. "It's little Nickleby! Shut the door, put out the candle, turn me up in the bedstead! Oh, dem, dem, dem!"

The woman looked first at Nicholas and then at Mr. Mantalini, as if uncertain on whom to visit this extraordinary behaviour, but Mr. Mantalini happening by ill-luck to thrust his nose from under the bed-clothes, in his anxiety to ascertain whether the visitors were gone, she suddenly and with a dexterity which could only have been acquired by long practice, flung a pretty heavy clothes-basket at him with so good an aim that he kicked more violently than before, though without venturing to disengage his head, which was quite extinguished.

The Kenwigses and Mr. Lillyvick are more like people described in the "Sketches," and extremely comic. Mr. Lillyvick, a pompous and rather rich water-rate collector and a bachelor, is uncle to Mrs. Kenwigs. The Kenwigses are a worthy, united couple, speaking in a strong London accent, devoted to the interests of their numerous children, to whom they confidently expect that Mr. Lillyvick will leave his money. But he unexpectedly marries an actress, Miss Petowker, who for a time seems engaged in Mr. Crummles' company and is most intimate with them; when the Kenwigses hear of this marriage, they are alike shocked, enraged, and grieved. But Mrs. Lillyvick soon elopes with a certain Captain, and the deserted husband returns to tell the news to the Kenwigses. The two speeches of Mr. Kenwigs before and after he hears of Mrs. Lillyvick's elopement are two masterpieces of equally comic indignation and comic forgiveness; while selfishness and devotion to his little ones prevail in both. Lillyvick, before telling of his wife's elopement, says:

"Kenwigs, . . . shake hands."

"Sir," said Mr. Kenwigs, "the time has been when I was proud to shake hands with such a man, as that man as now surweys me. . . . But now I look upon that man with emotion totally surpassing everything and I ask myself where is his honour, where is his straightforwardness, and where is his human nature?"

"Susan Kenwigs," said Mr. Lillyvick, turning humbly to his niece, "don't you say anything to me?"

"She's not equal to it, sir," said Mr. Kenwigs, striking the table emphatically. "What with the nursing of a healthy babby, and the reflections upon your cruel conduct, four pints of malt liquor a day is hardly able to sustain her."

"I am glad," said the poor collector meekly, "that the baby is a healthy one. I am very glad of that."

This was touching the Kenwigses on their tenderest point. Mrs. Kenwigs immediately burst into tears, and Mr. Kenwigs evinced great emotion.

"My pleasantest feeling all the time that child was expected," said Mr. Kenwigs mournfully, "was a thinking . . . 'if it's a boy what will his uncle Lillyvick say—what will he like him to be called—will he be Peter, or Alexander, or Diogenes, or what will he be?' And now when I look at him, a precious, unconscious, helpless infant; with no use in his little arms but to tear his little cap, with no use in his legs but to kick his little self . . . when I see him such a infant as he is, and think that that uncle Lillyvick, as was once a-going to be so fond of him, has withdrawed himself away, such a feeling of vengeance comes over me as no language can depicter, and I feel as if even that holy babe was a-telling me to hate him."

Mrs. Kenwigs then exclaims in tears, that she never will receive Mrs. Lillyvick, which causes Lillyvick to tell the truth that his wife has left him, finally exclaiming :

. . . " It was in this room that I first see Henrietta Petowker. It is in this room that I turn her off, for ever."

This declaration completely changed the whole posture of affairs.

Lillyvick continues that he means now to settle his money next day on the Kenwigs children, and this "noble and generous offer" completes the reconciliation.

"And now," said Mr. Lillyvick . . . "give me some supper. . . . I came up this morning and have been lingering about all day without being able to see you."

Then reverting to his runaway wife :

. . . " I humoured her in everything, she had her own way, she did just as she pleased, and now she has done this. There was twelve teaspoons and twenty-four pounds in sovereigns—I missed them first—it's a trial—I feel I shall never be able to knock a double knock again when I go my rounds—don't say anything more about it, please—the spoons were worth—never mind, never mind."

This chapter ends very cheerfully, however, with Mr. Kenwigs's happy reflections on Mr. Lillyvick's return :

"When I see that man," said Mr. Kenwigs, "a-mingling once again in the spear which he adorns, and see his affections deweloping themselves in legitimate sitiwations, I feel that his nature is as elewated and expanded as his standing afore society as a public character is unimpeached, and the woices of my infant children purvided for in life, seem to whisper to me softly, 'This is an ewent at which Evins itself looks down.'"[1]

The love-scene between Mrs. Nickleby and the old madman is almost too absurd for possibility, yet is most amusing, and admirably related. This old man looking over the wall of the place where he is confined, makes a confused sort of love to Mrs. Nickleby when walking with Kate. The latter at once suspects and fears him, as either mad or dangerous, while Mrs. Nickleby, herself little better than a fool practically, though an amiable one, persists in listening complacently to a long rambling set of speeches from the old madman till at length he comes to the point:

. . . "I am not a youth, ma'am, as you see, and although beings like me can never grow old, I venture to presume that we are fitted for each other."

"Really, Kate, my love," said Mrs. Nickleby faintly, and looking another way.

"I have estates, ma'am," said the old gentleman . . . speaking very fast, "jewels, lighthouses, fish-ponds, a whalery of my own in the North Sea and several oyster-beds of great profit in the Pacific Ocean. . . . I have enemies about me, ma'am," he looked towards his house and spoke very low, "who attack me on all occasions, and wish to secure my property. If you bless me with your hand and heart, you can apply to the Lord Chancellor, or call out the military if necessary—sending my toothpick to the commander-in-chief will be sufficient—and so clear the house of them before the ceremony is performed. After that love, bliss and rapture, rapture, love and bliss. Be mine, be mine."

. . . . .

"Kate, my dear," said Mrs. Nickleby, "I have hardly the power

[1] Chap. xx.

to speak, but it is necessary for the happiness of all parties that this matter should be set at rest for ever."

. . . . .

"Be mine, be mine," cried the old gentleman.

"It can scarcely be expected, sir," said Mrs. Nickleby, fixing her eyes modestly on the ground, "that I should tell a stranger whether I feel flattered by such proposals or not. . . ."

"Be mine, be mine," cried the old gentleman. "Gog and Magog, Gog and Magog. Be mine, be mine!"

"It will be sufficient for me to say, sir," resumed Mrs. Nickleby with perfect seriousness, "and I am sure you will see the propriety of taking an answer and going away—that I have made up my mind to remain a widow and to devote myself to my children. You may not suppose I am the mother of two children—indeed, many people have doubted it, and said that nothing on earth could ever make 'em believe it possible—but it is the case and they are both grown up. . . . It's a very painful thing to have to reject proposals, and I would much rather that none were made; at the same time this is the answer that I determined long ago to make, and this is the answer that I shall always give."

At this decisive reply, the keeper comes and pulls the amatory old gentleman by the legs from the wall, asks the ladies if he has been making love to them, and it is a plain fact he is out of his mind; Kate kindly asks if there is no hope for him, and the keeper's answer, though likely true, is peculiar:

. . . "He's a deal pleasanter without his senses than with 'em. He was the cruellest, wickedest, out-and-outered old flint that ever drawed breath. . . . I never came across such a vagabond, and my mate says the same. . . . Hope for *him*, an old rip! There isn't too much hope going, but I'll bet a crown that what there is, is saved for more deserving chaps than him anyhow."

He departs, but Mrs. Nickleby still believes in her old lover's sanity and gives her reasons to Kate:

"It's some plot of these people to possess themselves of his property—didn't he say so himself? He may be a little odd and flighty, perhaps, many of us are that, but downright mad! and express himself as he does, respectfully, and in quite poetical language, and making offers with so much thought and care and prudence—not as if he ran into the streets and went down upon his knees to the first chit of a girl he met, as a madman would! No, no, Kate, there's a great deal too much method in *his* madness; depend upon that, my dear."

Readers are forced to laugh constantly at these comic scenes which are so skilfully mingled with others of tragic interest in this story. There are more, perhaps, prominent characters in this book than in either "Pickwick" or "Oliver Twist." Dickens, instead of inclining decidedly to comic description, as in the former, or to the pathetic, as in the latter, indulges in both styles pretty equally in "Nickleby" by presenting cheerful and melancholy scenes and characters almost alternately, till at the end he kindly and wisely closes the story cheerfully, gratifying his readers, and probably himself also, by rewarding goodness and punishing evil as thoroughly as they usually are in a "good fairy" tale. Throughout this excellent story, as in some others, Dickens occasionally makes philosophical remarks. These observations well express the singular purity of his mind, united to a command of eloquent language, which might in some respects have fitted him for a writer on moral philosophy.

When Nicholas wonders that Smike feels no affection for his pretended father Snawley, whom Nicholas fears is his real one, Mr. Cheeryble, who evidently expresses Dickens's sentiments, replies:

"You fall into the very common mistake of charging upon Nature matters with which she has not the smallest connection, and for which she is in no sense responsible! Parents who never showed their love, complain of want of natural affection in their children—children who never showed their duty, complain of want of natural feeling in their parents—law-makers who find both so miserable that their affections have never had enough of life's sun to develop them, are loud in their moralising over parents and children too, and cry that the very ties of Nature are disregarded. Natural affections and instincts are the most beautiful of the Almighty's works, but, like other beautiful works of His, they must be reared and fostered, or it is as natural that they should be wholly obscured, and that new feelings should usurp their place, as it is that the sweetest productions of the earth left unattended should be choked with weeds and briers. I wish we could be brought to consider this, and, remembering natural obligations a little more at the right time, talk about them a little less at the wrong one."[1]

Of all Dickens's earlier works, none introduces more characters than "Nicholas Nickleby": it is a perfect hive of fanciful humanity, all working, busily indeed, for good or evil; virtue, vice, folly, and wisdom are mingled together, until their incarnations are finally disentangled and satisfactorily disposed of. Few readers would wish the least change in the final settlement of the different personages, except in one instance—the death of Smike—caused, partly, at least, from the effects of disappointed love. However, his survival might have involved him with his detestable father Ralph, who never discovers their relationship till soon after Smike's death, or, consistently with his ruling passion of hatred to Nicholas, he would either have restored him to Mr. Squeers or tormented him in some way himself. The chief impression left by "Nickleby," after a due amount of grateful admiration for its author, are, first, horrified astonishment at its exposure of some Yorkshire

[1] Chap. xiv.

schools; and secondly, sincere wonder at the profound and accurate knowledge it shows of London life and people. Except when describing Dotheboys and a short professional tour in the provinces, the story is laid entirely in London, and chiefly among the middle classes. No ladies and only two gentlemen of rank are described, and no clergymen or country gentlemen of any importance. There are no historical, classical, or political allusions, nor any theological discussions: neither are any of the villains, though bad enough in all conscience, in the same rank of life as Fagin or Sikes. No lawyers, good, bad, or indifferent, are introduced either in these pages, which, notwithstanding so many omissions, are of surprising interest throughout. While "Pickwick" caused so much laughter, and "Oliver Twist" such horror and sympathy, "Nickleby" inspired all these emotions, rather in a less degree, though singularly combined. But in its instructiveness when describing and sustaining an immense variety of characters with perfect consistency, it seems to rather surpass or at least fully equal its two celebrated predecessors.

CONCLUDING REMARKS ON DICKENS

CHAPTER III

CONCLUDING REMARKS ON DICKENS

IT is evident that reading aloud his works to large public audiences greatly fatigued Mr. Dickens's bodily powers, and probably hastened his death.[1] He always exerted himself so ardently in whatever he wrote or read, that when describing exciting or pathetic scenes, he felt, and even suffered, as if personally witnessing or enduring what he described with such extraordinary power. It is said by the philosopher Locke that all human ideas are derived from either observation or reflection. Throughout Dickens's works his powers of observation are, on the whole, perhaps, more original and remarkable than those of his reflection. The reason probably was that his observation was so wonderfully correct, as well as keen and intelligent, that he needed reflection less than most people in forming a judgment of men and things. Reflection usually follows as the assistant to erring observation, often slightly altering, and sometimes completely changing, previous impressions or ideas. But respecting Dickens, neither his own reflections nor those of others could usually have done otherwise than confirm the consistent, and almost unvarying, truth of his

[1] Forster's "Life of Dickens," vol. iii.

observation.[1] His personal appearance, perhaps, confirmed this estimate of his powers. His forehead, though high, was not very remarkable; but the keen brilliancy of his large, expressive eyes, and the intellectual force and power which their searching glance revealed, have probably been seldom equalled, either in pictures or in real life. They apparently proclaimed his mental powers, without the aid or confirmation of words. He understood characters with marvellous quickness, upon the slightest acquaintance, owing to his perceptive powers, and thus described them with such admirable accuracy. Whether he could have turned their various qualities to good account, like an able Prime Minister or general, is another question, and from his position in life was never proved. Except through the medium of literature he never acquired, or tried to acquire, much influence over others. He personally abstained altogether from politics, and seldom alludes to them in his books. The main objects of his writings were apparently to draw together the different classes of modern English society into a more friendly union than he found them; to expose legal mismanagement and abuses; to condemn harshness and cruelty to children especially, either in schools, workhouses, or in private life; and to check that engrossing spirit of avarice so common among an urban population, with which he himself was chiefly acquainted.

[1] "Out of his unequalled observation, his satire and his sensibility has produced a series of original characters, existing nowhere but in England, which will exhibit to future generations, not the record of his own genius only but that of his country and his times" (Forster's "Life of Dickens," vol. iii.).

Few, if any, novelists delight in describing children like Dickens, and, perhaps, none have ever made them so attractive. Shakespeare and Scott seldom introduce them. In the "Monastery" the little Glendinning brothers are both natural and interesting, but not described at great length. Nearly all Scott's imaginary children are either cheerful, good-natured, and sensible, or artful and mischievous, but he never described them so much "beyond their years" as Dickens does. For instance, Edward Glendinning, a quiet, thoughtful youth, is the natural beginning of the future monk and abbot; while the brave, impetuous little Halbert proclaims the future warrior. But Scott usually never makes heroes under age. Shakespeare likewise, in his matchless sketches of character, seldom described children, except in "King John" and "Richard the Third." In the latter his pathetic, yet spirited, descriptions of the two doomed young princes are wonderfully life-like, but all, unfortunately, very brief. Yet the strong sense and rising ambition of the elder prince in "Richard the Third," and the bright intelligence of his little brother, gave ample promise of future greatness, as their dangerous uncle, the Duke of Gloster, perceives and acknowledges.

When the two princes and their murderous uncle, the future Richard III., are before the fatal Tower of London, the eldest hearing that Julius Cæsar built it, asks,

> "Is it upon record, or else reported
> Successively from age to age, he built it?"

Buckingham replies:

> "Upon record, my gracious lord."

The prince exclaims :

> "But say, my lord, it were not register'd,
> Methinks the truth should live from age to age,
> As 'twere retail'd to all posterity,
> Even to the general all-ending day."

GLOSTER (*aside*). "So wise so young, they say, do never live long."

Prince Edward proceeds, evidently alluding to Cæsar's celebrated "Commentaries,"

> "That Julius Cæsar was a famous man ;
> With what his valour did enrich his wit,
> His wit set down to make his valour live :
> Death makes no conquest of this conqueror ;
> For now he lives in fame, though not in life.—
> I'll tell you what, my cousin Buckingham,
> . . . .
> An if I live until I be a man,
> I'll win our ancient right in France again,
> Or die a soldier, as I liv'd a king."

GLOSTER (*aside*). "Short summers lightly have a forward spring."

Richard III. Act iii.

In this fine scene Gloster twice mentions the belief, prevalent even now among some people, and verified in the cases of Paul Dombey and Little Nell, that children

> "So wise so young, they say, do never live long."

But Mr. Dickens, in describing his child-heroes and heroines, apparently relies chiefly, if not solely, on his own imagination, never saying that any are drawn from real life. Besides, in the cases of Little Nell, Oliver Twist, his friend Dick, and the two Dombeys, Mr. Dickens develops his favourite idea of superior and excellent children surrounded by harsh or worthless grown-up people in his rather inferior works, "Our Mutual Friend" and "Little Dorrit." In the former, the young heroine, Lizzie Hexam, and Jenny Wren are both complete and delightful contrasts to their parents. Little Jenny, moreover, calls her drunken father the "bad child," and constantly lectures him upon his duties while managing their joint abode, while Lizzie Hexam, a gentle, refined girl, is also a thorough contrast to her coarse, surly father.

These several instances of good, superior children among worthless parents and other grown-up persons alike illustrate Mr. Dickens's favourite and peculiar idea of reversing in fiction the natural order of things, by making children the moral teachers instead of the taught, the examples instead of the imitators. Yet such children seem to be what they are from intuition. Their characters and feelings are not only independent of surrounding circumstances, but are in direct opposition to them. All those good, tender, refined, and noble qualities usually implanted by judicious management and good example are by Dickens assigned to children born and bred among harsh, contemptible, wicked parents or associates, and placed in circumstances calculated to render them precisely the reverse of what they are. Yet he certainly succeeds in making them seem natural by describing them throughout with wonderful force and consistency; so that, if they could only have existed, they would probably have acted, spoken, and thought just as he makes them. The reader can fancy he has actually seen or heard them from the extreme ingenuity with which their conduct and characters are interwoven with other personages. Dickens evidently takes peculiar pleasure in describing these youthful favourites of his imagination, whom he has certainly succeeded in presenting to a world of real friends and admirers. Probably no other writer ever described such children before, and fortunate indeed are those parents who possess any like them.

It is remarkable that Dickens, after his first two joyous works, "Sketches" and "Pickwick," which diffused general merriment and laughter, began to dwell with great minuteness upon melancholy and pathetic incidents. "Oliver Twist," "Old Curiosity Shop," "Dombey and Son," &c., though all containing comic scenes and characters, leave a serious if not a melancholy impression on the reader. Dickens himself terms melancholy

> that cheapest and most accessible of luxuries,[1]

and certainly seems well acquainted with its nature in all its aspects and degrees. Unlike his great literary predecessor, Addison, who

> did not know what it was to be melancholy,[2]

or Scott, whose natural cheerfulness was never affected by his most tragic compositions, Dickens excited himself to the utmost in pathetic description, and, by his rare genius and taste, made his most melancholy scenes attractive even to the gayest of the gay. He shows such an exquisite moral purity, combined with the tenderest sympathy for all human sorrows, that the prosperous and the unfortunate, the cheerful and

[1] "Dombey and Son."

[2] "Spectator" ("Reflections in Westminster Abbey").

the sad, among his readers are alike irresistibly attracted by his powers of pathetic delineation.

Among the chief characteristics of Dickens's writings is his extreme detestation of all hypocrisy and affectation. From his first great work, "Pickwick," to his last, "Edwin Drood," inclusive, he exposes what is often termed "cant" in either religion or philanthropy, with, if possible, a deeper abhorrence than the subject requires. Doubtless, religious "humbugs," like the Rev. Mr. Stiggins, Mr. Pecksniff, Uriah Heep, and Chadband, or the false philanthropist, Mr. Honeythunder, deserve exposure and consequent condemnation. But it is scarcely possible that men like them would be able to do as much harm to the community as Dickens apparently believes, for their sphere must always be a limited one. They might for a time cheat and impose upon some ignorant or trustful individuals and families, but their utter roguery would surely be discovered sooner or later, and all would be over with them at once. It is a most remarkable fact that Dickens in all his works never describes a single religious fanatic or political zealot as willing to endure as to inflict torture or death for the sake of his own opinions. Lord George Gordon[1] is the only character at all resembling this class; but he is a very weak specimen, and an historical character, not the invention of Dickens, who represents him as led and ruled by the hypocrite Gashford, instead of associating him with any fierce, fanatical preachers, by whom such a man was more likely to be influenced and among whom, indeed, he was probably educated.

[1] "Barnaby Rudge."

Dickens apparently avoids the subject of sincere religious bigotry altogether in his works, and devotes himself to exposing with the keenest severity the contemptible vice of hypocrisy both in religion and philanthropy. No kings, prince, prelates, or Roman Catholic priests are ever mentioned in all his books, which may have caused some people to declare he could not have described them; but, as before observed, he never attempted their description, and, where there has been no attempt, it would surely be presumptuous to assume certain failure in so great a genius. Dickens took his wonderfully accurate and profound views of life and character chiefly from among the classes and during the period he knew himself by experience; hence he personally discovered the mischief done by religious hypocrites and impostors, whereas the fearful evils caused by religious fanatics were to him only matters of history. Had he known or lived in Ireland, or even in Scotland, he would probably have found the results of religious bigotry more injurious to the community, if not more revolting to common sense and justice, than either hypocrisy or imposture. Though such men as Stiggins, Pecksniff, Chadband, &c., have deceived many trustful people, perhaps to Dickens's own knowledge, which may have induced him to expose them at length; yet such contemptible impostors would acquire little influence in times of sincere religious controversy. They might not, indeed, be always counteracted by honest, sensible men, to whom Dickens usually entrusts their imaginary punishment; but they would assuredly be opposed to men as prejudiced in reality as they are in pretence, by men who deceive themselves, as well as others, in firmly believing their own opinions exclusively right, and those of all others unpardonably wrong. Such fanatics, even when not men of much ability, are proved by history to be far more influential in directing public opinion than the most able impostors, and have, in fact, done more harm.

No one, perhaps, knew this better than Sir Walter Scott; and men resembling his characters of Balfour, Macbriar, the Abbot of St. Cuthbert, &c., have, when in power, caused much more misery than all the Pecksniffs and Uriah Heeps of any age or country. It can hardly be maintained that this fanatical spirit is yet extinct, though it may be politically powerless; for signs of it constantly appear, not only in sermons and lectures, but in the deep religious prejudices which to this day alienate and divide Christians, even in Britain and Ireland, from each other. This intolerance, which formerly actuated the legislation of kings and governments, and which still prevails among many sincere Christians in private life, was never inspired by such impostors as Dickens describes. The mischievous influence of rogues like Pecksniff, Stiggins, Gashford, &c., could seldom extend beyond a few families, for their only objects are their own private and selfish gains. Dickens probably knew some such men, and, naturally indignant at them, eagerly devoted himself to their exposure and condemnation. He from personal experience, perhaps, knew little or nothing of sincere religious fanaticism, for otherwise his powerful pen would surely not have ignored so terribly fruitful a source of human injustice and suffering. He, indeed, alludes in strong language to this subject, but in a private letter,[1] saying that he

> held in unspeakable dread and horror these unseemly squabbles about the letter [of religion] which drew the spirit out of hundreds of thousands.

This view is natural, perhaps unavoidable, in a man of his intelligence and knowledge of character; but the dread and horror he intimated probably arose from historical impressions and reflections, rather than from personal experience, or he would have shown more interest on the subject of religious animosities which still actuate some people by no means destitute of sense, charity, or education.

It really seems that Mr. Dickens rather underrated the characters and motives of some religious zealots and persecutors. In his preface to "Barnaby Rudge" he says:

> What we call falsely a religious cry is easily raised by men who have no religion, and who, in their daily practice, set at nought the commonest principles of right and wrong—that it is begotten of intolerance and persecution, that it is senseless, besotted, inveterate, and unmerciful all history teaches us.

Of course, such a cry may be "easily raised" by such persons; but history proves that it is not those who "set at nought the commonest principles of right and wrong" that have been usually most successful in causing religious intolerance and persecution. On the contrary, the exemplary lives and complete sincerity of many religious persecutors even in Christian history have greatly increased their influence and power.[2]

[1] Forster's "Life of Dickens," vol. iii.

[2] See Buckle's remarks on this subject, "Civilisation in England," vol. i.

Religious intolerance is usually unmerciful indeed, but can hardly be termed altogether "senseless," when even to this day it is logically advocated by politicians and theologians of education and sincerity. The fact is that if these "religious cries" had been only excited by the morally bad and worthless, as Dickens implies, they would never have been so dangerous or so widely spread.

Unfortunately the persecuting laws and edicts at one time enacted in almost every Christian land were framed not by hypocrites, but by zealots; and a careful study of the religious history of Europe, even since the Protestant Reformation, surely proves that the evils caused by persecution are attributable to fanaticism, more than to imposture. In most Christian countries while religious disputes were agitating the most learned, estimable, and influential, those who violated "the commonest principles of right and wrong" were, doubtless, viewed by all parties alike as the common enemy. The nominal religion of such people, indeed, would signify little, except in making them the unscrupulous tools of whatever religious faction was in power. The danger to human happiness has chiefly been caused by persons of a very different kind, who, though possessing many qualities worthy of respect and reverence, were yet influenced by an intolerant spirit, with which their sincerity and enthusiasm inspired others. The chief Roman Catholic and Protestant persecutors in France, Spain, England, Scotland, and Ireland cannot certainly be termed "men who have no religion"; yet the intolerance they felt and inspired occasioned an amount of human misery and injustice which could hardly have been caused by the false and hypocritical. Their very virtues of sincerity and self-devotion have a moral influence over the opinions of others which no genius or talent could probably have obtained in the same degree or for the same purposes.

Thus a more extraordinary spectacle has never been presented by history than that of conscientious, noble-minded men treating each other with injustice and cruelty, during which wretched strife the criminal and worthless of religious denominations were employed as informers, jailers, or executioners. In this unnatural strife the best men of different religions cruelly persecuted each other, and were often as ready to endure as to inflict death or injustice, from a strength of religious conviction which apparently inspired every virtue except mercy. In another part of "Barnaby Rudge" Mr. Dickens writes:

> False priests, false prophets, false doctors, false patriots, false prodigies of every kind, veiling their proceedings in mystery, have always addressed themselves at an immense advantage to the popular credulity, and have, perhaps, been more indebted to that resource in gaining and keeping for a time the upper hand of truth and common-sense, than to any half-dozen items in the whole catalogue of imposture.[1]

Doubtless some hypocritical preachers, as well as quack-doctors and mercenary politicians, have done, and always will do, considerable mischief. But history teaches that far more evil to mankind has been caused by men who, instead of being *false*, were only too *sincere* in the most inveterate religious or political fanaticism. In fact, their sincerity, proved by readiness to endure the same penalties as they were eager

[1] Chap. xxxvii.

to inflict, gave them more influence than, perhaps, anything else could have done over the public mind. From this firm spirit of sincere, self-denying, and even heroic intolerance, have proceeded those relentless penalties for alleged religious error which have disgraced the statute-books of most Christian countries, Great Britain and Ireland included.

Sir Walter Scott, who studied all history attentively, especially that of his own country, has, therefore, most powerfully described the evils caused by *sincerely religious* persecutors, whose motives he always discusses with remarkable fairness and moderation. No one deplored the excesses of such misguided zeal more than Scott; while his steady good sense, and combined knowledge of human history and character, enabled him to do justice to the motives of those whose conduct he so regretted and censured. He seldom describes religious hypocrites; his Kettledrummles, Poundtexts, &c., though ridiculous, are all sincere; even Trusty Tomkins is a fanatic as well as a knave. Tony Foster and Trumbull are more like religious hypocrites than any of his characters; but even these rascals, Foster especially, are probably not destitute of some religious beliefs. Dickens's hypocrites, Gashford, Pecksniff, Heep, &c., are utter rogues, like Molière's Tartuffe, Fielding's Blifil, Sheridan's Joseph Surface and Dr. Cantwell, of a still older English comedy, and all seem incapable of religious convictions. Such men in times of religious warfare would probably vanish altogether, and leave the field of contention to sincere enthusiasts, like the Abbot of St. Cuthbert's, Eustace, Balfour, or Macbriar. It is, of course, accidental to what denominations such men may belong. The same intolerant spirit animates them alike; and history teaches that during and often long after the excitement of religious warfare, the spirit of fierce zealots, like the Abbot of St. Cuthbert's or Macbriar, overcomes the milder feelings of such men as Abbot Eustace or Warden in guiding public opinion. In the statute-books of Spain, Italy, France, Great Britain, and Ireland, till very recent years there existed the most cruel legal penalties against Christians of different denominations, enacted in precisely the same spirit, and avowedly for the same purpose of extinguishing what each sincerely believed were the fatal errors of the other. This spirit of sincere religious bigotry Dickens never mentions in his works, though in some, "Barnaby Rudge" especially, there were ample opportunities for illustrating its nature and tendency in imaginary characters; but it is, apparently, a subject which he systematically avoids.

In examining Dickens's chief works, from the "Sketches" to "Edwin Drood," the joyous wit and merriment of his first books seem to yield gradually to more serious thoughts and emotions. His keen sense of humour, indeed, remained to the last, but he used it chiefly to divert and relieve his readers after the more serious thoughts with which his later works on the whole inspired them; whereas the "Sketches" and "Pickwick" abound in wit and fun throughout, being only slightly varied by those grave feelings and emotions which predominated in his later writings. Though all his fictitious works refer to England, and chiefly to London, the two countries that most interested him, after his own, were evidently the United States of America and France. His "American Notes" and "Martin Chuzzlewit" to some extent refer to the former, and the "Tale of Two Cities" to the latter. He seldom or never mentions Scotland or Ireland; which is to be regretted, especially on account of Ireland, as that country never produced a Walter Scott to describe its peculiarities with perfect fairness. Of all his works, the last, "Edwin Drood," seems written in the most religious spirit. Though in all his writings he shows that love of virtue and hatred of vice which are the primary object and practical result of true religious convictions, he yet alludes more in "Edwin Drood" to the letter as well as to the spirit of religion, than in any other book.

It may be both interesting and instructive to compare his first works with his last, to perceive the effect which the lessons of life and experience produced upon a mind so powerful and observant; as he evidently retained unimpaired that keen wit and humour which had delighted the reading public for so many years, and especially the younger portion of them. His brilliant wit and gaiety certainly became more and more blended with serious thoughts and feelings towards the close or his remarkable and interesting life. Availing himself of his wonderful knowledge of character, he describes most of the vices, virtues, follies, and caprices of human nature, assigning them to fictitious persons, and developing their natural cause and influence in imaginary events. He generally follows the usual plan of novelists in making the most interesting characters persecuted or unfortunate for a long time in each story, till the reader's sympathy is thoroughly aroused, and then rewards virtue and punishes vice and cunning at the conclusion, thus relieving his readers and himself also. Dickens evidently felt as much love and hatred towards his good and bad characters as any of his most admiring readers could do. The intense interest in his imaginary personages he unfortunately indulged to a dangerous extent. When publicly reading the pathetic scenes in "Oliver Twist," and other books, his mental agitation was fearful; and it must always be regretted that he was not induced by earnest and respectful remonstrances to consider his own health, infinitely more valuable to the public than their temporary gratification at its own imminent risk.[1]

His sympathetic mind, so keenly alive to injustice, cruelty, and suffering, had evidently been severely tried and saddened during life's experience from early manhood to middle age. His keen sense of the ludicrous and his exquisite wit were, of course, inseparable from his nature through life; but his deep human sympathies induced him more and more to address the graver feelings of his readers, and to illustrate, in touching scenes and pathetic descriptions, the vast amount of suffering and misery which he knew by experience still existed even in the civilized, rich, and enlightened capital of England, and

[1] On the first night of the Sikes and Nancy scenes, his pulse went from 80 to 112, and on the second night to 118. From this through the six remaining nights it never was lower than 110 after the first piece read; and after the third and fourth reading of the Oliver Twist scenes it rose from 90 to 124 (Forster's "Life of Dickens,' vol. iii.).

thus to arouse those feelings of Christian charity which he found were professed by so many, yet which actuated comparatively so few.[1] To accomplish this excellent purpose his profound knowledge alike of human nature and the English public taste eminently fitted him. Thus his fanciful stories which amused, interested, and mentally absorbed all classes in English life, were many of them practically sermons to them all, though in an unusual form. The same principles which the best sermons can teach, Dickens, likewise, inculcated, through a medium more attractive, at least to the frivolous and thoughtless, who, besides being always a numerous class, really most need such instruction. The most selfish, stupid, or worldly minds seemed, as it were, arrested by his powerful genius, and forced by its admirable influence to secretly own

> How awful Goodness is,
> And Virtue in her shape how lovely,[2]

to feel the deepest sympathy for injured innocence, and the keenest abhorrence of all falsehood, cruelty, and hypocrisy.

Indeed, the moral effect of Dickens's works seemed to carry out and extend the influence of practical religious feelings among people of all religious denominations without distinction. Yet unhappily, owing to the intense religious prejudices, there are

[1] "I believe there has been in England since the days of the Stuarts no law so infamously administered, no law so often openly violated, no law habitually so ill-supervised (as the Poor Law)" (Dickens's postscript to "Our Mutual Friend").

[2] "Paradise Lost."

some excellent works calculated to improve every one, which are known to few beyond the author's own denomination, and are literally almost sealed books to all others. But to persons of all religions Dickens's books were alike acceptable. Their brilliant wit and humour cheered and interested the melancholy, the serious, and the thoughtless alike. All these different minds were amused and attracted by the first effect of his pages, while the moral good they instilled was the sure result of the intense interest they so universally aroused. Only the most unfeeling or stupid readers could study "Oliver Twist," "Nickleby," or "Dombey" without finding their better feelings aroused, strengthened, and gratified. The most frivolous, who only seek mere amusement in literature, will find in Dickens amusement, indeed, of the most attractive kind, yet inseparably blended with most valuable moral instructions and mental enlightenment. There is, perhaps, no more sublime moral spectacle than that of a man of the highest intellect, preeminently gifted with power to attract and interest others, steadily recognising and achieving through life the purpose for which he was so gifted by the universal Creator. This noble consciousness Dickens evidently shared with Shakespeare, Addison, Johnson, Walter Scott, and many other British writers, whose valuable works are so admirably described by Lord Macaulay as among

> the most splendid and the most durable of the many glories of England.[1]

Dickens's conscientious spirit seems, however, more

[1] "History of England," chap. i.

developed by the philosophy of his later writings; while the first abound with comic scenes and sketches only, varied by a few graver chapters, yet all are animated by the same purity of thought. Gradually, as Dickens felt his hold on public attention more secure, he became more serious and instructive in his style, while using his great comic powers chiefly to relieve his readers, and probably himself too, after the serious and depressing effects of pathetic narration. In his last chief works, "Dombey," "Copperfield," "Bleak House," and "Edwin Drood," Dickens appeals chiefly to the serious thoughts of his readers. The reflecting wisdom of middle age seems in these works not to exactly replace the wit and gaiety of his earlier writings, but to control and make them subservient to more important objects than mere amusement. While in "Pickwick" and the "Sketches" the thoughtful and pathetic scenes were quite exceptions among the mass of witty and humorous descriptions, the reverse rather marks his later writings, where comic scenes and personages only occasionally cheer and enliven their prevailing seriousness. He thus evidently preserved his great powers for lively and serious composition, from first to last, devoting them as he thought and found best suited to his purpose, of amusing and improving his readers at the same time. His last work, "Edwin Drood," reveals, perhaps, his religious feelings more than any other. The sentiments of Mr. Crisparkle, one of the best clergymen he ever described at length, with the Scriptural allusions at the end of the story, show that Dickens, at the close of his long and brilliant literary life, was reflecting in calm resignation upon the spirit of that religion which had so steadily actuated his motives and inspired his writings throughout. In his last will, written with remarkable clearness and force, he also reveals his religious feelings in few but most expressive words.[1] They are sufficient, however, if any such evidence was required, to prove how calmly and wisely this illustrious writer, though chiefly known to the world by works of imagination, reasoned and thought upon the solemn subject of sincere religious belief.

[1] "I commend my soul to the mercy of God through our Lord Jesus Christ, and I exhort my dear children humbly to try to guide themselves by the teaching of the New Testament in its broad spirit, and to put no faith in any man's narrow construction of its letter here or there" (Appendix to Forster's "Life of Dickens").

PART II

THACKERAY

CHAPTER I

THACKERAY STUDIED IN "VANITY FAIR"

THIS wonderfully clever novel, considered by many to be Mr. Thackeray's masterpiece, he calls "A novel without a hero"; yet Colonel William Dobbin, despite his awkwardness and plain looks, possesses most of the best qualities of one. This book was generally admired, though chiefly, perhaps, by men well acquainted with London society early in the nineteenth century. Among these the late Sir William Fraser, Bart., wrote:

> I read "Vanity Fair," not in numbers, but after the volume was complete. I allowed myself to read one chapter only each day; the food was too rich and nourishing to digest more. Nothing I have read since has at all approached the sensation which that glorious work gave me—not a line from beginning to end but what impressed me with its vigorous truth.[1]

The scene of the story is chiefly in London and the south of England, rather early in the nineteenth century, and begins at a Miss Pinkerton's seminary for young ladies. Among the latter are Miss Rebecca Sharp, the future heroine, or chief female character in this book, and Miss Amelia Sedley, who, though a comparative beauty, is altogether inferior to her

[1] Sir William Fraser's "Hic et Ubique" (Here and Everywhere), published 1893.

school companion in talents and accomplishments. Rebecca, or Becky, as Thackeray usually terms her, is certainly the most interesting and original personage in the whole story, and the author evidently takes special care in describing her extraordinary character and strange career.

The story begins where Amelia and Becky are leaving their school to begin the world on their own account. Of these two young ladies it is truly said that Miss Sharp is the impersonation of intellect without heart, and Amelia Sedley who has heart without intellect.[1] This brief description is alike true of both. Their governess, Miss Pinkerton, is almost a caricature of a stiff, formal, surprisingly ignorant, but not altogether ill-natured old lady, who views her two departing pupils with very opposite feelings. Thus she likes, almost loves, the gentle, pretty, rather silly Amelia Sedley, and detests Rebecca Sharp, small, clever, determined, and sharp indeed to the utmost, in nature as well as in name. Miss Pinkerton's sister, Miss Jemima, a quiet, simple person, quite overawed by her majestic sister, wishes to present both the departing pupils with gifts of Johnson's Dictionary, a learned work always given to departing scholars from this establishment. In seems that old Miss Pinkerton had formerly known the great Dr. Johnson, though how far their acquaintance extended is not mentioned. Miss Pinkerton now forbids this present to be made to the impudent little Becky Sharp. It happens that Becky is a good French scholar, pretending to be descended from an old French family, while old Miss Pinkerton does not very well under-

[1] Shaw's "Manual of English Literature."

stand French, her comparative ignorance of which often gives Becky an advantage over the dignified yet ignorant head-governess.

When the two pupils leave the Academy, there is a marked contrast between the sorrow of both fellow-pupils and servants at parting from the amiable Amelia Sedley and the saucy little Becky.

> Then came the struggle and parting below. Words refuse to tell it. All the servants were there in the hall—all the dear friends—all the young ladies—the dancing-master, who had just arrived, and there was such a scuffling and hugging and kissing and crying . . . as no pen can depict and as the tender heart would fain pass over. The embracing was over; they parted—that is, Miss Sedley parted from her friends, Miss Sharp had demurely entered the carriage some minutes before. Nobody cried for leaving *her*.

Miss Jemima, however, at the last moment brings Johnson's Dictionary, and in tears the kind creature gives it to Miss Sharp through the carriage window, exclaiming:

> . . . "You mustn't leave without that. Goodbye." . . . But lo and just as the coach drove off, Miss Sharp put her pale face out of the window and actually flung the book back into the garden. This almost caused Jemima to faint with terror.
>
> "Well, I never——" said she, "what an audacious——" Emotion prevented her from completing either sentence. The carriage rolled away. . . . The world is before the two young ladies.

The world was indeed then before them, and their relative positions therein are now explained by the author. Amelia is the only daughter of a worthy father and mother, her one brother, Joseph Sedley, is an official in India, and occasionally visits England. He is a vain, pompous, perfectly harmless man, rich and selfish, fated to be Becky's future victim, though not till the very end of the story.

Becky's early life is described as one of mingled hardship, cunning, and trickery, but in their drive from Miss Pinkerton's Academy the two pupils reveal a good deal of their real characters. Amelia, soft, kind, but not over wise, really loves Rebecca; while the latter, cold, calm, and resolute, yet always preserves a sort of liking or indulgence for Amelia, who remonstrates with her for her rudeness in spurning the present from kind Miss Jemima Pinkerton:

> "I hate the whole house,"

Miss Sharp exclaims when out of hearing.

> "I wish it were in the bottom of the Thames, I do; and if Miss Pinkerton were there, I wouldn't pick her out, that I wouldn't."

Thus exulting in her escape from the Academy, Becky declares that Amelia was the only one she liked in all the establishment.

> "I have never had a friend or a kind word except from you."

Then rejoicing in her knowledge of French, compared to old Miss Pinkerton's ignorance of it, Becky continues:

> . . . "She doesn't know a word of French and was too proud to confess it. I believe it was that which made her part with me, and so thank Heaven for French. *Vive la France! Vive l'Empereur! Vive Bonaparte!*"
>
> "O Rebecca, Rebecca, for shame!" cried Miss Sedley, for this was the greatest blasphemy Rebecca has as yet uttered, and in those days in England to say "Long live Bonaparte!" was as much as to say "Long live Lucifer!" "How can you—how dare you have such wicked, revengeful thoughts!"

To this remonstrance, Becky, always more truthful with the comparatively simple, trustful Amelia, replies with the shameless effrontery which never forsakes her,

"Revenge may be wicked, but it's natural. . . . I'm no angel";

and Thackeray confirms her by adding,

And to say the truth, she certainly was not.[1]

The parents of Becky and her early life are most carefully sketched. As their strange conduct and career greatly explain the character of their artful, energetic daughter, Thackeray's own words should be closely studied :—

Miss Sharp's father was an artist. . . . He was a clever man; a pleasant companion, a careless student, with a great propensity for running into debt and a partiality for the tavern. When he was drunk he used to beat his wife and daughter, and the next morning, with a headache, he would rail at the world for its neglect of his genius. . . .

As it was with the utmost difficulty that he could keep himself and as he owed money for a mile round Soho, where he lived, he thought to better his circumstances by marrying a young woman of the French nation, who was by profession an opera-girl. The humble calling of her female parent, Miss Sharp never alluded to, but used to state subsequently that the Entrechats were a noble family of Gascony and took great pride in her descent from them.

Thackerary continues with his usual calm sarcasm, in which, perhaps, no writer of fiction has surpassed or even equalled him :

. . . And curious it is that as she advanced in life this young lady's ancestors increased in rank and splendour.

---

[1] "The inimitable Becky was drawn from the companion of a wealthy and selfish old lady who lived in the neighbourhood of Kensington Square" (Melville's "Life of Thackeray," published 1910).

Rebecca's mother had had some education somewhere and her daughter spoke French with purity and a Parisian accent. It was in those days rather a rare accomplishment and led to her engagement with the orthodox Miss Pinkerton. For her mother being dead, her father finding himself not likely to recover after his third attack of *delirium tremens*, wrote a manly and pathetic letter to Miss Pinkerton recommending the orphan child to her protection, and so descended to the grave, after two bailiffs had quarrelled over his corpse.

Miss Sharp, the masterpiece as she may be considered of Thackeray's female characters, seems more or less his favourite, being sometimes called in a playful, half-comic manner "our darling Becky," despite her wholly unscrupulous character.[1] Her appearance would seem rather pleasing despite some natural disadvantages.

She was small and slight in person, pale, sandy-haired, and with eyes habitually cast down; when they looked up they were very large, odd, and attractive—so attractive that the Rev. Mr. Crisp, fresh from Oxford and curate to the Vicar of Chiswick, the Rev. Mr. Flowerdew, fell in love with Miss Sharp, being shot dead by a glance of her eyes which was fired all the way across Chiswick Church from the school-pew to the reading-desk.

The early life and training of Becky, thus humorously described, foreshadows with great truth and accuracy her future career in the pages of this practical novel. The author proceeds in his careful, often witty, delineation:

By the side of many tall and bouncing young ladies in this establishment [Miss Pinkerton's Academy] Rebecca Sharp looked

---

[1] It seems reasonably certain that Becky Sharp was drawn from an original, although the name of her prototype has been withheld. Lady Ritchie writes, "My father only laughed when people asked him" ("A Thackeray Dictionary," published 1910).

like a child. But she had the dismal precocity of poverty. Many a dun had she talked to and turned away from her father's door, many a tradesman had she coaxed and wheedled into a good humour and into the granting of one meal more. She sate commonly with her father, who was very proud of her wit, and heard the talk of many of his wild companions—often but ill-suited for a girl to hear. But she never had been a girl, she said—she had been a woman ever since she was eight years old.

Thackeray's happy yet peculiar expression, "the dismal precocity of poverty," should be well-remembered by readers of this work, as it forms indeed an explanation to a great extent of Becky's extraordinary and for a long time successful artfulness in dealing with both men and women, old and young. One of her first triumphs is over her old pompous and comparatively ignorant governess, Miss Pinkerton, who

in vain did battle against her and tried to overawe her. Attempting once to scold her in public, Rebecca hit upon the before-mentioned plan of answering her in French, which quite routed the old woman. In order to maintain her authority in her school, it became necessary to remove this rebel, this monster, this serpent, this firebrand; and hearing about this time that Sir Pitt Crawley's family was in want of a governess, she actually recommended Miss Sharp for the situation, firebrand and serpent as she was. . . . And as Miss Sedley, being now in her seventeenth year, was about to leave school and had a friendship for Miss Sharp ("'tis the only point in Amelia's behaviour," said Minerva [Miss Pinkerton] which has not been satisfactory to her mistress) Miss Sharp was invited by her friend to pass a week with her at home, before she entered upon her duties as governess in a private family.

Thus the world began for these two young ladies. . . . When Rebecca saw the two magnificent Cashmere shawls Joseph Sedley had brought home to his sister, she said with perfect truth, "that it must be delightful to have a brother," and easily got the pity of the tender-hearted Amelia for being alone in the world, an orphan without friends or kindred.

Becky, however, soon asks two important and practical questions, inquiring of Amelia with an apparent innocent frankness, which throughout the whole novel always deceives her simple friend till the very end:

> "Isn't he very rich? They say all Indian nabobs are enormously rich."
>
> "I believe he has a very large income."
>
> "And is your sister-in-law a nice, pretty woman?"
>
> "La! Joseph is not married," said Amelia. . . . Perhaps she had mentioned the fact already to Rebecca, but that young lady did not appear to have remembered it. . . . She was quite disappointed that Mr. Sedley was not married. . . . The meaning of the above series of queries, as translated in the heart of this ingenuous young woman, was simply this: "If Mr. Joseph Sedley is rich and unmarried, why should I not marry him?" . . . She redoubled her caresses to Amelia. . . . When the dinner-bell rang she went downstairs with her arm round her friend's waist, as is the habit of young ladies. She was so agitated at the drawing-room door, that she could hardly find courage to enter. "Feel my heart, how it beats, dear," she said to her friend.
>
> "No it doesn't," said Amelia. "Come in, don't be frightened. Papa won't do you any harm."

So ends the second chapter with one of those expressive little pictures which add much to the value and meaning of this work. Amelia Sedley and Becky stand beside each other—Amelia the taller, of course, quite naturally at her ease, with a protecting expression; Becky, small and timid-looking, pretending to be shy and frightened yet with a spirit as dauntless and a mind as artful, unscrupulous, and enterprising as is sometimes described in the real heroines of history. She is, perhaps, more like a French than an Englishwoman. It seems that Thackeray himself was told in France by "the best French literary authorities, that the character of Becky was so common in France that it would have excited no sensation there." [1]

Her first introduction to the simple and amiable Amelia's brother, Joseph Sedley, slightly reveals Becky's cunning power of deception, which Amelia, open, kind, and comparatively silly, never perceives or suspects. Jos, vain and conceited yet awkward and shy, shows nervousness at his first introduction to Miss Sharp, who whispers "rather loud" to Amelia:

"He's very handsome."

"Do you think so?" said the latter. "I'll tell him."

"Darling, not for worlds," said Miss Sharp, starting back as timid as a fawn.

Two such simple people as the Sedleys, brother and sister, are easy enough for Becky to completely outwit, deceive, and victimise throughout this whole novel. But she is soon to encounter two gentlemen of very different characters, both from each other and from the Sedleys. These are young George Osborne, only son of a rich London banker, and his friend, William Dobbin. This last personage, from his very name often associated with that of a quiet, obedient horse, usually a faithful drudge, is, except Becky Sharp, the most important character introduced, and is, indeed, almost the only one who without prejudice, like Miss Pinkerton, thoroughly understands Becky from the first, and is never deceived by her, during her rather long course of clever social intrigue and success. These two young men are both in love with Amelia,

[1] Sir William Fraser's "Hic et Ubique."

who more than returns Osborne's affection, while though liking Dobbin as a useful, agreeable friend, she has no idea of falling in love with him. Osborne is very handsome, very conceited and thoughtless. Dobbin is very plain, awkward, sincere, loving Amelia with almost the devotion of a worshipper; a man of firm principle and sound common sense. Both are in the army; but Osborne, when a boy at school, was cruelly tormented and bullied by an elder boy named Cuffe, whom Dobbin, a few years older than Osborne, thrashed in a hard-fought fight.[1]

A strong friendship arose after this battle between Osborne and Dobbin, which continues through the whole story. Though Thackeray calls this work "A novel without a hero," he is perhaps hardly fair to Dobbin in doing so. This man, despite his devotion to Amelia tempting him to wrongly advocate her father's trading interests at the expense of the public, is yet generous, kind, and courageous throughout. Dobbin and Becky Sharp in this book constantly represent good and evil characters, involved with others, all of whom without exception are their inferiors in ability, courage, and firm resolution. The sincere attachment between the brave, honest, awkward-looking Dobbin and the gay, handsome, frivolous George Osborne, during and ever since their boyhood, the author thus sarcastically describes:

He [Dobbin] flung himself down at little Osborne's feet and loved him. . . . He believed Osborne to be the possessor of every perfection, to be the handsomest, the bravest, the most active, the cleverest, the most generous of created boys. He shared his money

[1] Chap. v.

with him; bought him uncountable presents . . . the which tokens of merit George received very graciously as became his superior merit.

An amusing trip to Vauxhall Gardens is then described, the party consisting of Becky, Amelia, Osborne, Dobbin, and Jos Sedley. Of these people Thackeray writes as if rather contemptuous about all these creations of his:[1]

I must beg the good-natured reader to remember that we are only discussing at present about a stockbroker's family in Russell Square, who are taking walks, or luncheon, or dinner, or talking and making love as people do in common life and without a single passionate and wonderful incident to mark the progress of their loves. The argument stands thus: Osborne, in love with Amelia, has asked an old friend (Dobbin) to Vauxhall; Jos Sedley is in love with Rebecca. Will he marry her? That is the great subject now in hand. . . .

Let us then step into the coach with the Russell Square party and be off to the Gardens. There is barely room between Jos and Miss Sharp who are on the front seat, Mr. Osborne sitting bodkin opposite, between Captain Dobbin and Amelia. Every soul in the coach agreed, that night Jos would propose to make Rebecca Sharp Mrs. Sedley.

Jos's father views the possibility of his son's marriage with Rebecca in a peculiar spirit which he explains to his wife. In fact, both Jos's parents view their vain, conceited, rather stupid son with much the same contempt.

"Let Jos marry whom he likes; it's no affair of mine. . . . Better she, my dear, than a black Mrs. Sedley, and a dozen of mahogany grandchildren."

The party was landed at the Royal Gardens in due time. As the majestic Jos stepped out of the creaking vehicle the crowd gave a cheer for the fat gentleman, who blushed and looked very big and mighty as he walked away with Rebecca under his arm. George of

---

[1] Chap. vi.

course took charge of Amelia. She looked as happy as a rose in sunshine.

"I say, Dobbin," says George, "just look to the shawls and things, there's a good fellow."

And so while he paired off with Miss Sedley and Jos squeezed through the gate into the gardens with Rebecca at his side, honest Dobbin contented himself by giving an arm to the shawls and by paying at the door for the whole party.

This sketch in few words presents the relative positions and to some extent the separate characters of the entire party. The fat, consequential, harmless Jos Sedley, the gay, lively George Osborne, and the faithful Dobbin attending and worshipping Amelia Sedley at a distance; the kind, rather silly Amelia and the ever-cunning, watchful, and designing Becky, of whom Jos Sedley is the first of her many conquests, are alike presented to the reader's view. The utterly unrequited devotion of Dobbin to Amelia may seem exaggerated, but is maintained with steady consistency throughout the whole story and forms, indeed, one of its most interesting features.

. . . He carried about Amelia's white Cashmere shawl, and having attended while Mrs. Salmon performed the Battle of Borodino (a savage cantata against the Corsican upstart, who had lately met with his Russian reverses), Mr. Dobbin tried to hum it as he walked away and found he was humming the tune which Amelia Sedley sang on the stairs, as she came down to dinner. He burst out laughing at himself; for the truth is he could sing no better than an owl.

This Vauxhall expedition, however, turned out badly, as to Becky's private speculations; Jos becoming drunk and quarrelsome. He is ridiculed by Osborne and pitied by Dobbin, but soon leaves London sick and ashamed of himself, to the amusement and disappointment of the three—Osborne, Amelia, and Becky. Throughout this story, though laid early in the nineteenth century, Thackeray illustrates it according to the fashion of his own times, many years later, in the same century. To explain this, he makes a caricature of the older fashion and writes:

> I have not the heart to disfigure my heroes and heroines by costumes so hideous, and have, on the contrary, engaged a model of rank dressed according to the prevailing [1848] fashion.

CHAPTER II

THE Vauxhall adventure is in chapter vi. and chapter vii. introduces new scenes and characters.

Here are Sir Pitt Crawley, Baronet, of Queen's Crawley, Hampshire; his two grown-up sons, Pitt and Rawdon, his second wife, an invalid, and two young daughters by her, to whom Becky is to be governess. She accordingly goes to Sir Pitt's London mansion in Great Gaunt Street. Old Sir Pitt Crawley, M.P., supposed to live in the nineteenth century, bears some resemblance to Lord Macaulay's sketch of an English squire in the seventeenth:[1]

> His chief pleasures were commonly derived from field sports and from an unrefined sensuality. His language and pronunciation were such as we should now expect to hear only from the most ignorant clowns. His oaths, coarse jests, and scandalous terms of abuse were uttered with the broadest accent of his province. . . . He was a magistrate, and as such administered gratuitously to those who dwelt around him a rude patriarchal justice which, in spite of innumerable blunders and occasional acts of tyranny, was yet better than no justice at all. His ignorance and uncouthness, his low tastes and coarse phrases, would in our time be considered as indicating a nature and a breeding thoroughly plebeian.

Shakespeare's sketch of Justice Shallow, which doubtless Macaulay knew as far as "the innumerable blunders" are concerned, fully bears out this

[1] "History of England," chap. iii., published in 1849.

description. Shallow, though perhaps not tyrannical, when influenced by his roguish servant, Davy, is absurdly unjust and silly, though with a vague idea of doing right struggling against his age and infirmity. When asked by Davy to take the part of a certain William Visor against an unfortunate complainant, Shallow replies that to his own knowledge Visor is "an arrant knave." Davy's answer to his apparently doting master is a masterpiece of witty absurdity, which perhaps Shakespeare may have really heard:

"I grant your Worship that he is a knave, sir; but yet, Heaven forbid, sir, but that a knave should have some countenance at his friend's request. An honest man, sir, is able to speak for himself, when a knave is not."

This request Shallow at once complies with, replying in a weak, probably doting manner:

"Go to, I say he shall have no wrong."—*Henry IV.*, Part II.

Yet Thackeray's Sir Pitt Crawley would surely seem to many readers even of the author's time to be rather an exaggeration. Miss Sharp's ideas of country gentlemen were therefore utterly mistaken in Sir Pitt's instance, as she finds at once from his reception of her at his London house:

Rebecca had never seen a baronet, as far as she knew, and as soon as she had taken leave of Amelia and had counted the guineas which good-natured Mr. Sedley had put into a purse for her, as soon as she had done wiping her eyes with her handkerchief (which operation she concluded the very moment the carriage had turned the corner of the street), she began to depict in her own mind what a baronet must be. "I wonder does he wear a star?" thought she, "or is it only lords that wear stars? But he will be very handsomely dressed in a court suit with ruffles, and his hair a little powdered.

. . . I suppose he will be awfully proud and that I shall be treated most contemptuously. Still, I must bear my hard lot as well as I can—at least I shall be among *gentlefolks* and not with vulgar city people."

When reaching Sir Pitt's house in town, Becky's picturesque or romantic ideas of what a baronet should be are utterly mistaken, far more than she could have believed possible.[1] Yet Sir Pitt is described so naturally and consistently throughout, that Thackeray might be thought to have either known this most repulsive old character himself, or some reliable person whose description he heard. Becky, full of expectation, arrives at the door:

When the bell was rung . . . the door was opened by a man in drab breeches and gaiters with a dirty old coat, a foul old neckcloth lashed round his bristly neck, a shining, bald head, a leering red face, a pair of twinkling grey eyes, and a mouth perpetually on the grin. . . .

On entering the drawing-room by orders of the individual in gaiters, Rebecca found that apartment not more cheerful than such rooms usually are when genteel families are out of town. The faithful chambers seem, as it were, to mourn the absence of their masters. . . .

Two kitchen chairs and a round table and an attenuated old poker and tongs were, however, gathered round the fireplace, as was a saucepan over a feeble, sputtering fire. There was a bit of cheese and bread and a tin candlestick on the table, and a little black porter in a pot.

As this was not the sort of furniture Miss Sharp expected to find in a baronet's room at a London

[1] "That character is almost the only exact portrait in the whole book," Kingsley reports the author as saying. It has been said that Lord Rolle of Stevenstone was the original ("A Thackeray Dictionary").

house, she naturally inquires for Sir Pitt Crawley, when to her annoyance the shabby old individual in gaiters replies with a laugh:

"He, he! I'm Sir Pitt Crawley. . . . He, he! Ask Tinker if I ain't. Mrs. Tinker, Miss Sharp; Miss Governess, Mrs. Charwoman Ho, ho!"

The lady addressed as Mrs. Tinker at this moment made her appearance with a pipe and a paper of tobacco . . . and she handed the articles over to Sir Pitt who had taken his seat by the fire.

"Where's the farden?" said he. "I gave you three-halfpence. Where's the change, old Tinker?"

"There," cried Mrs. Tinker, throwing down the coin, "it's only baronets as cares about farthings."

"A farthing a day is seven shillings a year," answered the M.P., "seven shillings a year is the interest of seven guineas. Take care of your farthings, old Tinker, and your guineas will come quite nat'ral."

"You may be sure it's Sir Pitt Crawley, young woman," said Mrs. Tinker surlily, "because he looks to his farthings." . . .

Presently the baronet plunged a fork into the saucepan on the fire and withdrew from the pot a piece of tripe and an onion, which he divided into pretty equal portions and of which he partook with Mrs. Tinker.

"You see, Miss Sharp, when I'm not here Tinker's on board wages; when I'm in town she dines with the family. Haw, haw! I'm glad Miss Sharp's not hungry, ain't you, Tink?" And they fell to upon their frugal supper. . . .

Whatever Sir Pitt Crawley's qualities might be, good or bad, he did not make the least disguise of them. He talked of himself incessantly, sometimes adopting the tone of a man of the world.

Becky thus strangely placed among these utter strangers, alone, unprotected, unfriended, with none to counsel or advise her, seems never embarrassed, or frightened in the least; accustomed from childhood, as Thackeray previously describes, to many specimens of low company and naturally firm and self-reliant, she steadily maintains a fearless spirit that never forsakes her. The coarse rudeness of Sir Pitt and Mrs. Tinker rather amuse or interest than disgust or shock her. In fact, she keeps her own private interests and designs carefully concealed, never wavers, never falters, never hesitates, and even tries to be agreeable to the repelling old Mrs. Tinker, for Becky always tries to be civil to every one.

Rebecca lay awake for a long, long time, thinking of the morrow and of the new world into which she was going and of her chances of success there.

In this room were

two little family pictures of young lads, one in a college gown and the other in a red jacket like a soldier. When she went to sleep Rebecca chose that one to dream about.

The saying "Coming events cast their shadows before" seems verified in this little instance, the soldier lad being destined to be her future husband; but at present Miss Becky Sharp is merely the young governess for Sir Pitt's two little daughters, and with him she drives off in a coach the next day to Queen's Crawley, the baronet's country home. From this strange and not very pleasant country mansion Becky writes most intelligent letters to her trustful young friend, Amelia Sedley. Her epistles describe all she meets, thinks, and hears with amusing exactness. Her spirits never flag, she never seems to know what it is to be shocked, saddened, or even much surprised at anything. She is now beginning real life in practical earnest, without wise friends or relatives; yet her career is entirely in private life and chiefly among people of little if any political influence as yet. Had her lot been cast among kings, statesmen, or distinguished people, her extraordinary knowledge of character, firmness, intelligence, and utter unscrupulousness would perhaps have raised her to great, if short-lived, power or authority. Her private letters reveal her character with peculiar interest. She thoroughly knows, despises, yet rather likes her simple, gentle school friend, Amelia, and thus with assumed sentimentalism, while full of private plots and plans, she writes:

With what mingled joy and sorrow do I take my pen to write to my dearest friend! Oh, what a change between to-day and yesterday! *Now* I am friendless and alone; yesterday I was at home in the sweet company of a sister whom I shall ever, *ever* cherish! *You* went on Tuesday to joy and happiness, with your mother and *your devoted young soldier* by your side, and I thought of you all night dancing at the Perkins's, the prettiest, I am sure, of all the young ladies at the ball. I was brought by the groom in the old carriage to Sir Pitt Crawley's town house. . . . Sir Pitt is not what we silly girls, when we used to read "Cecilia" at Chiswick, imagined a baronet must have been. . . . Fancy an old, stumpy, short, vulgar, and very dirty man in old clothes and shabby old gaiters, who smokes a horrid pipe and cooks his own horrid supper in a saucepan. . . . A carriage and four splendid horses covered with armorial bearings, however, awaited us at Mudbury, four miles from Queen's Crawley, and we made our entrance to the baronet's park in state. . . .

"There's an avenue," said Sir Pitt, "a mile long. There's six thousand pounds of timber in them there trees. Do you call that nothing?" He pronounced avenue—*evenue*, and nothing—*nothink*, so droll; and he had a Mr. Hodson, his hind from Mudbury, into the carriage with him. . . .

I remarked a beautiful church spire rising above some old elms in the park. . . . "Is that your church, sir?" I said.

"Yes, hang it," said Sir Pitt (only he used, dear, a *much wickeder word*), "how's Buty, Hodson? Buty's my brother Bute, my dear—

my brother the parson. Buty and the Beast I call him, ha, ha." Hodson laughed too, and then, looking more grave and nodding his head, said,

" I'm afraid he's better, Sir Pitt. He was out on his pony yesterday, looking at our corn."

"Looking after his tithes, hang 'un" (only he used the same wicked word). "Will brandy and water never kill him? He's as tough as old What-d'ye-call-'em, old Methusalem."

Mr. Hodson laughed again . . . and I have no doubt from this that the brothers are at variance, as brothers often are, and sisters too. . . .

I was interrupted last night by a dreadful thumping at my door; and who do you think it was? Sir Pitt Crawley in his nightcap and dressing-gown, such a figure! As I shrank away from such a visitor, he came forward and seized my candle: " No candles after eleven o'clock, Miss Becky," said he. " Go to bed in the dark, you pretty little hussy" (that is what he called me), "and unless you wish me to come for the candle every night, mind and be in bed at eleven," and with this he and Mr. Horrocks, the butler, went off laughing. . . .

Half an hour after our arrival the great dinner-bell was rung and I came down with my two pupils (they are very thin, insignificant little chits of ten and eight years old). . . . We all assembled in the little drawing-room where Lady Crawley sits. She is the second Lady Crawley and mother of the young ladies. She was an ironmonger's daughter. . . . She looks as if she had been handsome once and her eyes are always weeping for the loss of her beauty. She is pale . . . and has not a word to say for herself evidently. Her stepson, Mr. Crawley, was likewise in the room. He was in full dress, as pompous as an undertaker. He is pale, thin, ugly, silent; he has thin legs, no chest, hay-coloured whiskers and straw-coloured hair. . . .

At ten the servants were told to call Sir Pitt and the household to prayers. Sir Pitt came in first, very much flushed and rather unsteady in his gait; after him the butler . . . Mr. Crawley's man and three other men, smelling very much of the stable, and four women, one of whom I remarked was much over-dressed, and who flung me a look of great scorn as she plumped down on her knees.

Becky's long, amusing letter ridicules the whole Crawley establishment with mingled wit and bitterness. Everything she writes is more or less sarcastic, though keenly observant of every one and everything around her. Witty sarcasm is, indeed, always Thackeray's strong point, especially throughout this masterpiece of his novels. Yet he now offers the following explanation of his peculiar style of descriptive writing, which, despite his apparent fear of the contrary effects, eminently delighted the public at large:

> My kind reader will please to remember that this history has "Vanity Fair" for its title, and that Vanity Fair is a very vain, wicked, foolish place, full of all sorts of humbugs and falsehoods and pretensions. . . .
>
> And as we bring our characters forward, I will ask leave as a man and a brother not only to introduce them, but occasionally to step down from the platform and talk about them, if they are good and kindly to love them and shake them by the hand, if they are silly to laugh at them confidentially in the reader's sleeve, if they are wicked and heartless to abuse them in the strongest terms which politeness admits. Otherwise you might fancy it was I who was sneering at the practice of devotion, which Miss Sharp finds so ridiculous; . . . whereas the laughter comes from one who has no reverence except for prosperity and no eye for anything beyond success. Such people there are living and flourishing in the world—faithless, hopeless, charityless. Let us have at them, dear friends, with might and main. Some there are, and very successful too, mere quacks and fools, and it was to combat and expose such as these, no doubt, that laughter was made.[1]

---

[1] Chap. viii.

CHAPTER III

IN the next chapter (ix.), Thackeray describes the Crawley family at some length. He mentions the second Lady Crawley as a weak person in humble station, who had given up her former lover, Peter Butt, a man about her own station in life, and married the brutal, selfish old Sir Pitt, to whose treatment of her he thus alludes:

> When her husband was rude to her she was apathetic. Whenever he struck her, she cried.

Thackeray then appeals to his readers with keen good sense and kind feeling on this subject:

> O Vanity Fair, Vanity Fair! This might have been but for you a cheery lass—Peter Butt and Rose a happy man and wife, in a snug farm. . . . But a title and a coach and four are toys more precious than happiness in Vanity Fair, and if Harry the Eighth or Bluebeard were alive now and wanted a tenth wife, do you suppose he could not get the prettiest girl that shall be presented this season?

The author now describes Sir Pitt's sons, Pitt and Rawdon. These brothers are complete contrasts to one another, and each is on the whole superior to their degraded, odious old father. Pitt the elder, though pompous and pedantic, always seems to the present writer to deserve more praise than blame, yet Thackeray evidently dislikes him, and inclines readers to do so also. But despite his occasional meanness and prosy way of talking, he on the whole does his duty, and, in fact, does more good *generally* than almost any other man in this story, not excepting Dobbin—which, indeed, may not be saying much. He is as obedient and respectful to his disreputable father as that disgraceful old man's conduct permits him to be. He is alone of all the Crawley family considerate to and kind to his ill-used stepmother.

For many years his was the only kindness she ever knew, the only friendship that solaced in any way that feeble, lonely soul.[1]

He proves also kind and practically forgiving throughout the story to his bullying, profligate younger brother. Indeed, the relative conduct and behaviour of the brothers are really that of insult and bullying on one side, and quiet endurance with occasional generosity on the other. Yet Thackeray himself seems rather to prefer the younger. Even while describing the strong Rawdon's bullying and scorning his weaker brother when at school, and young Pitt's steady, harmless conduct there, Thackeray writes with calm sarcasm indicating little if any preference for either:

At Eton he [Pitt] was called Miss Crawley. . . . But though his parts were not brilliant, he made up for his lack of talent by meritorious industry and was never known during eight years at school to be subject to the punishment which it is generally thought none but a cherub can escape.

Pitt when grown up does all in his power to establish order and respectability amongst his father's

[1] Chap. xiv.

servants and household in and about Queen's Crawley. In short, he does usually what is right towards every one, except in one instance only, where he is certainly treacherous to his drunken cousin, Jim Crawley. Yet all he does is in such a pompous, disagreeable way, that it makes him rather disliked by readers, really more than his practical conduct and character deserve, considering the degraded state of his family, which, though in an unpleasing way, he is always trying to improve and inspire with right feelings.

Thus Thackeray describes him usually in the right, but provoking in his style of being so :

> When he grew to man's estate . . . be began to reform the slackened discipline of the Hall, in spite of his father, who stood in awe of him. . . . He was a man of such rigid refinement that he would have starved rather than have dined without a white neckcloth . . . and Sir Pitt never swore at Lady Crawley while his son was in the room.

Thackeray's lengthened description of old Sir Pitt [1] would surely seem exaggerated, yet it is thoroughly consistent throughout:

> He was unluckily endowed with a good name and a large though encumbered estate, both of which went rather to injure than to advance him. He had a taste for law which cost him many thousands yearly, and being a great deal too clever to be robbed, as he said, by any single agent, allowed his affairs to be mismanaged by a dozen whom he all equally mistrusted. He was such a sharp landlord that he could hardly find any but bankrupt tenants, and such a close farmer as to grudge almost the seed to the ground, whereupon revengeful Nature grudged him the crops which she granted to more liberal husbandmen. . . . In disposition he was sociable and far from being proud . . . he was fond of drink, of

[1] Chap. ix.

swearing, of joking with farmers' daughters; he was never known to give away a shilling or to do a good action, but was of a pleasant, sly, laughing mood, and would cut a joke and drink his glass with a tenant, and sell him up the next day. . . . In a word, the whole baronetcy, peerage, commonage of England did not contain a more cunning, mean, selfish, foolish, disreputable old man.

The reason why this degraded and degrading old wretch stood in awe of his eldest son is thus explained, but though the younger Pitt's conduct and influence are nearly always on the right side, and certainly meant to improve all about him, Thackeray gives him very little credit for good intentions, despite of all the good he does, and tries to do :

The Baronet owed his son money out of the jointure of his mother, which he did not find it convenient to pay; indeed, he had an almost invincible repugnance to paying anybody and could only be brought by force to discharge his debts. . . . "What's the good of being in Parliament," he said, "if you must pay your debts?" Hence, indeed, his position as a senator was not a little useful to him.

Here Thackeray pauses in his narration to appeal, as it were, to the civilised public generally and to suggest, though somewhat vaguely, some change in British education or opinion without advocating anything like revolution, yet his language is strong, vehement, and powerful :

Vanity Fair, Vanity Fair! Here was a man who could not spell and did not care to read—who had the habits and the cunning of a boor . . . who never had a taste or emotion, or enjoyment, but what was sordid and foul, and yet he had rank and honour and power somehow and was a dignitary of the land and a pillar of the State.[1] He was high sheriff and rode in a golden coach. Great

[1] "Sir Pitt Crawley certainly diverges so far from the ordinary type of English country gentlemen, that one suspects him to be a portrait from life" ("The Writings of Thackeray," by Leslie Stephen).

ministers and statesmen courted him, and in Vanity Fair he had a higher place than the most brilliant genius or spotless virtue.

The odious old Sir Pitt's unmarried half-sister, Miss Crawley, is now described; she is rich, selfish, and to her unlucky humble lady-companion, Miss Briggs, rather cruel. She much prefers her wild young nephew, Rawdon Crawley, to his brother Pitt, meaning to make the former her heir, and has more than once paid his debts. Miss Crawley, owing entirely to her money, neither valuing nor caring to inspire any esteem, is courted by all the Crawleys, who are on the whole a very mean, degraded family, and a disgrace to their class. Her wealthy position and selfish, arrogant temper make her both flattered and feared by all the Crawleys, more or less. Upon this subject Thackeray displays his satirical powers to the utmost, in a rather comic appeal to his readers. He describes, in his most amusing style, what his own behaviour and feelings would be, were this old Miss Crawley, the creature of his imagination, a living reality of his acquaintance:

She has a balance at the banker's which would have made her beloved anywhere.

What a dignity it gives an old lady, that balance at the banker's! How tenderly we look at her faults if she is a relative (and may every reader have a score such). . . . What a good fire there is in her room when she comes to pay you a visit, although your wife laces her stays without one! The house during her stay assumes a festive, neat, warm, jovial, snug appearance not visible at other seasons. . . . Even the servants in the kitchen share in the general prosperity. . . . Ah, gracious powers! I wish you would send me an old aunt, a maiden aunt—an aunt with a lozenge on her carriage and a front of light coffee-coloured hair—how my children should work workbags for her, and my Julia and I would make her comfortable! Sweet, sweet vision! Foolish, foolish dream![1]

Miss Sharp's wonderful success in dealing with and describing the Queen's Crawley family forms the subject of the two next chapters. Friendless and alone in this strange family, surrounded by selfish, vulgar, mean people, without a single really respectable person among them except young Mr. Pitt to some extent, she yet holds her own, and by degrees more than her own, among all of them. Though nominally only the governess of old Sir Pitt's two little daughters, she contrives to attract, please, and influence the baronet himself, and both his sons in succession. The young Pitt, though both self-conceited and self-righteous, is the best of all the Crawleys morally and intellectually, and does, or tries to do, more good to all about him than any other of the Crawley party.

In some respects this man may not be altogether unlike the Rev. Mr. Collins in Miss Austen's famous novel.[2] Miss Sharp has now old Miss Crawley to deal with, who comes on a visit to her half-brother, Sir Pitt. Becky's own words, whether in letters or spoken to herself, reveal her real character, conduct, hopes, and motives with peculiar clearness. Thackeray thus sarcastically introduces some of her natural remarks:

Being received as a member of the amiable family, whose portraits we have sketched in the foregoing pages, it became naturally Rebecca's duty to make herself, as she said, agreeable to her benefactors and to gain their confidence to the utmost of her power. . . .

---

[1] Chap. ix.

[2] "Pride and Prejudice."

"I am alone in the world," said the friendless girl, "I have nothing to look for but what my own labours can bring me, and while that little pink-faced chit Amelia, with not half my sense, has ten thousand pounds and an establishment secure, poor Rebecca has only herself and her own wits to trust to. . . . Not that I dislike poor Amelia: who can dislike such a harmless, good-natured creature—only it will be a fine day when I can take my place above her in the world—and why, indeed, should I not?"

Thackeray continues in a cool, critical way, pretending to be always rather fond of Rebecca:

Thus it was that our little romantic friend formed visions of the future for herself—nor must we be scandalised that in all her castles in the air, a husband was the principal inhabitant. . . . So she wisely determined to render her position with the Queen's Crawley family comfortable and secure, and to this end, resolved to make friends of every one around her who could at all interfere with her comfort.

Becky's success with the Crawleys, though short-lived, is nearly as complete as she could wish for a time. Indeed, her knowledge of character and keen insight into the dispositions of others are among her most remarkable gifts, and she contrives to make friends of old Sir Pitt, his two sons, even of her two pupils to some extent, and finally of old Miss Crawley. Her success, however, over young Mr. Pitt, though very amusing, is the least complete of her triumphs, and is owing entirely to his personal vanity:

With Mr. Crawley, Miss Sharp was respectful and obedient . . . and was often affected even to tears by his discourses of an evening, and would say, "Oh, thank you, sir," with a sigh and a look up to heaven that made him occasionally condescend to shake hands with her. "Blood is everything, after all," would that aristocratic religionist say. "How Miss Sharp is awakened by my words, when not one of the people here is touched. I am too fine for them—too delicate. I must familiarise my style—but she understands it. Her mother was a Montmorency."

Indeed, it was from this famous family, as it appears, that Miss Sharp by the mother's side was descended. Of course, she did not say that her mother had been on the stage; it would have shocked Mr. Crawley's religious scruples. . . .

He took Rebecca to task once or twice about the propriety of playing backgammon with Sir Pitt, saying that it was a godless amusement and that she would be much better engaged in reading "Thrump's Legacy" or "The Blind Washerwoman of Moorfield," or any work of a more serious nature; but Miss Sharp said her dear mother used to play the same game with the old Count de Trictac and the venerable Abbé du Cornet, and so found an excuse for this and other worldly amusements.

The success with which Becky, for some time at least, manages to really outwit the Queen's Crawley family, despite their quarrels, and the influence which she practically acquires over them, and indeed over most people whom she meets, induces the author to make an interesting explanation; in which, however, perhaps many readers will think cunning a more correct name than clever for her character. Rebecca is endowed from the first with a rare knowledge of human nature, great powers of deception and a firm resolution to promote her own interests without shame or scruple, which in political life might have given her vast influence with many people. In her peculiar and rather obscure position in life, she is yet enabled to triumph over a succession of people, most rather richer than herself, by a consistent course of private intrigue, among a variety of persons nearly all inferior to her, both in ability and resolution. So great and so surprising is her success, indeed, in deceiving very different people that Thackeray emphatically says in explanation:

A system of hypocrisy which lasts through whole years, is one seldom satisfactorily practised by a person of one-and-twenty, however our readers will recollect that though young in years, our heroine was old in life and experience, and we have written to no purpose if they have not discovered that she was a very clever woman.

Yet it must be owned that the selfish, quarrelsome Crawley family were none of them really wise, or even sensible people, so that a woman of Becky's ability found it not a very difficult task to deceive them more or less all in turn.

The two brothers, Pitt and Rawdon, disliked each other, and except in selfishness had scarcely any feeling in common. Their old aunt, Miss Crawley, possessing £70,000, paid an annual visit to her half-brother, Sir Pitt, and both his sons were most respectful to her, for pecuniary reasons. She disliked the elder and much preferred Rawdon, a drinking, sporting, gambling duellist. Sir Pitt's advice to his eldest son and his reply, upon the occasion of Miss Crawley's visit and Thackeray's own comment, explain their characters and motives with peculiar clearness, and with a wit which few if any authors could rival.

"Shut up your *sarmons*, Pitt, when Miss Crawley comes down," said his father. "She has written to say that she won't stand the preachifying."

"O sir! Consider the servants."

"The servants be hanged!" said Sir Pitt, and his son thought even worse would happen were they deprived of the benefit of his instructions.

"Why, hang it, Pitt!" said the father to his remonstrance, "you wouldn't be such a flat as to let three thousand a year go out of the family?"

"What is money, compared to our souls, sir?" continued Mr. Crawley.

"You mean that the old lady won't leave the money to you?"—and who knows but it *was* Mr. Crawley's meaning?

Old Miss Crawley was certainly one of the reprobates. She had a snug little house in Park Lane. . . . She read Voltaire and had Rousseau by heart, talked very lightly about divorce and most energetically of the rights of women. . . .

This worthy old lady took a fancy to Rawdon Crawley when a boy . . . always used to pay his debts after his duels, and would not listen to a word that was whispered against his morality.

"He will sow his wild oats," she would say, "and is worth far more than that puling hypocrite of a brother of his."

Pitt Crawley, however, despite vanity and bigoted self-righteous ideas, cannot fairly be called a hypocrite, as among all the Crawley family he seems the only one who tries, though in a disagreeable, conceited way, to keep everybody and everything in good order. The Queen's Crawley family, of whom he is certainly the most respectable, are a truly odious party, well deserving Thackeray's keen sarcasm about them:[1]

These honest folks at the Hall (whose simplicity and sweet rural purity surely show the advantage of a country life over a town one).

Sir Pitt's brother, the Rev. Bute Crawley, and his sharp, practical little wife are now introduced, and if Sir Pitt is a wretched sample of a country squire, the Rev. Bute is equally unfavourable as a sample of a country parson. Mr. Bute is a low, coarse, sporting man, perhaps resembling Macaulay's

[1] Chap. xi.

poetical sketch of a country clergyman in a hunting district :

> Dr. Nimrod, whose orthodox toes
> Are seldom withdrawn from the stirrup.[1]

But though a fine athlete, bold, cheerful, and strong, he has none of the generous, kindly feelings which often accompany these manly qualities. He is mean and selfish, constantly in money troubles:

> His wife was a smart little body, who wrote this worthy divine's sermons. . . . She ruled absolutely within the rectory, wisely giving her husband full liberty without . . . Mrs. Crawley was a saving woman and knew the price of port wine. . . . In spite of her care, however, he was always in debt. . . . His sister helped him with a hundred, now and then, but of course his great hope was in her death—when " Hang it " (as he would say), " Matilda must leave me half her money."

A more repulsive, detestable family than the Crawleys can hardly be imagined and has rarely been described. Sir Pitt and his clergyman brother dislike each other as much as the baronet's two sons dislike each other. Rawdon rather resembles his uncle the rector, though there is no friendship between them; but neither of Sir Pitt's sons, with all their faults, is as utterly low and degraded as their father. Miss Crawley, the rich maiden sister and aunt among these hardened, mean people, is of course a bone of contention between them, as she herself, as shrewd and as selfish as any of them, very well knows.

The author makes the following bitter, and it

[1] " Miscellaneous Writings."

may be hoped exaggerated, reflection on such people:

> These money transactions—these speculations in life and death—these silent battles for reversionary spoil—make brothers very loving towards each other in Vanity Fair. I for my part have known a five-pound note to interpose and knock up half a century attachment between two brethren, and can't but admire as I think what a fine and durable thing Love is among worldly people.

Among such a hard and selfish family as the Crawleys is placed the artful, resolute little orphan, Miss Sharp. As cold-hearted and worldly as any of them, yet possessing superior intelligence, with a natural wit and a rare power of amusing others altogether above and beyond the capacity of any of the Crawleys, she has also another advantage to aid her in intrigues among them. Unlike Mrs. Bute, who has her own daughters to think of and provide for, and unlike the young Crawley brothers, the elder striving to keep up "appearances" in a dissolute family and the younger devoted to reckless dissipated habits, yet a favourite of his rich old aunt; unlike also the selfish, wealthy old Miss Crawley, and her degraded old brother, Sir Pitt—Miss Becky has only her own interests to think of. She is absolutely without fortune, alliance, or influential friends of any kind, and is therefore exposed to all the jealousy, rudeness, and suspicions aroused by her lonely, unfriended position. Fortunately, however, for herself, in a worldly sense, Becky is never either shocked at or ashamed of anything other people can do or say about her. She therefore studies the Crawley family as being the social world in miniature for the present, though doubtless hoping to mix with far more important and distinguished people through time. At present, however, concealing all future hopes or speculations, she sets herself steadily to study and indirectly to profit by those immediately around her to the utmost of her power and opportunity.

Mrs. Bute Crawley, an envious, shrewd, active little woman, far superior to her coarse, reckless husband, who is quite under her rule, becomes very uneasy and suspicious about Becky's increasing influence and position at Queen's Crawley. Hearing that Becky had been a pupil of Miss Pinkerton, her own former governess, Mrs. Bute writes a letter to that old lady at Chiswick, and receives an answer from her about Miss Sharp. Both these epistles are most amusing in their way, when, after exchanging rather fulsome compliments, Mrs. Bute, inquiring for one of her pupils as a governess and Miss Pinkerton naming two, the real cause and spirit of their correspondence are alike revealed in their respective postscripts. Thus Mrs. Bute concludes:

PS.—Mr. Crawley's brother, the baronet, with whom we are not, alas! upon those terms of *unity*, in which it *becomes brethren to dwell*, has a governess for his little girls, who I am told had the good fortune to be educated at Chiswick. I hear various reports of her . . . and as I long to be attentive to *any pupil of yours*, do, my dear Miss Pinkerton, tell me *the history* of this young lady, whom for *your sake* I am most anxious to befriend.

To this question comes a prompt reply. Miss Pinkerton, after recommending two of her pupils, one of whom she frankly owns "is twenty-nine, her face is much pitted with small-pox. She has a halt in her gait, red hair, and a trifling obliquity of vision," gives the really desired answer in a postscript. This is indeed a masterpiece of covert dislike and damaging suspicion, though conveyed in formal, guarded language.

PS.—The Miss Sharp whom you mention as governess to Sir Pitt Crawley, M.P., was a pupil of mine and I have nothing to say in her disfavour. Though her appearance is disagreeable, we cannot control the operations of nature, and though her parents were disreputable (her father being a painter, several times bankrupt, and her mother, as I have since learned with horror, a dancer at the Opera), yet her talents are considerable and I cannot regret that I took her in *out of charity*. My dread is lest the principles of the mother, who was represented to me as a French Countess, forced to emigrate in the late revolutionary horrors but who, as I have since found, was a person of the *very lowest order and morals*—should at any time prove to be *hereditary* in the unhappy young woman whom I took as *an outcast*.

Next follows an amusing descriptive letter from Becky herself to her old friend, Amelia Sedley, whom she rather trusts and to some extent even likes, though despising her weak character. This letter is long but most amusingly written, and if discovered by the inmates of Humdrum Hall, as she calls it, would likely have caused her speedy expulsion therefrom. Her conquest of old Sir Pitt she thus briefly and truly describes. Sir Pitt is apparently falling in love with her already, though his poor, delicate wife, Lady Crawley, being still alive, marriage is impossible. Becky writes very frankly:

I believe the old wretch likes me as much as it is in his nature to like any one. . . . Miss Crawley has arrived . . . the great, rich Miss Crawley with seventy thousand pounds in the five per cents., whom, or I had better say *which*, her two brothers adore. She looks very apoplectic, the dear soul; no wonder her brothers are anxious about her. You should see them struggling to settle her cushions, or to hand her coffee. "When I come into the country," she says (for she has a great deal of humour), "I leave my toady, Miss Briggs, at home. My brothers are my toadies here, my dear, and a pretty pair they are!" . . . What a charming reconciler and peacemaker money is!

Another admirable effect of Miss Crawley and her seventy thousand pounds is to be seen in the conduct of the two brothers Crawley. I mean the baronet and the rector . . . who hate each other all the year round, become quite loving at Christmas. . . . When Miss Crawley arrives there is no such thing as quarrelling heard of—the Hall visits the Rectory and *vice versa*—the parson and the baronet talk about the pigs and the poachers, and the County business in the most affable manner and without quarrelling in their cups, I believe."

Becky then proceeds to describe Sir Pitt's second son, Rawdon Crawley, with whom she is fated to be involved and whose portrait she had dreamed about, when first at Sir Pitt's London house:

Our sermon-books are shut up when Miss Crawley arrives, and Mr. Pitt, whom she abominates, finds it convenient to go to town. On the other hand the young dandy—*blood* I believe is the term—Captain Crawley makes his appearance. . . . He is a very large young dandy. He is six feet high, and speaks with a great voice and swears a great deal and orders about the servants, who all adore him nevertheless, for he is very generous of his money. . . . He has a *dreadful reputation among the ladies*. . . . Shall I tell you a compliment the Captain paid me? I must, it is so pretty. . . . Well, I heard him say "By Jove, she is a neat little filly," meaning your humble servant, and he did me the honour to dance two country dances with me. . . . He says the country girls are *bores*—indeed, I don't think he is far wrong. You should see the contempt with which they look down on poor me! . . .

I wish you could have seen the faces of the Miss Blackbrooks . . . when Captain Rawdon selected poor me for a partner.

The rector, Mr. Bute Crawley, and his shrewd little wife are now described, or rather they describe themselves, in a familiar talk together about Sir Pitt's family, and especially about Miss Crawley, whom they are all trying to please while she is on a visit to the old baronet. The Rev. Bute bitterly abuses his nephew Rawdon, though rather resembling him in some respects, but then he has young sons of his own, and the whole Crawley family are evidently the incarnations of selfishness.

. . . "Why did you ask that scoundrel Rawdon Crawley to dine?" said the Rector to his lady, "*I* don't want the fellow. . . . He's never content unless he gets my yellow-sealed wine, which costs me ten shillings a bottle, hang him! Besides, he's such an infernal character—he's a gambler—he's a drunkard—he's a profligate in every way. He shot a man in a duel—he's over head and ears in debt and he's robbed me and mine of the best part of Miss Crawley's fortune. . . ."

"I think she's going," said the Rector's wife. "She was very red in the face when we left dinner. I was obliged to unlace her."

"She drank seven glasses of champagne," said the reverend gentleman in a low voice, "and filthy champagne it is too that my brother poisons us with. . . .

"She drank cherry-brandy after dinner," continued his Reverence, "and took curacoa with her coffee. . . . She can't stand it, Mrs. Crawley—she must go—flesh and blood won't bear it! and I lay five to two Matilda drops in a year."

Indulging in these solemn speculations and thinking about his debts and his son Jim at college and Frank at Woolwich and the four girls who were no beauties, poor things, and would not have a penny, but what they got from their aunt's expected legacy, the Rector and his lady walked on for a while.[1]

They continue fretting, scolding, and abusing all the other Crawleys except their own children, when at

[1] Chap. xi.

last Mrs. Bute, much the most intelligent of the two, frankly tells her husband that

> he is intoxicated as usual. And the next morning, when the Rector woke and called for small beer, she put him in mind of his promise to visit Sir Huddleton-Fuddleston on Saturday, and as he knew he should have a *wet night*, it was agreed that he might gallop back again in time for church on Sunday morning.

After this revelation of selfish meanness and utter want of right principle in two brothers who are expected to set a respectable example, when neither could plead ignorance or any excuse for their odious conduct and thoughts, Thackeray addresses his readers with calm sarcasm:

> Thus it will be seen that the parishioners of Queen's Crawley were equally happy in their Squire and in their Rector.

Miss Sharp's success in pleasing or deceiving all the Crawley family is complete though short-lived. Miss Crawley, though shrewd and observant, becomes delighted with Becky's agreeable way of talking and insists on almost openly preferring her to any one else she meets. She enthusiastically exclaims to her brother, old Sir Pitt, when insisting upon Becky dining at table:

> "Why, she's the only person fit to talk to in the County."

She even praises the little governess to her face, comparing her favourably to the Crawley family, with Sir Pitt and the Rev. Bute and not excepting her own humble companion, Miss Briggs, over whom she is a constant tyrant. She

> ordered that Rawdon Crawley should lead her into dinner every day and that Becky should follow with her cushion. "We must

sit together," she said. "We're the only three Christians in the County, my love" [and here Thackeray shrewdly remarks]: "In which case it must be confessed that religion was at a very low ebb in the county of Hants."

Meantime Rawdon Crawley quite loses his heart to Becky who, always lively and clever, in reality cares nothing for him, nor indeed for any one or anything except her own interests:

. . . The Captain had written her notes (the best that the great blundering dragoon could devise and spell). . . . But when he put the first of the notes into the leaves of the song she was singing, the little governess, rising and looking him steadily in the face, took up the triangular missive daintily . . . popped the note into the fire, and made him a very low curtsey, and went back to her place and began to sing away again as merrily as ever.

"What's that?" said Miss Crawley, interrupted in her after-dinner doze by the stoppage of the music.

"It's a false note," Miss Sharp said, with a laugh, and Rawdon Crawley fumed with rage and mortification.

This flirtation between the artful Miss Becky and the bold yet comparatively stupid Rawdon Crawley is amusingly sketched, during an evening walk they take together, but he is evidently an easy conquest for the clever little adventuress.

"O those stars, those stars!" Miss Rebecca would say, turning her twinkling green eyes up towards them. "I feel myself almost a spirit when I gaze upon them."

"O—ah—Gad—yes, so do I exactly, Miss Sharp," the other enthusiast replied. "You don't mind my cigar, do you, Miss Sharp?" Miss Sharp loved the smell of a cigar out of doors beyond everything in the world—and she just tasted one too . . . and restored the delicacy to the Captain, who twirled his moustache . . . and swore, "Jove—aw—Gad—aw—it's the finest segaw I ever smoked in the world, aw," for his intellect and conversation were alike brilliant and becoming to a heavy young dragoon.

It is the silent influence of old Miss Crawley, however, that enables the young couple to continue their flirtation without opposition from the rest of the Crawley family, Sir Pitt declaring:

"that if it wasn't for Miss Crawley, he'd take Rawdon and bundle 'un out of doors, like a rogue as he was." He owns this to Horrocks, his steward, who replies: "He *be* a bad'n, sure enough, and his man Flethers is wuss and have made such a row in the housekeeper's room about the dinners and hale, as no lord would make . . . but I think Miss Sharp's a match for'n, Sir Pitt" [and Thackeray thus confirms this opinion]: "And so in truth she was—for father and son too."

CHAPTER IV

THE author now leaves Miss Sharp making a rapid conquest both of Sir Pitt and of Rawdon Crawley, and describes at some length the devoted, unrequited love of Dobbin for Amelia Sedley, who is in love with George Osborne, the only son of a rich London banker, a purse-proud, arrogant old gentleman, with two unmarried daughters now living with him. George is a handsome, conceited young dandy; his sisters are proud and worldly, and none of the Osborne family really understands the true character of poor gentle little Amelia. Yet George hitherto returns her affection as far as his proud, selfish nature permits him to care for any one but himself. His sisters are about equally proud and selfish, yet are made rather amusing by the skill of their inventor:

> . . . When young Bullock . . . who had been making up to Miss Maria the last two seasons, actually asked Amelia to dance, could you expect that the former young lady should be pleased? And yet she said she was . . . "I'm so delighted you like dear Amelia," she said quite eagerly after the dance. "She's engaged to my brother George . . . at home we're all *so* fond of her." Dear girl! who can calculate the depth of affection expressed in that enthusiastic *so*?"

The Miss Osbornes have a formal yet rather sly governess, Miss Wirt. This person appears in another of Thackeray's works,[1] and is apparently much the same character while in the same profession. These three not very amiable ladies, the governess and her two pupils, alike despise poor Amelia, the sisters constantly telling George that he is far above and at least socially too good for her. He agrees to some extent, yet

> gave himself up to be loved with a good deal of easy resignation.

Dobbin, a wonderfully devoted friend to both George and Amelia, is slightly despised by each of them, though they alike make free use of him as an obliging friend. He preserves an almost unaccountable love for Miss Sedley, thinks more of her happiness than that of any one else, and is always trying to keep the lively, gay young Osborne faithful to her. The detailed account of Dobbin's unrequited devotion to them both takes up much of this book, and is, perhaps, not a very cheerful part of it, while presenting an interesting contrast to the intrigues of Becky Sharp, which are certainly far more enlivening to read about. It is Dobbin's fate to be undervalued or misunderstood by nearly every one, except his inventor. Not only is he despised, though rather liked by Amelia and George; but he is mistaken by the Miss Osbornes who have little idea of his love for Amelia, while one of them would even accept him herself. His own mother and sisters also ridicule Miss Sedley. Yet despite of almost every discouragement, Dobbin steadily tries to promote Amelia's marriage with Osborne, while longing to wed her

[1] "A Visit to some Country Snobs" in "The Snobs of England."

himself. The timid Amelia is naturally frightened at the scornful manner of all the Osborne family towards her. At one time her father, Mr. Sedley, was friendly with Mr. Osborne, but that friendship quite declined when Sedley became poorer, while the stern old Osborne was increasing in wealth, influence, and family ambition. Mr. Osborne, in his richly furnished Russell Square mansion, completely rules his two daughters, while his only son George he scolds and indulges alternately, though very proud of the handsome, selfish young man, who seems to care little, if anything, for anybody but himself. Among this not very agreeable family Dobbin labours to further Amelia's wishes and objects, and she coolly thanks and likes him, but apparently scarcely understands his deep affection for herself. Dobbin, with a devotion rare indeed, if possible, desires to promote her happiness far more than his own, and makes her, in fact, the idol of his mind and of his life. To her he throughout devotes his time, thoughts, and efforts. Though his conduct is noble and self-denying to the utmost, his love for Amelia tempts him, in spite of his high principles, to be practically unfair to the general public. Thus, when her father becomes almost ruined, Dobbin still warmly recommends old Sedley's bad wines to the general public for Amelia's sake alone.[1] Were it not for his love for Amelia, which might be called unscrupulous in disregarding all other considerations, William Dobbin well deserves to be called the real hero of this book, a title, however, which Thackeray denies him. Meanwhile, the way in which Amelia is snubbed, to use a common phrase,

[1] Chap. iii. in vol. ii.

may be amusing to read of, but painful to witness for any compassionate person.

While, however, the two school-friends, Becky and Amelia, are now separated and carrying on their own matrimonial schemes, Miss Sharp captivating Rawdon Crawley and Amelia trying, not quite in vain, to induce George Osborne to return her own sincere affection, Thackeray turns aside a little to mention public affairs. Napoleon I. is still the dread and the aversion of all Britain at this time. His very name was said sometimes to frighten children, and to induce simple recruits for enlistment in the rather doubtful yet tempting words :

"Perhaps a recruit might chance to shoot Great General Bonaparte."

After Napoleon's abdication

peace was declared, Europe was going to be at rest, . . . and Lieutenant Osborne's regiment would not be ordered on service. That was the way in which Miss Amelia reasoned. The fate of Europe was Lieutenant George Osborne to her. . . . She thought about him the very first moment on waking and his was the very last name mentioned in her prayers. . . . What were her parents doing not to keep this little heart from beating so fast? Old Sedley did not seem much to notice matters. He was graver of late and his City affairs absorbed him. Mrs. Sedley was of so easy and uninquisitive a nature that she was not even jealous. Mr. Jos was away, being besieged by an Irish widow at Cheltenham. Amelia had the house to herself—ah ! too much to herself sometimes, not that she ever doubted ; for, to be sure, George must be at the Horse Guards . . . and when he is with the regiment, he is too tired to write long letters.

Thus while Osborne's letters to Amelia were brief, those from her to him were many indeed, and an amusing picture is here given of Osborne lighting his cigar with "ardent love-letters."

Dobbin always keeps a strict watch on him in Amelia's behalf, while some younger officers, Ensigns Spoony and Stubbles, greatly admire the gay George, calling him

"a regular Don Giovanni, by Jove!"

Osborne, selfish and extravagant, often borrows money from Dobbin, whom he quarrels with for trying to keep him true to Miss Sedley. Dobbin once exclaims in indignant remonstrance to his profligate, thoughtless young friend:

. . . "I've told you you were neglecting a sweet girl, George. I've told you that when you go to town you ought to go to her and not to the gambling-houses about St. James'!"

"You want your money back, I suppose?" said George, with a sneer.

"Of course I do—I always did, didn't I?" says Dobbin. "You speak like a generous fellow."

"No, hang it, William, I beg your pardon," here George interposed in a fit of remorse. "You *have* been my friend in a hundred ways, Heaven knows. You've got me out of a score of scrapes. . . . And I say—Dob—don't be angry with me, and I'll give you a hundred next month, when I know my father will stand something handsome . . . and I'll go to town and see Amelia to-morrow—there now, will that satisfy you?"

"It is impossible to be long angry with you, George," said the good-natured captain; "and as for the money, old boy, you know if I wanted it you'd share your last shilling with me."

"That I would, by Jove, Dobbin," George said, with the greatest generosity;

but here Thackeray shrewdly observes, briefly revealing Osborne's true character:

though, by the way, he never had any money to spare,

and the author proceeds, amusingly contrasting the characters of these two young officers. Osborne, to show that he would be as good as his word, prepared to go to town, thereby incurring Captain Dobbin's applause.

. . . "I should have liked to make her a little present," Osborne said to his friend in confidence, "only I am quitè out of cash until my father tips up." But Dobbin would not allow this good-nature and generosity to be balked and so accommodated Mr. Osborne with a few pound notes, which the latter took after a little faint scruple.

And I dare say he would have bought something very handsome for Amelia, only getting off the coach in Fleet Street, he was attracted by a handsome shirt-pin in a jeweller's window which he could not resist.

George, after this purchase, made himself very agreeable to Amelia, and she dined with his father and sisters at their house in Russell Square, and was in excellent spirits. His stern old father, however, was in a gloomy state of mind; he had heard too true rumours of old Sedley's affairs going wrong, and aware of his son's attachment to Amelia, resolves to firmly oppose his marriage. When this old gentleman returns home to dinner he finds Amelia there with his two daughters:

. . . He looked round gloomily at his eldest daughter who, comprehending the meaning of his look, which asked unmistakably, "Why the devil is she here?" said at once:

"George is in town, papa, and has gone to the Horse Guards and will be back to dinner."

"O, he is, is he? I won't have the dinner kept waiting for *him*, Jane," with which this worthy man lapsed into his particular chair.

The old gentleman's temper is not improved by his son's being late for dinner, to which he, his two daughters, Amelia and the governess, Miss Wirt, now sit down, all the ladies being alike frightened and awed by the surly master of the house. Amelia trembled.

"Soup?" says Mr. Osborne, clutching the ladle, fixing his eyes on her, in a sepulchral tone, and having helped her and the rest did not speak for a while.

"Take Miss Sedley's plate away," at last he said. "She can't eat the soup nor more can I. It's beastly. Take away the soup, Hicks, and to-morrow turn the cook out of the house, Jane."

At length, and before dinner is quite over, George arrives in good spirits, and after the ladies are gone he begins praising his father's wine.

That was generally a successful means of cajoling the old gentleman.

Mr. Osborne had heard with pride of his son's now associating with fashionable people, and wishes therefore to prevent the intended marriage of him and Amelia, whose poor father's affairs are verging towards bankruptcy. Old Osborne's almost slavish respect for high rank, despite his proud, sullen nature, Thackeray amusingly describes:

Whenever he met a great man he grovelled before him and my lorded him as only a free-born Briton can do. . . . He fell down prostrate, and basked in him, as a Neapolitan beggar does in the sun.

Therefore his vanity is so gratified at George being now in high society, that he lavishes his money on him freely to enable him to keep in it.

George held up a little token which had been netted by Amelia and contained the very last of Dobbin's pound notes.

Osborne then exclaims in a sort of worldly enthusiasm :

> "You shan't want, sir. The British merchant's son shan't want, sir. My guineas are as good as theirs, my boy, and I don't grudge 'em. Call on Mr. Chopper as you go through the city to-morrow ; he'll have something for you. I don't grudge money when I know you're in good society."

It must be owned that the Osborne family, father, son, and two daughters, are most unamiable people, and poor little affectionate Amelia Sedley among them is naturally both despised and misunderstood, while her father's affairs get worse and worse. The more unfortunate Sedley is, the more stern and unfeeling old Osborne becomes towards him while in his own well-furnished, gloomy house in Russell Square. The harsh father, his proud, dull daughters and wild, conceited son are all rather depressing to read about. There is little if any wit or merriment among the Osbornes—little else, indeed, but purse-proud, haughty selfishness.

Thus the next chapter (xiv.), reverting to Becky Sharp's doings, is an enlivening, if not cheerful, change.

CHAPTER V

MISS CRAWLEY and Becky return to the former's London house, while poor delicate Lady Crawley dies; but neither her fate nor her character attract much interest, she being what is often called a complete nonentity. But the sudden influence of the cunning little Miss Sharp confounds Miss Crawley's former confidants, the meek companion, Miss Briggs, and the more shrewd housekeeper, Mrs. Firkin, who accordingly discuss Becky's character together and wonder helplessly at the artful way in which the little governess has superseded them both in the favour of the capricious old lady, whose whims and wishes they are always trying to gratify. Miss Briggs asks:

"What sort of a person is this Miss Sharp, Firkin? I little thought . . . to find a stranger had taken my place in the affections of my dearest, my still dearest, Matilda."

Mrs. Firkin replies with mingled wonder and jealous indignation, as well as a little suspicion:

"Miss B., they are all infatyated about that young woman . . . and I think somethink has bewidged everybody."

Miss Crawley herself is now nursed, flattered, and

managed by Miss Sharp in the former's house in Park Lane, but old Sir Pitt had become more and more attached to Becky. This doting folly of Sir Pitt his sister-in-law, Mrs. Bute Crawley, hints to her nephew Rawdon, warning him that Becky may yet become his father's wife. Rawdon, vain and shameless as he is, is no match for Becky in either intelligence or self-control, as Miss Sharp in the following scene sufficiently proves. When Rawdon actually ventured to hint about his father's liking for her:

. . . She flung up her head scornfully, looked at him full in the face and said:

"Well, suppose he *is* fond of me. I know he is and others too. You don't think I am afraid of him, Captain Crawley? You don't suppose I can't defend my own honour," said the little woman, looking as stately as a queen.

"O, ah, why—give you fair warning—look out, you know, that's all."

"You hint at something not honourable, then?" said she, flashing out.

"O — Gad — really — Miss Rebecca," the heavy dragoon interposed.

"Do you suppose I have no feeling of self-respect, because I am poor and friendless, and because rich people have none? . . . I'm a Montmorency. Do you suppose a Montmorency is not as good as a Crawley?"

When Miss Sharp was agitated and alluded to her maternal relatives, she spoke with ever so slight a foreign accent, which gave a great charm to her ringing voice. "No," she continued, kindling as she spoke to the Captain. "I can endure poverty but not shame — neglect, but not insult, and insult from — from *you*."

Her feelings gave way and she burst into tears. "Hang it, Miss Sharp—Rebecca—by Jove—I wouldn't for a thousand pounds. Stop, Rebecca!" She was gone. She drove out with Miss Crawley that day. . . Skirmishes of this sort passed perpetually during that little campaign—tedious to relate and similar in result.

The Crawley heavy cavalry was maddened by defeat and routed every day.

Becky meantime had made herself both useful as well as agreeable at Queen's Crawley, so that when she was comfortably settled with Miss Crawley in the latter's snug house in Park Lane, old Sir Pitt wrote constantly, entreating her to return. Miss Briggs and Mrs. Firkin, the companion and the maid, though not dismissed, yet found themselves fast losing influence compared to the increasing power of Miss Sharp. Rawdon Crawley, who often visits at his partial aunt's, now through Rebecca makes acquaintance not only with Miss Sedley but renews it with her admirer, George Osborne, whom Rawdon Crawley, far more cunning than that vain young coxcomb, had cheated before and wished to cheat again, while dreading Dobbin, always Osborne's friend, who had tried to separate the dupe from the knave before, sometimes in vain. Old Miss Crawley is delighted with pretty, simple little Amelia, partly from her gentle manner, while the conceited fop Osborne, tries to patronise Miss Sharp, but gets a complete repulse when he says:

"Ah, Miss Sharp, how d'ye do?" held out his left hand towards her, expecting that she would be quite confounded at the honour. Miss Sharp put out her right forefinger, and gave him a little nod, so cool and killing that Rawdon Crawley, watching the operations from the other room, could hardly restrain his laughter as he saw the Lieutenant's entire discomfiture, the start he gave, the pause and the perfect clumsiness with which he at length condescended to take the finger which was offered for his embrace.

"She'd beat the devil, by Jove!" the Captain said in rapture. . .

Though Rebecca had had the better of him, George was above the meanness of tale-bearing, or revenge upon a lady; only he could not help cleverly confiding to Captain Crawley next day some notions of his regarding Miss Rebecca, that she was a sharp one, a dangerous one, a desperate flirt, and in all of which opinions Crawley agreed laughingly, and with every one of which Miss Rebecca was made acquainted with before twenty-four hours were over. They added to her original regard for Mr. Osborne and she esteemed him accordingly.

George, who is no match for the cunning of either Becky or Rawdon, actually tells his lover Amelia that he thought it right to have warned Crawley

against that little sly, scheming Rebecca.

"O George, what *have* you done?" Amelia said. For her woman's eyes, which Love had made far-sighted, had in one instant discovered a secret which was invisible to Miss Crawley, to poor virgin Briggs, and above all to the stupid peepers of that young whiskered prig, Lieutenant Osborne."

Meantime the death of poor delicate Lady Crawley occasions some curious changes in the Crawley family. Old Miss Crawley takes the news quietly, hoping and thinking her half-brother will never marry again; when to her surprise the old gentleman arrives at her house door, asking to see her, she sends Becky to refuse his request, saying she is too unwell to receive him, when Sir Pitt Crawley replies:

"So much the better, Miss Becky,"

and when alone together the baronet makes her a comical but quite sincere offer of marriage.

"I can't git on without you. . . . The house all goes wrong. . . .

All my accounts has got muddled agin. You *must* come back. Do come back. Dear Becky, do come."

"Come as what, sir?" Rebecca gasped out.

"Come as Lady Crawley, if you like," the baronet said, grasping his crape hat. "There! will that zatusfy you? Come back and be my wife. You're vit vor't. Birth be hanged! You're as good a lady as ever I see. You've got more brains in your little vinger than any baronet's wife in the county. Will you come? Yes or no? . . . I'll make you happy, see if I don't. You shall do what you like, spend what you like, and 'av it all your own way. I'll make you a zettlement. I'll do everything reg'lar. Look year," and the old man fell on his knees and leered at her like a satyr.

Rebecca started back, a picture of consternation.

Miss Sharp, the rare consummate little actress as she may well be called, is now in her turn greatly surprised and sincerely disappointed; she seems never to have expected this offer, and yet she had studied the whole Queen's Crawley family with the keenest attention. She had, in fact, deceived them more or less all round, for none of them understood her real character and at this time all the family, except the Bute Crawleys, admired or trusted her. But she is now quite taken aback, being utterly unprepared for the scene before her.

Thackeray continues with emphatic force:

In the course of this history we have never seen her lose her presence of mind, but she did now, and wept some of the most genuine tears that ever fell from her eyes.

"Oh, Sir Pitt!" she said. "Oh, sir — I — I'm *married already*."

The accompanying illustration of this scene, showing Sir Pitt on his knees before Becky, is perhaps the best likeness of her in the book. Her demure, shrinking, yet artful expression, and the coarse, half-doting look of the odious old man express their relative feelings almost as clearly as in words. Becky then in turn goes down on her knees, asking Sir Pitt to let her be his daughter. Old Miss Crawley, when told of this scene by her two satellites, Miss Briggs and Mrs. Firkin, who after listening at the door inform their astounded old mistress, recovers promptly from illness, sails into the room and hears the truth from Sir Pitt. She then in wondering indignation asks Becky:

"Pray, Miss Sharp, are you waiting for the Prince Regent's divorce, that you don't think our family good enough for you?"

Becky now acts her part admirably, and in answer to Miss Crawley, while seeming deeply grieved, replies with dignified composure:

"My attitude, when you came in, ma'am, did not look as if I despised such an honour as this good—this noble man deigned to offer me. Do you think I have no heart? Have you all loved me and been so kind to the poor orphan—deserted—girl, and am *I* to feel nothing? O my friends! O my benefactors! may not my love, my life, my duty try to repay the confidence you have shown me? Do you grudge me even gratitude, Miss Crawley? It is too much—my heart is too full," and she sank down in a chair so pathetically that most of the audience present were perfectly melted with her sadness.

Of this audience, however, the shrewd Mrs. Firkin seems the most incredulous, for she writes to Mrs. Bute Crawley

by that very night's post. . . . Sir Pitt has been and proposed for Miss Sharp, wherein she has refused him, to the wonder of all.

Meantime, the self-indulgent old Miss Crawley and her poor, humble companion, Miss Briggs, talk over the late scene together, the unfeeling old lady tyrannising over her simple companion and each fancying that Becky has some "previous attachment":

. . . "You poor friendless creatures are always having some foolish *tendre*," Miss Crawley said. "You yourself, you know, were in love with a writing-master (don't cry, Briggs—you're always crying, and it won't bring him to life again)."

Miss Crawley then wonders who is Becky's husband, longing to find out and having no idea of the truth, for Becky resolutely keeps that a secret while thanking, blessing, and praising Miss Crawley for all her kindness to her, who, completely deceived, believes Becky to be

a dear, artless, tender-hearted, affectionate, incomprehensible creature.

Thackeray proceeds in his amusing, witty style, in which, indeed, few novelists much resemble him, to very gradually unfold to the readers the great secret to which hitherto Miss Sedley had partly given hints, which no one except the two interested parties know of in this story. He thus commences an address to his readers:

What think you were the private feelings of Miss, no (begging her pardon) of Mrs. Rebecca? . . .

Well, then, in the first place Rebecca gave way to some very sincere and touching regrets that a piece of marvellous good fortune should have been so near her and actually obliged to decline it. . . .

But Rebecca was a young lady of too much resolution and energy of character to permit herself much useless and unseemly sorrow for the irrevocable past . . . she wisely turned her whole attention towards the future, which was now vastly more important to her. And she surveyed her position and its hopes, doubts, and chances. In the first place she was *married*—that was a great fact and Sir Pitt knew it. . . . How Miss Crawley would bear the news was the great question. Misgivings Rebecca had, but she remembered all Miss Crawley had said; the old lady's avowed contempt for birth; her daring liberal opinions; her general romantic propensities; her almost doting attachment to her nephew, and her recently expressed fondness for Rebecca herself. She is so fond of him, Rebecca thought, that she will forgive him anything; she is so used to me that I don't think she could be comfortable without me. . . . At all events, what use was there in delaying? the die was thrown, and now or to-morrow the issue must be the same. And so, resolved that Miss Crawley should have the news, the young person debated in her mind as to the best means of conveying it to her and whether she should face the storm that must come, or fly and avoid it, until its first fury was blown over In this state of meditation, she wrote the following letter:—

"Dearest Friend,—The great crisis which we have debated about so often is come. Half of my secret is known, and I have thought and thought until I am quite sure, that now is the time to reveal *the whole of the mystery*. Sir Pitt came to me this morning and made, what do you think?—*a declaration in form!* Think of that! Poor little me. I might have been Lady Crawley. . . .

"Sir Pitt knows I am married, and not knowing to whom is not very much displeased as yet. *Ma tante* is *actually angry* that I should have refused him. But she is all kindness and graciousness. . . . She dotes upon you so (you naughty and good-for-nothing man) that she would pardon you anything. . . . Dearest! something *tells me* we shall conquer—you shall leave that odious regiment, quit gaming, racing and *be a good boy* and we shall all live in Park Lane and *ma tante* shall leave us all her money."

After these cheerful expectations, Becky asks her correspondent to come next day to "your own R." and directs her letter to

> Miss Eliza Styles, at Mr. Barnet's, Sadler, Knightsbridge.

Then comes the revelation, which most readers must have expected or guessed, that the Miss Styles ("an old schoolfellow," Rebecca said) was indeed no other than Captain Rawdon Crawley.

Becky now sincerely regrets her recent hasty marriage, and wishes it had been with old Sir Pitt. Whether in reality it is likely or even possible that a very young, intelligent woman like her would have preferred an old, rough, ugly, coarse man to his handsome, gay young son some readers may perhaps incline to doubt. Yet Thackeray describes her as truly and sincerely regretting her refusal of Sir Pitt, whom evidently she would have accepted had the old gentleman not been forestalled by his lively military son. Becky's private marriage so concealed from every one Thackeray amusingly describes:[1]

> . . . My belief is that one day when Miss Sharp had gone to pass the forenoon with her dear friend, Miss Amelia Sedley, in Russell Square, a lady very like her might have been seen entering a church in the city in company with a gentleman with dyed mustachios, who after a quarter of an hour's interval, escorted her back to the hackney coach in waiting, and that this was a quiet bridal party.

There can be no doubt of Thackeray's correct belief in this important instance, but Rebecca now

[1] Chap. xvi.

takes a step which, though after due consideration, proves rather unfortunate for her interests in the end. She resolves to secretly leave Miss Crawley's house, take lodgings elsewhere with her husband, leaving a letter in her room announcing her marriage, directed to Miss Briggs, but intended for Miss Crawley. In this letter Becky entreats Briggs to intercede with Miss Crawley, owning that "Miss Crawley's Rawdon is *my* Rawdon" and begging forgiveness. At this time, unluckily for Becky, Mrs. Bute Crawley arrives, to whom Briggs and Firkin tell the news of Becky's marriage, her rejection of old Sir Pitt and her subsequent flight. They tell all this unexpected news to old Miss Crawley, who, overwhelmed with surprise and vexation, actually faints away, upon which Mrs. Bute immediately takes charge of the house, quite overruling Miss Briggs, and proving herself the strictest of all possible companions to poor old Miss Crawley, now quite helpless.

One fit of hysterics succeeded another. The doctor was sent for —the apothecary arrived. Mrs. Bute took up the post of nurse by her bedside. "Her relations ought to be round about her," that amiable woman said.

Meanwhile the news of his son's marriage enrages old Sir Pitt, who

broke out into a fury of language which it would be no good to repeat in this place.

Becky, however, still keeps up her spirits as well as those of her loving yet comparatively stupid husband.

"Suppose the old lady doesn't come to," Rawdon said to his little wife, as they sat together in the snug little Brompton lodgings . . . "suppose she don't come round, eh, Becky?"

"I'll make your fortune," she said, and Delilah patted Samson's cheek.

"You can do anything," he said, kissing the little hand. "By Jove, you can, and we'll drive down to the 'Star and Garter' and dine, by Jove."

CHAPTER VI

THE next chapter[1] announces the ruin of Mr. Sedley, Amelia's father, and a general sale of the unlucky old bankrupt's goods. Among these Dobbin selects Amelia's piano and secretly buys it for her. Rawdon and Becky are at this sale, where Dobbin awaits them, while Jos Sedley, still at Cheltenham, sends some money to relieve his distressed parents, but does not visit them. Meanwhile the sly, artful little Mrs. Bute Crawley has quite established herself in Becky's place at Miss Crawley's house, and begins to tyrannise over the old invalid under the pretence of nursing her. On the whole, therefore, Miss Crawley was certainly much happier when Becky was in the house, but for some time she was helplessly in the power of Mrs. Bute.

The old aunt was long in "coming to." A month had elapsed. Rawdon was denied the door by Mr. Bowls; . . . his letters were sent back unopened. . . . Crawley and his wife both of them augured evil from the continued presence of Mrs. Bute.

"Gad! I begin to perceive now why she was always bringing us together at Queen's Crawley," Rawdon said.

"What an artful little woman!" ejaculated Rebecca.

"Well, I don't regret it, if you don't," the Captain said, still in an amorous rapture with his wife.

But Rebecca's steady contempt for him, which never

[1] Chap. xvii.

alters, is an amusing, perhaps some would say a melancholy, contrast to his admiration for her and her cleverness.

"If he had but a little more brains," she thought to herself, "I might make something of him," but she never let him perceive the opinion she had of him, listened with indefatigable complacency to his stories of the stable and the mess.

Thus Rawdon and his wife get on very well together at present, despite their many embarrassments, but the story now[1] turns to some extent to the historical events of the period (1815). Napoleon had returned to France from Elba, and again all Europe was alarmed at this ambitious warrior's return to his martial nation, of which, indeed, he was the popular idol and almost absolute ruler. The ruin of old Sedley occurs at this time, and Amelia's parents are now more than ever indignant at the selfishness and extravagance of George Osborne. Indeed, at this part of the story the success of Becky and the ruin of her old schoolfellow Amelia are strongly contrasted. Old Mr. Osborne now cannot endure the thoughts of his son marrying Amelia, whose true and devoted friend Captain Dobbin, though never quite appreciated by her, yet takes her part in every way and with everybody. Even his two sisters, very unlike their noble-minded brother, openly sneer at the unfortunate Amelia in their private talk with him :

"Hadn't you better, now that Miss Sedley is free, propose for her yourself, William?" Miss Ann asked sarcastically. "It would be a most eligible family connection. He! he!"

"I marry her!" Dobbin said, blushing very much and talking

[1] Chap. xviii.

quick. "If you are so ready, young ladies, to chop and change, do you suppose *she* is? Laugh and sneer at that angel. She can't hear it, and she's miserable and unfortunate and deserves to be laughed at. Go on joking, Ann. You're the wit of the family and the others like to hear it. But men don't talk in this way; it's only women who get together and hiss and shriek and cackle. There, get away—don't begin to cry—I only said you were a couple of geese," Will Dobbin said, perceiving Miss Ann's pink eyes were beginning to moisten as usual. "Well, you're not geese, you're swans—anything you like, only do leave Miss Sedley alone!"

Anything like William's infatuation about that silly little flirting, ogling thing was never known, the mamma and sisters agreed together in thinking.

It is thus Dobbin's strange, hard fate to be completely devoted to Miss Sedley, and be despised or blamed by all his relations as well as her acquaintances for his love to her, and which Amelia herself never returns or seems to understand till very late in the story. This part of the book, when Sedley's ruin is announced, Thackeray records without discussing Napoleon's again heading the French army against the chief Powers of Europe, while the British army, including Osborne, Rawdon, and Dobbin, are soon to go abroad to resist the heroic warrior, or dangerous usurper, as he was severally termed by friends and foes. Amelia, however, thinks it right to free George Osborne from his engagement to her, considering the ruined state of her parents; while Dobbin, who loves her infinitely more than anything or anybody else, does all in his power to promote her secret desire to wed George Osborne. This giddy, vain, thoughtless, yet not cold-hearted young man is now firmly, through Dobbin's influence, determined to marry Amelia, despite the stern, unrelenting opposition of his father, whose conduct towards the unfortunate Sedleys since their misfortunes is one of the most odious parts of his harsh, stern, but not altogether ungenerous character.

Amelia, therefore, writes to Osborne, giving up her engagement to him, in great grief, and ends her pathetic note by thanking him for sending her piano, which Dobbin himself had bought for her, unknown to all but himself, at the sale of her ruined old father's effects. In fact, Dobbin's consistent nobleness is well contrasted with Osborne's conceited selfishness throughout, though to do George justice he has yet to encounter a terrible storm of reproach and indignation from his proud, obstinate father. But this story, which is continually alternating between Miss Sharp's cunning intrigues and Amelia's trials, now [1] reverts again to poor Miss Crawley, terribly oppressed by Mrs. Bute, whose only object is to watch and completely control the rich old invalid for her own family's interests. Like some other eager, energetic people, however, Mrs. Bute has only her own sense and spirit to depend upon, and gets little if any help even from her reckless, dissipated husband :

"If that poor man of mine had a head on his shoulders," Mrs. Bute Crawley thought to herself, "how useful he might be under present circumstances to this unhappy old lady. He might make her repent of her shocking, free-thinking ways, . . . and he might induce her to do justice to my dear girls and the two boys, who require, and deserve, I am sure, every assistance which their relatives can give them."

And as the hatred of vice is always a progress towards virtue, Mrs. Bute Crawley endeavoured to instil into her sister-in-law a

---

[1] Chap. xix.

proper abhorrence for all Rawdon Crawley's manifold sins, of which his uncle's wife brought forward such a catalogue as would indeed have served to condemn a whole regiment of young officers. . . . But if a fault may be found with her arrangements it is this, that she was too eager, she managed rather too well; undoubtedly she made Miss Crawley more ill than was necessary, and though the old invalid succumbed to her authority, it was so harassing and severe, that the victim would be inclined to escape at the very first chance which fell in her way.

Mrs. Bute keeps her shut up in a dark room till the apothecary, Mr. Clump, remonstrates and urges that poor old Miss Crawley should be allowed a drive out sometimes. To this idea Mrs. Bute makes the following objection, with vicious allusions to the Rawdon Crawleys:

"The sight of her horrid nephew casually in the Park, where I am told the wretch drives with the brazen partner of his crimes," Mrs. Bute said (letting the cat of selfishness out of the bag of secrecy), "would cause her such a shock that we should have to bring her back to bed again. She must not go out, Mr. Clump."

"Upon my word, madam," Mr. Clump now said bluntly, "I won't answer for her life if she remains locked up in that dark room."

Though Mr. Clump understands Mrs. Bute's character and objects, he yet has to be rather reserved, but he and Dr. Squills have a private talk ("over a bottle of wine") which reveals at once their knowledge of the invalid and of her present nurse:

"What a little harpy that woman from Hampshire is, Clump," Squills remarked, "that has seized upon old Tilly Crawley. Devilish good Madeira."

"What a fool Rawdon Crawley has been," Clump replied, "to go and marry a governess." . . . "The old girl will fling him over," said the physician, and after a pause added, "She'll cut up well, I suppose." "Cut up," says Clump with a grin, "I wouldn't have her cut up for two hundred a year." "That Hampshire woman will kill her in two months, Clump, my boy, if she stops about her," Dr. Squills said. "Old woman, full pulse, nervous subject, palpitation of the heart; pressure on the brain; apoplexy; off she goes. Get her up, Clump; get her out, or I wouldn't give many weeks' purchase for your two hundred a year."

Mrs. Bute is at length, as if frightened by the doctors, induced to take Miss Crawley out for a carriage drive, and as Mrs. Bute had predicted, they met the Rawdon Crawleys also driving, and took no notice of them:

It was a gallant and decided triumph for Mrs. Bute,

yet she dreads the danger of more chance meetings and advises Miss Crawley to try a change to Brighton.

The story now returns to Dobbin trying all he can to promote Amelia's marriage with Osborne, despite his own secret and unreturned love for her himself. This singular yet consistent conduct of his occupies a great part of this book, Thackeray dwelling constantly upon it, as if a relief, or pleasing contrast, to the equally consistent, but utterly unscrupulous, conduct and career of Becky Sharp. The enmity between the two old men, Sedley and Osborne, father and father-in-law of his beloved Amelia, is one of Dobbin's many difficulties to deal with, but it is beyond his power to reconcile them either to each other or to their children's marriage. Mr. Osborne, purse-proud, harsh, and arrogant to an odious degree, wishes his son to marry a rich half-negress, or something like one from her pictures, a certain Miss Swartz, who is a good-natured old friend of Amelia, but who apparently cares as little for George Osborne as he cares for her. Old Osborne has no idea of his son's determination to marry Amelia, and thinks he can either persuade or frighten him into giving up his engagement to her altogether. Hitherto his almost despotic rule over his son and his two daughters naturally made him expect that George would obey him, but in this idea the old gentleman finds himself mistaken in the end, as the wealthy Miss Swartz has no attraction for Captain George.

" What a match for George she'd be " (the sisters and Miss Wirt agreed) "and how much better than that insignificant little Amelia."

Thackeray then draws a brief sketch of old Osborne's temper.

When the elder Osborne gave what he called "a hint," there was no possibility for the most obtuse to mistake his meaning. He called kicking a footman downstairs a hint for the latter to leave his service. . . . He gave George, finally, such another hint regarding the heiress, and ordered him to marry her out of hand, as he would have ordered his butler to draw a cork, or his clerk to write a letter.

This imperative hint disturbed George a good deal. . . . The junior Osborne was quite as obstinate as the senior; when he wanted anything quite as firm as his resolution to get it, and quite as violent when angered as his father in his most stern moments.[1]

Dobbin, ever devoted to Amelia's interests and happiness, is now resolved to do all he can to reconcile old Osborne to his son's marrying her. This old gentleman's desire for George to wed Miss Swartz, the dark heiress, is doomed to disappointment. George is anything but attracted by this stupid, plain, but rather good-natured young lady.

[1] Chap. xxi.

She is, indeed, far inferior to Amelia both in beauty and sense, but is very fond of her, and was her schoolfellow at Miss Pinkerton's.

One of the best pictures in this book is that of Miss Swartz, turning hastily round on her music-stool and praising Amelia before the Osbornes, when she sees Miss Sedley's name on some songs. But she had utterly failed to attract George before this scene.

> Her bejewelled hands lay sprawling on her amber-satin lap. Her tags and ear-rings twinkled, and her big eyes rolled about. . . . "Dammy," George said to a confidential friend, "she looked like a China doll, which has nothing to do all day long but to grin and wag its head. By Jove, Will, it was all I could do to prevent myself from throwing the sofa cushion at her." He restrained that exhibition of sentiment, however.

The explosion now soon comes between the hot-tempered Osborne gentlemen, father and son, rather like each other in selfish obstinacy. At length, after some violent language on both sides, the elder Osborne trying to insist on his son's giving up his intended marriage with Miss Sedley, old Osborne urges or rather orders George to marry Miss Swartz, saying she'll be an heiress with eight thousand a year, or else to leave the house. To this peremptory language George replies with indignant and satirical scorn :

> "Marry that mulatto woman? . . . I don't like the colour, sir. Ask the black that sweeps opposite Fleet Market, sir. *I'm* not going to marry a Hottentot Venus."

At this haughty refusal Osborne orders his son out of the house, who departs and rejoins his friend

Dobbin, and after relating what had passed exclaims, now resolved to marry Amelia, out of love for her and anger against his father combined:

> "I'll marry her to-morrow," he said with an oath; "I love her more every day, Dobbin."

George's marriage with Amelia takes place, Dobbin aiding, abetting, and hastening it with all his might. The noble conduct of this generous man is carefully narrated through all this book, yet nobody seems to quite understand him, not even Amelia or George, while availing themselves freely, the one of his money and the other of his friendship. After the wedding the bride and bridegroom drive off. As the carriage, splashing mud, drove away,

> Dobbin stood in the church porch looking at it, a queer figure. The small crew of spectators jeered at him. He was not thinking about them or their laughter. . . . It was all over. They were married and happy, he prayed God.

In about ten days after their marriage the Osborne newly wedded pair, the Rawdon Crawleys, and Dobbin are together at Brighton, a town which here, and in other books,[1] Mr. Thackeray highly praises, and evidently likes greatly. The news comes here that the army is ordered off to Belgium. George, Rawdon, and Dobbin are all three now to be on the move:

> This news of war could not but come with a shock upon our lovers and cause all three gentlemen to look very serious.[2]

---

[1] "The Newcomes."

[2] Chap. xxii.

CHAPTER VII

IN the next chapter (xxiii.) Dobbin resolutely sets himself to the desperate task of trying to reconcile Mr. Osborne to his son's marriage with Amelia. He first solicits Miss Jane Osborne, little guessing, apparently, that this lady is inclined to be in love with himself, while he is always utterly indifferent to every one except Amelia. George knows about his sister's feeling,

having often bantered him gracefully and said, "Hang it, Will, why don't you take old Jane? She'll have you if you ask her. I'll bet you five to two she will."

Dobbin's interview with Miss Osborne is an amusing failure. He earnestly justifies George's marrying Amelia, and at last asks

with atrocious astuteness:

"What would you feel if a man were faithless to you?"

"I should perish—I should throw myself out of window—I should take poison and should pine and die, I know I should," Miss cried, who had nevertheless gone through one or two affairs of the heart without any idea of suicide.

Dobbin continues to plead vainly, for it is not really in Miss Osborne's power, though she is not altogether ill-disposed, to make her father relent, and Dobbin finally tells her of George's actual marriage with Miss Sedley. Dobbin's next attack is upon the feelings of old Osborne himself. The Captain approaches the subject cautiously, earnestly hoping to reconcile father and son, but when the irritable old gentleman hears Amelia's name he gives way to a storm of rage, and abuses her and her father in such insulting words that the patient Dobbin himself loses temper, and announces the irrevocable fact of George's marriage. Mr. Osborne on hearing this news sinks back in his chair without speaking and Dobbin departs, knowing he can do no good by further argument or entreaty. Old Osborne this evening [1] actually effaces his son's name from the old family Bible, and sends a letter, through his clerk, to his offending son, whom he now no longer receives as a member of his family, allowing him about two thousand pounds, and refuses to receive any further communication from him whatever.[2] This note is received by George in Brighton, where he still is with the Rawdon Crawleys, and he immediately reproaches Dobbin for not making better terms for him, and exclaims to his true friend:

. . . "It was all your doing. You were never easy until you had got me married and ruined. What the deuce am I to do with two thousand pounds? Such a sum won't last two years. I've

---

[1] Chap. xxiv. [2] Chap. xxv.

lost a hundred and forty to Crawley at cards and billiards since I've been down here. A pretty manager of a man's affairs *you* are, forsooth."

Dobbin admits that George's position is a hard one, adding "with a bitter smile," while for a moment referring to his unselfish self:

" There are some men who wouldn't mind changing with you." . . . The dispute ended, as many scores of such conversations between Osborne and his friend had concluded previously—by the former declaring there was no possibility of being angry with Dobbin long, and forgiving him very generously after abusing him without cause.

While Dobbin, however, tries all he can to promote Amelia and George's happiness at Brighton, a fatal foe to poor Amelia's felicity appears in the ever-artful Mrs. Becky, who gradually attracts Osborne more and more, while privately nicknaming him Cupid, and urging her equally artful and dishonest, though less intelligent, husband to win all the money he can from the vain dupe at cards. But the near approach of real warfare now begins to engage the thoughts of both knave and dupe alike at this time:

" I say, what'll Mrs. O. do when O. goes out with the regiment?" Crawley said. . . .

" I suppose she'll cry her eyes out," Becky answered. . . .

" You don't care, I suppose," Rawdon said, half-angry at his wife's want of feeling.

" You wretch! don't you know that I intend to go with you?" Becky replied. " Besides, you're different. You go as General Tufto's aide-de-camp. *We* don't belong to the line," Mrs. Crawley said, throwing up her head, with an air that so enchanted her husband that he stooped down and kissed it.

She then practically alludes to financial matters:

> "Rawdon, dear—don't you think—you'd better get that—money from Cupid before he goes?" Becky continued. . . . She called George Osborne Cupid. . . . She watched over him kindly at écarté of a night when he would drop in to Rawdon's quarters for half an hour before bed-time. She had often called him a horrid, dissipated wretch and threatened to tell Emmy of his wicked ways and naughty, extravagant habits.

A picture, drawn like all the rest by the author, accompanies this scene, George and Rawdon playing cards together, while Becky, leaning with a cunning smile on Osborne's chair, is watching the game, which means, of course, constant loss to Osborne and gain to the roguish Crawleys. Some time after:

> Rawdon got a little family note from his wife. . . . "Great news," she wrote, "Mrs. Bute is gone. Get the money from Cupid to-night, as he'll be off to-morrow most likely. Mind this.—R." . . .
>
> Rawdon touched Osborne on the elbow and said gracefully, "I say, Osborne, my boy, if quite convenient, I'll trouble you for that 'ere small trifle." It was not quite convenient, but nevertheless George gave him a considerable present instalment in banknotes.

At this time Mrs. Bute is away from old Miss Crawley, but Becky contrives to meet the poor, humble companion, Miss Briggs, while both are bathing, and wins her over to her side. Becky then dictates a very dutiful letter for Rawdon to send his old aunt, but unluckily Becky's brilliant, clever style of writing, which Miss Crawley knows Rawdon incapable of composing, is at once detected by the sharp, suspicious old lady, who never forgives him for his marriage, though truly thankful to be freed from Mrs. Bute. Becky intrusts her note to Rawdon to deliver, who owns he had not gone with it into his aunt's house, which he perhaps might have done. At hearing this Becky loses temper with him for the first time, apparently, in their married life:

> "*You didn't go in, Rawdon!*" screamed his wife.
>
> "No, my dear. I'm hanged if I wasn't afraid when it came to the point."
>
> "You fool! you ought to have gone in, and never come out again," Rebecca said.
>
> "Don't call me names," said the big Guardsman, sulkily. "Perhaps I *was* a fool, Becky, but you shouldn't say so."

This sulky allusion to his own marriage Becky never notices, but makes a peaceful reply, still urging him to see and if possible to reconcile his offended and formerly most indulgent old aunt. But no reconciliation ever takes place. Perhaps had Rawdon followed his shrewd little wife's advice and visited Miss Crawley, the old lady might yet have been won over by the pleading and the excuses of the handsome young man. She, however, never sees him again, and the whole party, the two Rawdon Crawleys and the two Osbornes, with Amelia's conceited brother, Jos Sedley, leave Brighton for London. Here George at once begins to lavish away most of the little money he has. But now the war on the Continent is soon attracting the whole party to Belgium, where the great battle of the future is destined to be fought.

The aggressive ambition of Napoleon I., whom

Thackeray often mentions but never, unfortunately, describes, is now alarming all Europe Apparently Thackeray dreads personally describing this wonderful man, though a writer of his genius and profound knowledge of human nature in its minutest points might perhaps have rivalled Walter Scott in faithfully describing historical personages. But he steadily avoids the subject, and consistently follows the interesting fortunes of the private and politically unimportant personages of his invention, and about whom he certainly instructs, as well as interests, all readers who need or desire enlightenment about the English social world in the beginning and middle of the nineteenth century. Major and Mrs. O'Dowd, Irish people, as their name implies, are now introduced.[1]

Mrs. O'Dowd, a kind, courageous, shrewd woman, likes and befriends Amelia, but distrusts Mrs. Becky, from the first time she knows the two ladies. But the stormy political history of this period now forces the imaginary persons in this book into immediate action. The scene is now in Brussels ; Amelia happy as ever with her George, who all the time is gradually being estranged from her by the artful Mrs. Becky, while the ever-faithful Dobbin keeps a constant though useless watch on the giddy young Osborne, completely victimised by the two Rawdon Crawleys, who are practically a pair of clever, shameless swindlers.

"When do you intend to give up play, George, as you have

[1] Chap. xxvii.

promised me any time these hundred years?" Dobbin said to his friend a few days after the night at the Opera.

" When do you intend to give up sermonising?" was the other's reply.

These two brief questions are very explanatory of the conduct of both these gentlemen and of their relations to each other.

The extraordinary mixture of gaiety and joyousness among the British at this awful period in Brussels, while daily expecting a terrific battle with the French under Napoleon, is thus described by Thackeray, while ably connecting the fearful realities of this eventful time with his own imaginary characters, though, unlike Sir Walter Scott, he never even attempts to introduce a historical one. He writes impressively:[1]

There never was since the days of Darius such a brilliant train of camp-followers[2] as hung round the Duke of Wellington's army in the Low Countries in 1815, and led it dancing and feasting, as it were, up to the very brink of battle. A certain ball which a noble Duchess gave at Brussels on the 15th of June in the above-named year is historical. . . . I have heard from ladies who were in that town at the period that the talk and interest of the persons of their own sex regarding the ball was much greater even than in respect of the enemy in their front.

Becky is now attracting general attention by her wit, cleverness, and partly by the idea which she industriously circulates that she is one of the old Montmorency family, and she is certainly an excellent

[1] Chap. xxix.

[2] "The camp of Darius was crowded with 277 cooks, 29 waiters, 87 cupbearers" (Lemprière's "Classical Dictionary").

French scholar. Poor Amelia, on the contrary, becomes more and more depressed and sad at seeing her husband becoming quite captivated by her former little friend, while Dobbin continues to be her constant friend and well-wisher. During the eventful historical ball an imaginary incident occurs, briefly mentioned here, yet which indicates important future events in this novel :

> George danced with Rebecca twice or thrice, how many times Amelia scarcely knew. She sat quite unnoticed in her corner, except when Rawdon came up with some words of clumsy conversation and later in the evening when Captain Dobbin made so bold as to bring her refreshments and sit beside her. . . .
>
> At last George came back for Rebecca's shawl and flowers. . . . George went away then with the bouquet, but when he gave it to the owner there lay a note coiled like a snake among the flowers. Rebecca's eye caught it at once. She had been used to deal with notes in early life. . . . He saw by her eyes as they met that she was aware what she would find there.

The real meaning and secret of this mysterious note, so admirably likened in its hidden danger to a snake coiled among flowers, though concealed from readers at present, may, perhaps, be guessed. Becky is winning over Osborne more and more to her from his neglected wife, whom nobody pities but the faithful Dobbin. He, except when engaged in his military duties, remains as devoted as ever to both the Osbornes, as much almost to George as to Amelia. Dobbin is always vainly trying to keep the young profligate George from drinking and card-playing, till at last the need of all such warnings comes to an end. Dobbin, finding George drinking and gambling at this critical time, brings news which at once puts an end to all such folly :

" Come out, George," said Dobbin still gravely, " don't drink."

" Drink! there's nothing like it. Drink yourself and light up your lantern jaws, old boy. Here's to you."

Dobbin went up and whispered something to him, at which George, giving a start and wild hooray, tossed off his glass . . . and walked away speedily on his friend's arm. " The enemy has passed the Sambre," William said, " and our left is already engaged. Come away. We are to march in three hours."

Away went George, his nerves quivering with excitement. . . . What were love and intrigue now? . . . He thought over his brief married life. . . . How wild and reckless he had been! Should any mischance befal him, what was then left for her? Why had he married her? He was not fit for marriage. Why had he disobeyed his father who had always been so generous to him? Hope, remorse, ambition, tenderness, and selfish regret filled his heart. He sat down and wrote to his father, remembering what he had once said before, when he was engaged to fight a duel. Dawn faintly streaked the sky as he closed this farewell letter.

He goes to Amelia's room and is described showing more affection for her than ever, and as if for the time forgetting Becky, his dangerous temptress:

A bugle from the Place of Arms began sounding clearly and was taken up through the town, and amidst the drums of the infantry and the shrill pipes of the Scotch the whole city awoke.[1]

Thackeray even at this exciting moment avoids describing the historical characters of this eventful time, and admits so doing, saying:[2]

We do not claim to rank among the military novelists. Our place is with the non-combatants.

Thackeray here contrasts the worthy Major O'Dowd

[1] Chap. xxix. [2] Chap. xxx.

and his gallant, devoted wife with the unprincipled Rawdon Crawleys. Despite his brave, reckless character Rawdon is appalled, rather than alarmed, at the coming danger:

. . . Rawdon's gravity became such that Becky rallied him about it in a manner which rather hurt the feelings of the Guardsman. "You don't suppose I'm afraid, Becky, I should think," he said with a tremor in his voice. "But I'm a pretty good mark for a shot, and you see if it brings me down, why I leave one and perhaps two behind me whom I should wish to provide for. . . . It is no laughing matter *that*, Mrs. C., anyways."

Rebecca, by a hundred caresses and kind words, tried to soothe the feelings of the wounded lover . . . she could soon put on a demure face: "Dearest love," she said, "do you suppose I feel nothing?" and hastily dashing something from her eyes, she looked up in her husband's face with a smile.

Rawdon, though a reckless, unprincipled duellist, is yet not an unfeeling man, and now makes a short, singular will:

He pleased himself by noting down with a pencil, in his big schoolboy handwriting, the various items of his portable property which might be sold for his widow's advantage—as, for example, "My double-barril by Manton, say 40 guineas, my driving cloak lined with sable fur £50, my duelling pistols in rosewood case (same which I shot Captain Marker) £20, my regulation saddle-holsters and housings . . . and so forth, over all of which articles he made Rebecca mistress.

He had really loved his artful, heartless wife with a depth and sincerity of which she was incapable of returning or perhaps understanding.

Indeed, the fascinating powers of Mrs. Becky over most people she meets would seem rather exaggerated, but the author certainly describes her successive triumphs over various and differing characters with such steady and perfect consistency that her social career is a very interesting study. Her ascendancy over her reckless husband is almost complete, even at this time of danger.

. . . This famous dandy of Windsor and Hyde Park went off on his campaign with a kit as modest as that of a sergeant and with something like a prayer on his lips for the woman he was leaving.

And Rebecca, as we have said, wisely determined not to give way to unavailing sentimentality on her husband's departure. She waved him an adieu from the window. . . . There had been no rest for her that night. She was still in her pretty ball-dress, her fair hair hanging somewhat out of curl on her neck and the circles round her eyes dark with watching. "What a fright I seem," she said, examining herself in the glass, "and how pale this pink makes me look!" So she divested herself of this pink raiment, in doing which a note fell out from her corsage, which she picked up with a smile and locked into her dressing-box.

This note was evidently

the snake coiled in the flowers

which George Osborne had given her and which is again to make its appearance at the end of this book. Becky for the present keeps it safe and unknown, while she calmly awaits whatever fate may befall either of her admirers. Rawdon and Osborne are now rushing into battle, while she remains safe, calculating, and observant. Respecting Becky's wonderful composure, knowledge of character, and resolute spirit at this trying time, Thackeray emphatically writes:

If this is a novel without a hero, at least let us lay claim to a heroine. No man in the British army which has marched away, not the great Duke himself, could be more cool or collected in the presence of doubts and difficulties.

Thackeray now recalls the vain, fat, cowardly Mr. Jos Sedley, whom the faithful Dobbin is vainly trying to persuade to attend to Amelia, should anything befall her husband, and she be left a poor, helpless widow, disliked and disowned by the Osborne family. George, despite his thoughtlessness, cannot help being moved at leaving his young wife, as he rushes impetuously off to join his regiment :

. . . His pulse was throbbing and his cheeks flushed ; the great game of war was going to be played and he was one of the players. What a fierce excitement of doubt, hope, and pleasure ! . . . What were all the games of chance he had ever played compared to this one? Into all contests requiring athletic skill and courage, the young man from his boyhood upwards had flung himself with all his might. The champion of his school and his regiment, the bravos of his companions had followed him everywhere ; from the boys' cricket match to the garrison races, he had won a hundred of triumphs ; and wherever he went women and men had admired and envied him.

Here the author makes a remarkable reflection, arising out of his literary studies and personal knowledge of the world combined. Thackeray does not very often pause in his story's steady narration to make such reflections, which are perhaps the more interesting if not more important on that account :

. . . What qualities are there for which a man gets so speedy return of applause as those of bodily superiority, activity, and valour? Time out of mind, strength and courage have been the theme of bards and romances; and from the story of Troy down to to-day, poetry has always chosen a soldier for a hero. I wonder is it because men are cowards in heart, that they admire bravery so much and place military valour so far beyond every other quality for reward and worship?

CHAPTER VIII

THE story now reverts to the stupid, pompous, and timid Jos Sedley, whose revealed cowardice is ridiculed even by his foreign, cunning valet Isidor. The ever-artful Mrs. Becky, now, in the absence of both her husband and lover, Rawdon and Osborne, resolves to regain her influence over Jos, whom she understood thoroughly and whose dull, vain nature made him an easy prey, throughout all this story, to her arts and designs, whenever she cared to employ them against him. She accordingly, wishing to keep him in Brussels, begins thus complaining to Jos of her poor, absent husband:[1]

"Captain Crawley left me this morning as gay as if he were going to a hunting party. What does he care? What do any of you care for the agonies and tortures of a poor forsaken woman?"

Then she says to herself:

. . . ("I wonder whether he *could* really have been going to the troops, this great, lazy gourmand.") "Oh, dear Mr. Sedley, I have come to you for comfort—for consolation. I have been on my knees all the morning. I tremble at the frightful danger into which our husbands, our friends, our brave troops and others are rushing."

She then gently insinuates that her husband is jealous of her:

[1] Chap. xxxi.

"The only unkind words I have ever had from him (I will do Captain Crawley that justice) have been about you—and most cruel, cruel words they were." . . .

All Jos's blood tingled with delight, as he surveyed this victim of his attractions. . . . From Solomon downwards, have not wiser men than he been cajoled and befooled by women? "If the worst comes to the worst," Becky thought, "my retreat is secure and I have a right-hand seat in the barouche."

At this time Becky's influence over the three gentlemen—her husband, George Osborne, and Joseph Sedley—is almost at its height, yet for all these men she has much the same practical indifference, though, of course, despising the cowardly Jos Sedley, when compared with the two handsome, gay young officers, Osborne and Crawley. Jos's thoughts were, after this interview with Becky,

now glowing, maddening, upon the contemplation of the enchanting Rebecca; anon shrinking guiltily before the vision of the jealous Rawdon Crawley, with his curling fierce mustachios and his terrible duelling pistols loaded and cocked.

After captivating the vain, timid Jos Sedley, Becky, certainly a most inveterate mischief-maker and successful deceiver, betakes herself to her former friend and present rival, Amelia, whom she finds grieving helplessly about Osborne's danger, weakly accusing Becky of tempting him away from her and exclaiming with tearful reproaches, suspecting the truth but not sure of it:

. . . "Why did you come between my love and me? . . . Do you think you could love him as I did? His love was everything to me. You knew it, and wanted to rob me of it. . . . You did not succeed, but you tried. Ask your heart if you did not."

"She knows nothing," Rebecca thought.

In this thought Becky probably refers to the secret note,

coiled among the flowers,

from Osborne to her, and of which Becky tells Amelia nothing about as yet, while carefully keeping it concealed in her own possession. The tender-hearted, trustful Amelia continues fretting about George to Becky, knowing nothing of what her companion could tell her of his falsehood contained in the hidden note, which, for the present, Becky never reveals, while carefully keeping it with a calculating eye on the possible future.

" Look," said Amelia, " this is his sash—isn't it a pretty colour? " and she took up the fringe and kissed it. . . . She had forgotten her anger, her jealousy, the very presence of her rival seemingly. For she walked silently and almost with a smile on her face towards the bed and began to smooth down George's pillow. . . .

Rebecca was of a good-natured and obliging disposition and she rather liked Amelia than otherwise. Even her hard words, reproachful as they were, were complimentary—the groans of a person stinging under defeat. Meeting Mrs. O'Dowd . . . and informing her that poor Mrs. Osborne was in a desperate condition,

she sends

the good-natured Irishwoman straight to see if she could console her young favourite.

Mrs. O'Dowd, however, thoroughly understands and detests Becky's heartless nature, though hardly, perhaps, aware as yet of the extent of her deceit and artfulness. She comes now to console and comfort poor, sad little Amelia, scornfully observing of Becky's heartlessness with reference to the decisive battle of Waterloo, now at hand:

"It's not *you* that will cry your eyes out with grief, anyway."

The sound of distant cannon is now heard, and chapter xxxii. describes the terrible excitement and anxiety in Brussels at this most eventful moment, historically true indeed, which Thackeray makes produce a very different effect on his imaginary persons now in that city. Jos Sedley, always a pompous coward, takes to flight, while the brave young wounded officer, Tom Stubble, arrives helpless, and Mrs. O'Dowd kindly takes charge of him. This courageous, honest Irish lady comforts and cheers the wounded youth, whom she won't leave, scornfully refusing to accompany or follow Jos in his flight from the apprehended danger of a French triumph. She exclaims to Stubble just before Jos's flight from Brussels:

"No harm shall come to you while *I* stand by. I don't budge till I get the word from Mick [her husband]. A pretty figure I'd be, wouldn't I, stuck behind that chap on a pillion?" This image caused the young patient to burst out laughing in his bed, and even made Amelia smile.

Jos makes a last vain effort to tempt his sister to accompany him, and finally sets off on his ignominious flight from the scene of danger. Thackeray proceeds:

All that day from morning until past sunset the cannon never ceased to roar. It was dark when the cannonading stopped all of a sudden. . . .

No more firing was heard at Brussels—the pursuit rolled miles away. Darkness came down on the field and city; and Amelia was praying for George, who was lying on his face, dead, with a bullet through his heart.[1]

Thackeray now leaves the scene of war, which he describes briefly indeed, yet with great power and force, indicating that he might have been an able historian, but he always preferred fiction, of which this great work proved him such a successful master. He returns, therefore, to the rich, selfish old Miss Crawley, constantly watched and worried by greedy, expectant relations as her age increases, while her poor, bullied companion, Miss Briggs, is always faithful to her. Rawdon, however, sends his aunt a letter with some so-called relics from the battle; but the well-expressed letter is soon detected by the sharp old lady as being Becky's composition. Thackeray then reveals that Becky had really bought the alleged "relics of the war," epaulets, a Cross of the Legion of Honour, and the hilt of a sword,

for a few francs, from one of the innumerable pedlars who immediately began to deal in relics of the war. The novelist who knows everything knows this also.[2]

Miss Crawley now sees little or nothing of her half-brother, Sir Pitt. This coarse old profligate squire becomes more and more ill-conducted and disreputable since Becky left the Hall. He apparently makes or tries to make Miss Bessy Horrocks, his butler's daughter, his mistress, as Thackeray hints at in his expressive and comically picturesque style:

. . . The ribbons in Miss Horrocks's cap became more splendid than ever. The polite families fled the Hall and its owner in terror.

---

[1] "Thackeray never wrote anything finer than the Waterloo Chapters of 'Vanity Fair'" (Melville's "Life of Thackeray").

[2] Chap. xxxiii.

Sir Pitt went about tippling at his tenants' houses. . . . He drove the family coach and four to Southampton with Miss Horrocks inside, and the county people expected every week; as his son did in speechless agony, that his marriage with her would be announced in the provincial paper.

His conduct, naturally enough, horrifies his eldest son Pitt, who, though priggish and pedantic, is practically far the most respectable of the Crawley family ; yet Thackeray evidently dislikes him, perhaps rather too much, and easily makes his readers do so too. Pitt is often preaching or giving moral lectures under difficult and certainly discouraging circumstances, for which he is not responsible ; yet the author ridicules rather than pities him :

. . . His eloquence was praised at the missionary meetings and other religious assemblies in the neighbourhood . . . for he felt when he rose that the audience said, "That is the son of the old reprobate, Sir Pitt, who is very likely drinking at the public-house at this very moment." And once when he was speaking of the benighted condition of the king of Timbuctoo, and the number of his wives who were likewise in darkness, some gipsy miscreant from the crowd asked, "How many is there at Queen's Crawley, young Squaretoes?" to the surprise of the platform and the ruin of Mr. Pitt's speech.

Yet, despite Pitt's occasional meanness and pedantry, he certainly does more good than harm in all his dealings with others, except in the case of his drunken young cousin, Jim Crawley, whom he meanly exposes later on.

He is in love with a Lady Jane Sheepshanks, whom he marries, second daughter of the Earl and Countess of Southdown. The Countess is a grim old, bigoted lady, while Lady Jane, though not often introduced, is perhaps the most consistently amiable and dutiful of all the female characters in this book. Pitt wisely persuades Lady Southdown to allow Lady Jane to visit old Miss Crawley, in the hope, of course, that the invalid lady will remember her, if not himself, in her will. Lady Emily, the elder sister, more like her austere mother, wishes to send Miss Crawley no end of tracts, but Pitt prudently suggests that the quiet, gentle Lady Jane would please the old lady much more than the religious enthusiast Lady Emily.

The “strong-minded Lady Southdown,” far more worldly than she seems, quite agrees with Pitt, exclaiming:

> “Most certainly, Emily would ruin everything.”
>
> . . . Lady Southdown, we say, for the sake of the invalid's health, or for the sake of her soul's ultimate welfare or for the sake of her money, agreed to temporise.

Lady Jane accordingly visits and greatly pleases the invalid Miss Crawley, who is perfectly delighted with her kind manners and gentle nature. Meantime the Bute Crawleys, also on the eager look-out for Miss Crawley's fortune, are naturally alarmed at Lady Jane's visit, and resolve in an evil hour to send their wild young son James also on a visit to his aunt, hoping that Jim, being young, lively, and good-looking, may please his aunt, for a similar ultimate purpose.[1] But the Bute Crawleys never made a greater mistake. Jim, though wishing to please, is indeed a very different guest to meek, demure Lady Jane. Smoking, drinking, and watch-

[1] Chap. xxxiv.

ing prize-fights are among his chief and favourite habits.

At first his youth and liveliness rather please the old aunt, but her wine, of which he partakes far too freely, soon undoes the first rather good impression he made. His cousin Pitt, not only dreading young Jim's rivalry to him in this contest for Miss Crawley's good graces, encourages the foolish boy in drinking with a mean, hypocritical cunning, which really seems hardly consistent with his usual respectable and well-meaning character. He then succeeds in tempting his young cousin to become quite drunk, when they are alone together after dinner, by declaring what he knows to be utterly untrue:

> "The chief pleasure which my aunt has, is that people shall do as they like in her house. This is Liberty Hall, James, and you can't do Miss Crawley a greater kindness than to do as you please, and ask for what you will. Here's the fresh bottle."

For a moment, and only a moment, James seems to suspect the truth, and replies:

> "No jokes, old boy—you want to trot me out, but it's no go. *In vino veritas*, old boy, Mars, Bacchus, *Apollo virorum*, hey? I wish my aunt would send down some of this to my governor, it's a precious good tap."

Poor foolish young Jim the next day falls completely into his artful cousin's snare. He gets more and more drunk, offers to fight Pitt, and disgusts both his aunt and Lady Jane. An alarming bill is brought to Miss Crawley from a public-house, stating what drink Jim, with some pugilists, had drunk there, on his arrival at Brighton.

The landlord, fearing lest the account should be refused altogether, swore solemnly that the young gent had consumed personally every farthing's worth of the liquor. Had he drunk a dozen bottles of claret the old spinster could have pardoned him. Mr. Fox and Mr. Sheridan drank claret. Gentlemen drank claret. But eighteen glasses of gin consumed among boxers in an ignoble pot-house—it was an odious crime and not to be pardoned readily.

This day, too, the unlucky boy's modesty had likewise forsaken him. He was lively and facetious at dinner: he drank as much wine as upon the previous day:

Pitt was not pleased altogether perhaps, but still not unhappy in the main. Poor Jim had his laugh out and staggered across the room with his aunt's candle, and offered to salute her with the blandest tipsy smile, and went upstairs to his bedroom perfectly satisfied with himself. Once up in the bedroom one would have thought he could not make matters worse, and yet this unlucky boy did.

Jim, attracted to the window by the romantic appearance of the ocean and the heavens, thought he would further enjoy them by smoking.

Nobody would smell the tobacco, he thought, if he cunningly opened the window and kept his head and pipe in the fresh air. This he did; but, being in an excited state, poor Jim had forgotten that his door was open all this time, so that, the breeze blowing inwards and a fine through draught being established, the clouds of tobacco were carried dowstairs, and arrived with quite undiminished fragrance to Miss Crawley and Miss Briggs.

The pipe of tobacco finished the business, and the Bute-Crawleys never knew how many thousand pounds it cost them.

When warned by Mr. Bowls, Miss Crawley's servant, rushing upstairs to the room, that his mistress couldn't endure tobacco, poor Jim can only exclaim,

> "Missis needn't smoke," with a frantic, misplaced laugh,

but next morning an express and decisive note was brought to him in the writing of Miss Briggs, saying that Miss Crawley had endured a bad night owing to the smell of smoke, and politely turning him out of her house.

> And herewith honest James's career as a candidate for his aunt's favour ended.

Pitt and Lady Jane, at least to a great extent, were now left high and unrivalled in Miss Crawley's favour. Thackeray, after detailing Jim's failure, returns to Becky and Rawdon, now in Paris. Among French society Becky's success was great, and, in recording it, the author makes a curious remark, which would seem perhaps founded on his personal knowledge:

> All the French ladies voted her charming. She spoke their language admirably. Her husband was stupid certainly—all English are stupid—and, besides, a dull husband in Paris is always a point in a lady's favour. She was the gayest and most admired of Englishwomen, and had a little European congress on her reception night. Famous warriors rode by her carriage in the Bois, or crowded her modest little box at the Opera. Rawdon was in the highest spirits. There were no duns in Paris as yet.

While the lady adventuress was pleasing society by her wit and charm of manner, her roguish husband was employing and enjoying himself in an equally unscrupulous though more practical way.

Play was plentiful and his luck good.

So in fêtes, pleasure, and prosperity the winter of 1815–16 passed away with Mrs. Rawdon Crawley, who accommodated herself to polite life, as if her ancestors had been people of fashion for centuries past—and who from her wit, talent, and energy, indeed merited a place of honour in Vanity Fair.

During this eventful period in Europe many writers might have been tempted to describe some distinguished persons in real life. But Thackeray adheres steadily throughout to his chosen group of imaginary people, whom he describes with such interesting and thorough consistency that perhaps few readers would regret his adhering to what suited him best, and which was eminently suited to his very peculiar genius, as he himself avows in another work.[1] Yet a sketch of Napoleon from his pen would probably have been most interesting; but, though laying his story during that wonderful man's life, Thackeray never attempts the least personal notice of him.

Early in 1816 Mrs. Rawdon Crawley produces a son and heir, and this family event greatly raises the Crawley family. Old Miss Crawley now transfers both present love and future money to Lady Jane, and Pitt and she never again see the Rawdon Crawleys. This rich, selfish old lady, the latter part of whose life had been so tormented by her Crawley relations, all hoping to get her money, while caring nothing for herself, never again appears in this story, and ends her life under the care of the really good and amiable Lady Jane. This lady is indeed a very pleasing contrast, whenever she appears, to nearly all the

[1] See his remarks about his own peculiar style and genius in his "Journey from Cornhill to Cairo."

other women introduced in this work, which, however, describes both Becky and Amelia far more at length.

The death of the wild, brave, giddy young officer George Osborne at Waterloo proves a great shock to all the proud, worldly-minded, rich Osborne family. The stern old father, who never forgave his son's marriage with Amelia, says little, but is evidently greatly stunned, if not saddened, by the news of his only son's death. The faithful Dobbin vainly tries to intercede for Amelia with the relentless old man, telling him that Amelia will soon be a mother, is very poor and broken-hearted. She gives birth to a son, whom she names "George," after his father. To him she transfers all her love, only regarding her real lover, Dobbin, with friendly acknowledgment. He leaves soon for India.

His parting with Amelia, while nursing her beloved infant, is one of the most touching parts of this story. Amelia, quite absorbed in recollections of her late beloved yet faithless husband, never seems to really understand the depth or the truth of Dobbin's love for herself. In taking leave of Dobbin, while the child is sleeping in her lap, she calmly says:

> "I'll write to you about Georgy; dear William, how good you have been to him and to me. Look at him. Isn't he like an angel?" He bent over the child and mother. He could not speak for a moment. And it was only with all his strength that he could force himself to say a God bless you. "God bless you," said Amelia, and held up her face and kissed him.
>
> "Hush! Don't wake Georgy!" she added as William Dobbin went to the door with heavy steps. She did not hear the noise of his cab-wheels as he drove away: she was looking at the child, who was laughing in his sleep.[1]

[1] Chap. xxxv.

Had the child been some years older and known the real truth about his father and Dobbin, the falsehoods of the former and the nobleness of the latter towards his mother and himself, he might perhaps have laughed in real earnest if sardonically inclined.

And so Dobbin departs for India, leaving his heart behind him, devoted while life lasts to Amelia.

CHAPTER IX

THE story now reverts to the swindling campaign of the Rawdon Crawleys in Paris, where their joint success in French society comes somewhat suddenly to a close. The lady's triumph among gay society, though naturally delightful to Becky, is not so practically valuable as that of her knavish husband, in different games, at the expense of others for a time. But a complete end comes to their roguish success. This artful couple play into each other's hands, Rawdon being a great gambler, and his wife pretending to be shocked. Their odious cunning in gambling ruined some people.

At Crawley's charming little reunions of an evening this fatal amusement was commonly practised—much to good-natured little Mrs. Crawley's annoyance.[1] She spoke about her husband's passion for dice with the deepest grief; she bewailed it to everybody who came to the house. She besought the young fellows never, never to touch a box. . . .

Other officers, chiefly young—for the young fellows gathered round Mrs. Crawley—came from her parties with long faces, having dropped more or less money at her fatal card-tables. Her house began to have an unfortunate reputation. The old hands warned the less experienced of their danger. . . . In spite of Rawdon's undoubted skill and constant successes, it became evident to Rebecca, considering these things, that their position was but a precarious one, and that even although they paid scarcely anybody, their little capital would end one day by dwindling into zero. "Gambling,"

[1] Chap. i. vol. ii.

she would say, "dear, is good to help your income, but not as an income itself. Some day people may be tired of play and then where are we?"

It was, indeed, their success at play which was mainly supporting this couple in temporary luxury when the news of old Miss Crawley's death hurried them away from Paris to London, to find that Miss Crawley had left nearly everything to Pitt and Lady Jane Crawley. Becky, caring little, if anything, for her young child, of whom Rawdon, to do him justice, is very fond, leaves him almost entirely in the care of a French nurse, who accompanies them to London. Here she and Rawdon resume their social life, and by every art and device, cordially helping each other, strive, hitherto in strict alliance, to live in London and enjoy its pleasures. When Rebecca is occasionally slighted or insulted by some people, who know, or guess, her real character, she, with a sort of good-humour, exhorts her rather fiery duelling husband to keep his temper and never resent anything, but to devote himself with her to maintaining their rather difficult social and fashionable position.[1]

"You can't shoot me into society," she said good-naturedly. "Remember, my dear, that I was a governess, and you, you poor silly old man, have the worst reputation for debt and dice and all sorts of wickedness. . . . You were in such a fury you were ready to murder your brother, you wicked Cain you, and what good would have come of remaining angry? All the rage in the world won't get you your aunt's money, and it is much better that we should be friends with your brother's family than enemies. . . . When your father dies Queen's Crawley will be a pleasant house for you and me to pass the winter in. If we are ruined, you can carve and take

[2] Chap. ii. vol. ii.

charge of the stable and I can be a governess to Lady Jane's children. I will get you a good place before that, or Pitt and his little boy will die and we will be Sir Rawdon and My Lady. While there is life there is hope, my dear, and I intend to make a man of you yet. Who sold your horses for you? Who paid your debts for you?"

Rawdon was obliged to confess that he owed these benefits to his wife and to trust himself to her guidance for the future. When the Rawdon Crawleys are established in London, they get on friendly terms with Pitt and Lady Jane, who were not then in town. Becky now soon receives gay company in her London house. Among her visitors are the old Marquis of Steyne and the young Earl of Southdown, Lady Jane's brother; the latter is an easy-going, kindly little man, while Lord Steyne is perhaps the most inveterately wicked man in the whole book. In fact, three more odious samples of an English peer, an English country squire, and an English banker could hardly be found than Lord Steyne, Sir Pitt Crawley, and Mr. Osborne. These three most unamiable, nay repulsive, old gentlemen never meet in this story, and perhaps hardly know each other; Steyne makes one brief and scornful allusion to Sir Pitt, but may not have been acquainted with him. Becky, after her comparatively easy conquests of Jos Sedley, old Sir Pitt, and young Rawdon Crawley, had now a far more difficult and dangerous card to play in dealing with such a man as Lord Steyne, as she finds eventually. At first the old lord appears at her pleasant little London house, while Rawdon is playing cards, as usual winning money, with poor good-natured young Lord Southdown. Lord Steyne, old, self-indulgent, and nearly as crafty as Mephistopheles, is a thorough man of the world, rich and influential, yet is amused, and even for some time deceived, by the artful Mrs. Becky. Though neither so coarse as old Sir Pitt Crawley nor so arrogantly rude as Mr. Osborne, Steyne is really the most hardened and dangerous man of the three.[1]

He is a man of some polish and apparent refinement, founded evidently on a classical education, often alluding to classical subjects, but none of his great social or educational advantages make him, in reality, a better man than either. His wife is a Roman Catholic; and Lord Steyne,

> a good scholar and amateur casuist,

shows his cynical nature in causing arguments between the Rev. Mr. Trail, his son's Protestant tutor, and Lady Steyne's spiritual director, Father Mole. He cried:

> "Bravo, Latimer!" "Well said, Loyola," alternately.

He promised Mole a bishopric if he would come over, and vowed he would use all his influence to get Trail a cardinal's hat if he would secede.

Becky one evening declared playfully she must have a sheep-dog, meaning a lady companion, while Lord Steyne, with witty sarcasm, remarks of her

[1] "The wicked Lord Steyne was the Marquis of Hertford. I think Thackeray did a great deal to malign Lord Hertford and he did not quite deserve it. The society he lived in, his great wealth, and his epicurean tendencies all combined to make him exceptional in his passions and unscrupulous in his mode of gratifying them." ("Countess of Cardigan's Recollections," published 1909).

knavish husband's card-playing at this moment, when Rawdon exclaims to his victim, Lord Southdown :

"I take your three to one." "Hark at Melibœus,[1] he's pastorally occupied too, he's shearing a Southdown. What an innocent mutton, hey? Damme, what a snowy fleece!"

Rebecca's eyes shot gleams of scornful humour.

"My lord," she said, "you are a knight of the order."

He had the collar round his neck, indeed—a gift of the restored princes of Spain.

Lord Steyne had been, in early life, notorious for his daring and success at play. He had won his marquisate, it was said, at the gaming-table; but he did not like the allusion to those bygone *fredaines*. Rebecca saw the scowl gathering over his heavy brow.

With her usual clever, astute sharpness, Becky resolved at once to conciliate so valuable an acquaintance.

"Yes," she said, "I must get a watch-dog. But he won't bark at *you*."

She then sings some French songs

in such a charming, thrilling voice, that the mollified nobleman . . . might be seen nodding his head, and bowing time over her.

Rawdon and his friend meanwhile played écarté until they had enough. The Colonel won—his wife having all the talk and all the admiration, and he sitting outside the circle, not comprehending a word of the jokes, the allusions, the mystical language within.

[1] A shepherd mentioned in Virgil's "Eclogues."

"How is Mrs. Crawley's husband?" Lord Steyne used to say to him, by way of a good day when they met; and, indeed, that was now his avocation in life. He was Colonel Crawley no more. He was Mrs. Crawley's husband.

Rawdon's little son, named after himself, is greatly neglected by Becky, and is perhaps the more endeared to his reckless father, who naturally pities and loves the child as he gradually sees less and less of his gay little wife, associating chiefly with brother officers and rather avoiding his home. Becky literally cares nothing about her little son.

Sometimes—once or twice a week—that lady visited the upper regions in which the child lived. She came like a vivified figure out of the "Magasin de Modes," blandly smiling in the most beautiful new clothes—wonderful scarfs and jewels glittered about her. . . . When she left the room an odour of rose or some other magical fragrance lingered about the nursery. She was an unearthly being in his eyes, superior to his father—to all the world, to be worshipped and admired at a distance.[1]

Rawdon would seem at this time to have rather agreed with his child in estimation of Mrs. Becky.

"Hang it, I ain't clever enough for her—I know it. She won't miss me,"

he used to say: and he was right, his wife did not miss him.

Rebecca was fond of her husband. She was always perfectly good-humoured and kind to him. He was her upper servant—he went on her errands, obeyed

[1] "It is hinted that Becky may have been the Madame Rebecque, whose appearance in the opera of 'La Dame Blanche,' at Strasburg, in 1830, gave rise to a furious uproar in the theatre there" (Melville's "Life of Thackeray," chap. xii.).

her orders without question—took her to the opera box—and came punctually back to fetch her when due.

"Hang it, you know, she is so clever," he said, "and I'm not literary and that, you know." For, as we have said before, it requires no great wisdom to be able to win at cards and billiards, and Rawdon made no pretensions to any other sort of skill.

His wife urged him to dine abroad :

"Don't stay and stupefy yourself at home to-night, my dear," she would say . . . "and now I have a sheep-dog I need not be afraid to be alone."

"A sheep-dog—a companion! Becky Sharp with a companion! Isn't it good fun?" thought Mrs. Crawley to herself. The notion tickled hugely her sense of humour.

While the Rawdon Crawleys are cultivating the dangerous society of Lord Steyne, and getting more and more among fashionable people, the story reverts[1] to the sorrows and trials of the poor, affectionate, unhappy little widow Amelia Crawley. Her parents are almost ruined, and her father, old Mr. Sedley, becomes a wine-merchant as a sort of despairing enterprise. In this attempt to make a fortune Sedley is, for a short time, greatly aided by Major Dobbin, whose intense devotion to Amelia, it must be owned, tempts him to be unjust, if not unscrupulous, towards others. It has been said that Thackeray seldom, or never, describes any character without some fault, and the kind Major Dobbin's conduct in spreading what may be called charitable falsehoods about Sedley's affairs seems, indeed, the

[1] Chap. iii. vol. ii.

only fault discoverable in him during the progress of this book, of which, despite its title, he seems the true and worthy hero. When in India, at Madras:

Dobbin furiously canvassed the Governor, the Commander-in-chief, the judges, the regiments, and everybody whom he knew in the Presidency, and sent home to Sedley & Co. orders for wine which perfectly astonished Mr. Sedley. But no more orders came after that first burst of good fortune; the curses of the mess-room assailed Major Dobbin for the vile drinks he had been the means of introducing there, and he bought back a great quantity of the wine, and sold it at public outcry, at an enormous loss to himself.

At this time poor Amelia's troubles are great indeed. Her father is ruined, while her brother, the comparatively rich, pompous Jos Sedley, is more angry with his unlucky father for his misfortunes than very sympathising. His selfish pride was irritated by his father's applications for orders for his evidently inferior wine, and he

wrote back contumeliously to the old gentleman, bidding him to mind his own affairs.

Dobbin is all the time sending the poor Sedleys presents from India for Amelia and her little son George, now growing up to be proud and selfish like his father, and a great trouble to his mother, though she is quite devoted to him and indulges him in everything. As if to complete Mrs. Osborne's trials, Dobbin's sisters, who seem proud and selfish, and very unlike their generous brother, call on her one day

with news which they were *sure* would delight her—something very interesting about their dear William.

This news is that he is about to marry a Miss Glorvina O'Dowd,

> " a very beautiful and accomplished girl, everybody said."
>
> Oh, Amelia was very, *very* happy indeed. . . . And, by some impulse, of which I cannot explain the meaning, she took George in her arms and kissed him with an extraordinary tenderness. Her eyes were quite moist when she put the child down—though she was so very happy indeed.

Evidently poor Amelia is anything but happy at the news, for she had always received and treated Dobbin as a kind, useful friend, quite devoted to her interests, but without ever returning his love. She still and always adores the memory of her comparatively good-for-nothing husband, while transferring much love and every attention to her little spoilt boy.

CHAPTER X

THACKERAY calls the next chapter (iv., Vol. II.) a cynical one, and it certainly is perhaps the most so of all, though the whole book, from beginning to end, seems more or less of a cynical nature.

The story now turns to Hampshire and the two Crawley families, of the Squire and the Rector, both odious samples indeed of their classes, which it may be devoutly hoped are usually of a better kind, or they could never have been so long influential, honoured, and respected in English society or public opinion.

While the Rector—Bute Crawley—and his sharp little wife, after their wild son Jim's failure to please his aunt, vainly try to promote the marriages of their daughters, old Sir Pitt's habits at the Hall go from bad to worse, His eldest son, Pitt, with his wife, Lady Jane, pay a remarkable visit to the paternal abode, an event described in the author's most graphic style.

That was an awful and unfortunate visit, never to be thought of by the family without horror. Pitt begged his wife, with a ghastly countenance, never to speak of it. . . . As they drove up the avenue of the park in their neat and well-appointed carriage, Pitt remarked with dismay and wrath great gaps among the trees—his trees—which the old Baronet was felling entirely without licence. The park wore an aspect of utter dreariness and ruin. . . . The library looked out on the front walk and park, Sir Pitt had opened one of the windows and was bawling out thence to the postilion and Pitt's servant, who seemed to be about to take the luggage down. "Don't move none of them trunks," he cried, pointing with a pipe which he held in his hand. "It's only a morning visit, Tucker, you fool. . . . How do, Pitt? How do, my dear? Come to see the old man, hey? Gad! you've a pretty face too. You ain't like that old horse-godmother, your mother. Come and give old Pitt a kiss like a good little gal."

The embrace disconcerted the daughter-in-law somewhat. . . . "Pitt has got vat," said the Baronet after this mark of affection. "Does he read ee very long sermons, my dear? Hundredth Psalm, Evening Hymn, hay, Pitt? Go and get a glass of Malmsey and a cake for my Lady Jane, Horrocks, you great big booby, and don't stand staring there like a fat pig. I won't ask you to stop, my dear, you'll find it too stoopid, and so should I too along a Pitt."

"I perceive, sir," said Pitt, with a heightened voice, "that your people will cut down the timber."

"Yees, yees, very fine weather, and seasonable for the time of year," Sir Pitt answered, who had suddenly grown deaf. . . .

Pitt once more brought the conversation back to the timber; but the Baronet was deaf again in an instant.

"I'm getting very old, . . . I sha'n't be here now for long; but I'm glad ee've come, daughter-in-law. I like your face, Lady Jane . . . and I'll give ee something pretty, my dear, to go to Court in." And he shuffled across the room to a cupboard, from which he took a little old case containing jewels of some value. "Take that," said he, "my dear; it belonged to my mother. . . . Pretty pearls—never gave 'em the ironmonger's daughter. No, no. Take 'em and put 'em up quick," said he, thrusting the case into his daughter's hand, and clapping the door of the cabinet to, as Horrocks entered with a salver and refreshments.

The real reason for this eager hurry on the part of the dissolute, weak old man is then explained clearly enough in the author's shrewd, expressive way.

"What have you a-been and given Pitt's wife?" said the individual in ribbons, when Pitt and Lady Jane had taken leave of the old gentleman. It was Miss Horrocks, the butler's daughter —the cause of the scandal throughout the country—the lady who reigned now almost supreme at Queen's Crawley.

The rise and progress of those Ribbons had been marked with dismay by the county and family.

Thackeray then half-comically relates the guilty influence of this young mistress of the degraded old Squire; the way in which he is blamed and avoided by all his fellow country squires, and the special horror of his son and heir, the sedate and correct Mr. Pitt.

He trembled daily lest he should hear that the Ribbons was proclaimed his second legal mother-in-law.[1] After that first and last visit, his father's name was never mentioned in Sir Pitt's polite and genteel establishment. . . . The Countess Southdown kept on dropping per coach at the lodge-gate the most exciting tracts, which ought to frighten the hair off your head. Mrs. Bute at the Parsonage nightly looked out to see if the sky was red over the elms behind which the Hall stood and the mansion was on fire. . . .

Miss Horrocks was installed as housekeeper at Queen's Crawley, and ruled all the domestics there with great majesty and rigour. All the servants were instructed to address her as "Mum" or "Madam," and there was one little maid, on her promotion, who persisted in calling her "my Lady" without any rebuke on the part of the housekeeper. "There has been better ladies, and there has been worser, Hester," was Miss Horrocks's reply to this compliment of her inferior. One day the Baronet surprised "her Ladyship," as he jocularly called her, seated at the piano with the utmost gravity, and squalling to the best of her power. . . . The little kitchen-maid on her promotion was standing at her mistress's side . . . and wagging her head up and down and crying, "Lor', Mum, 'tis bittiful!" just like a genteel sycophant in a real drawing-room."

---

[1] The author should surely have written "stepmother.'

But Miss Horrocks's reign is soon over, for old Sir Pitt has a dangerous fit after a late carouse with Horrocks, whose daughter, while trying to open some boxes and desks, is grievously surprised by the sudden arrival of the active, lively Mrs. Bute Crawley, with her husband and son Jim, who, detecting Miss Horrocks, threaten her with handcuffs and jail. The unlucky Ribbons vainly tries to excuse herself, protesting that old Sir Pitt, now insensible, had given her a bunch of keys, which she now throws down, entreating little Hester, her former admirer, to confirm her words. But times are changed, and the former fawning little flatterer now tells the likely truth, though scarcely for the truth's sake:

> "Law, Betsy! how could you go for to tell such a wicked story?" said Hester; "and to Madam Crawley, so good and kind, and his Rivrince" (with a curtsy), "and you may search all *my* boxes, Mum. . . . And here's a candle, Mum, if you please, Mum. I can show you her room, Mum, and the press in the housekeeper's room, Mum, where she keeps heaps and heaps of things, Mum," cried out the eager little Hester with a profusion of curtsies.

Horrocks and his daughter now have to leave the Hall, completely frightened by the Bute Crawleys, and soon after Pitt, the heir to Queen's Crawley, and his wife arrive at the Hall, and are of course now supreme there. The old invalid, Sir Pitt, is in charge of the mean, treacherous little Hester. His present condition, but for his odious life and character, would arouse pity. The kind Lady Jane, however, the most amiable of the Crawley family, proves a deserving favourite with him.

> He used to nod many times to her when she came in and utter

inarticulate deprecatory moans when she was going away. When the door shut upon her he would cry and sob, whereupon Hester's face and manner, which was always exceedingly bland and gentle while her lady was present, would change at once, and she would make faces at him and clench her fist, and scream out, " Hold your tongue, you stoopid old fool ! " and twirl away his chair from the fire which he loved to look at. . . . At last a day came when the nurse's occupation was over. Early one morning, as Pitt Crawley was at his steward's and bailiff's books in the study, a knock came to the door and Hester presented herself, dropping a curtsy, and said :

" If you please, Sir Pitt, Sir Pitt died this morning, Sir Pitt ! " . . . and she dropped another curtsy.

This news, told totally without feeling, of the death of one who seems to have had none either for anybody, was received by the listening successor with a cold, suppressed relief, hardly to be wondered at or blamed considering old Sir Pitt's disgraceful life and degraded character.[1]

" What was it that made Pitt's pale face flush quite red ? . . . " I'll clear the estate now with the ready money," he thought, and rapidly calculated its encumbrances and the improvements he would make.

Rawdon Crawley and Becky are invited to the Hall despite the angry opposition of old Lady Southdown. Pitt, formerly so meek and subservient to her, now resolves to establish and maintain his supreme authority. He calmly, but firmly, reminds his arbitrary mother-in-law that he is now the head of the Crawley family.

[1] " In ' Vanity Fair ' the author declared that Sir Pitt Crawley was the only exact portrait in the book ; it has later been asserted that a former Lord Rolle sat for the character " (Melville's " Life of Thackeray ").

Despite his prim formality, the young Sir Pitt really acts right, generally speaking, to all with whom he has to deal. He desires his wife, the quiet little Lady Jane, who admires him and obeys him in everything, to inform the Rawdon Crawleys of Sir Pitt's death, and to invite them to the Hall.

This amusing pair of swindlers receive the invitation in a rather different spirit. Becky wishes to accept it, while Rawdon at first makes a slight opposition, but she overrules him as usual, and is making plans and schemes for their own profit at the expense of others. She exclaims:

> "Hurray!" and waving the note of invitation round her head. "You don't mean to go?" Rawdon interposed. "Of course I mean to go. I mean that Lady Jane shall present me at Court next year. I mean that your brother shall give you a seat in Parliament, you stupid old creature. I mean that Lord Steyne shall have your vote and his, my dear old silly man."

Rawdon wishes their little son to go with them, but to this Becky objects, replying:

> "No such thing; why pay an extra place? He's too big to travel bodkin between you and me. Let him stay here in the nursery and Briggs can make him a black frock. Go you and do as I bid you. And you had best tell Sparks, your man, that old Sir Pitt Crawley is dead and that you will come in for something considerable. . . . He'll tell this to Raggles, who has been pressing for money, and it will console poor Raggles." And so Becky began sipping her chocolate.

The Marquis of Steyne is now becoming more and more infatuated with the Rawdon Crawleys.[1] He

[1] "The Marquis of Steyne is plainly sketched from the notorious third Marquis of Hertford" ("Thackeray Dictionary," published 1910).

calls and finds Becky with her simple, quiet companion, Miss Briggs,

busy cutting, ripping, snipping, and tearing all sorts of black stuffs available for the melancholy occasion. "Miss Briggs and I are plunged in grief and despondency for the death of our papa," Rebecca said. "Sir Pitt Crawley is dead, my lord. We have been tearing our hair all the morning and now we are tearing up our old clothes."

"Oh, Rebecca, how can you!" was all that Briggs could say as she turned up her eyes,

and then stops, shocked at Rebecca's falsehoods, yet too meek and timid to say more, while Steyne, understanding Rebecca, and knowing something of the late Sir Pitt, scornfully repeats Miss Briggs's words:

"'Oh, Rebecca, how can you!' So that old scoundrel's dead, is he? He might have been a peer if he had played his cards better—but he ratted always at the wrong time."!

Miss Briggs, quiet, innocent, and unsuspicious, becomes, indeed, completely a victim to the Rawdon, Crawleys as the author then narrates:

Briggs was the house-dog whom Rebecca had provided as guardian of her innocence and reputation. Miss Crawley had left her a little annuity.

When she found how her friend was situated and how, having a snug legacy from Miss Crawley, salary was no object to our gentle woman, Becky instantly formed some benevolent little domestic plans concerning her. This was just the sort of companion that would suit her establishment.

Mrs. Bowls, formerly Mrs. Firkin, housekeeper in the late Miss Crawley's service, vainly warns Miss Briggs against trusting Mrs.

Becky, saying prophetically, "Wherein you will rue it, Miss B., as sure as my name is Bowls. . . ." And Briggs promised to be very cautious. The upshot of which caution was that she went to live with Mrs. Rawdon Crawley the next week and had lent Rawdon Crawley six hundred pounds upon annuity before six months were over.[1]

---

[1] Chap. v. vol. ii.

CHAPTER XI

THE Rawdon Crawleys now pay their visit to Sir Pitt and Lady Jane Crawley, who are restoring the neglected old home of the Crawley family to a proper state. The stern Lady Southdown becomes partly reconciled to Becky, who not only speaks as the old lady likes upon religious matters, but at night actually takes some medicine from her, probably a very small dose, which the grim old Countess is always glad to administer to her unfortunate acquaintances. Even this unpleasing episode the witty Becky turns to both pleasure and profit, as—

Lord Steyne and Lady Southdown's son in London had many a laugh over the story when Rawdon and his wife returned to their quarters in Mayfair. Becky acted the whole scene for them. She put on a night-cap and gown. She preached a great sermon in the true serious manner, she lectured on the virtue of the medicine which she pretended to administer, with a gravity of imitation so perfect that you would have thought it was the Countess's own Roman nose through which she snuffled. "Give us Lady Southdown and the black dose" was a constant cry amongst the followers in Becky's little drawing-room in Mayfair. And for the first time in her life the Dowager Countess of Southdown was made amusing.

While staying at the renovated old hall Mrs. Rawdon Crawley indulges alone in thoughtful reflections upon her own past history and her present social position and future prospects.

"It isn't difficult to be a country gentleman's wife," she thought. "I think I could be a good woman if I had five thousand a year." She remembered her thoughts and feelings seven years back and contrasted them with those which she had at present, now that she had seen the world and lived with great people, and raised herself far beyond her original humble station.

"I have passed beyond it because I have brains," Becky thought, "and almost all the rest of the world are fools. I could not go back, and consort with those people now whom I used to meet in my father's studio. Lords come up to my door with stars and garters instead of poor artists with screws of tobacco in their pockets. I have a gentleman for a husband, and an earl's daughter for my sister, in the very house where I was little better than a servant a few years ago. But am I much better to do now in the world than I was when I was the poor painter's daughter, and wheedled the grocer round the corner for sugar and tea? Heigho! I wish I could exchange my position in society and all my relations for a snug sum in the three per cent. Consols."

Thackeray here makes important, interesting reflections, which he not often does, apart from the immediate interest of his book, which are the more valuable and worthy of notice as they must arise from his personal, exact, and penetrating knowledge of humannature, though it may be hoped his sarcasm may be too severe.

I believe that remorse is the least active of all a man's moral senses—the very easiest to be deadened when wakened, and in some never wakened at all. We grieve at being found out, and at the idea of shame or punishment, but the mere sense of wrong makes very few people unhappy in Vanity Fair.[1]

---

[1] Chap. vi. vol. ii.

Readers of this able work may well remember these remarks. They aid in greatly explaining the singular character and career of Becky Sharp. She is witty, agreeable, even fascinating, not altogether ungenerous nor particularly vindictive, yet artful and designing to an extraordinary, if not impossible, degree. She is not even incapable, apparently, of committing deliberate murder, without hesitation or remorse, not for the sake of revenge, but simply in merciless, unscrupulous pursuit of her worldly interests. She, of course, easily deceives the kind, perhaps rather dull, Lady Jane and her prim, pedantic, rather vain brother-in-law.

> " How happy you will be to see your darling little boy again ! " Lady Crawley said, taking leave of her kinswoman. "Oh, so happy ! " said Rebecca, throwing up her green eyes. She was immensely happy to be free of the place and not loath to go. Everybody had been dull, but had been kind in their way. " It is all the influence of a long course of Three per Cents.," Becky said to herself and was right very likely.

The next chapter[1] reverts to the purse-proud, vain Osborne family in Russell Square. Mr. Osborne, always harsh and arrogant, is certainly very different from what a gentleman is usually supposed to be in his conduct and his manner towards his two not very amiable daughters, Jane and Maria, who are both rather ill-natured, even to each other. Osborne had finally consented to the marriage of Miss Maria with a Mr. Frederick Bullock, a young man always very eager for money.

[1] Chap. vii.

Osborne said Fred had agreed to take his daughter with twenty thousand, and he should bind himself to no more. Fred might take it and welcome, or leave it and go and be hanged. Fred, whose hopes had been raised when George had been disinherited, thought himself infamously swindled by the old merchant. Jane Osborne condoled with her sister Maria during the family feud. "I always told you, Maria, that it was your money he loved and not you," she said soothingly. "He selected *me* and my money, at any rate: he didn't choose you and yours," replied Maria, tossing up her head.

The Bullocks, however, quarrel with Mr. Osborne without entirely breaking with him, but greatly offend the irritable old gentleman by only inviting him and his unmarried daughter to what he thinks are their second-rate parties. While driving home from one of these parties Osborne exclaims, with amusing though really violent passion :—

"So she invites her father and sister to a second day's dinner, and to meet City folk and literary men, and keeps the earls and the ladies and the honourables to herself. Honourables? Damn honourables! I am a plain British merchant, I am, and could buy the beggarly hounds over and over."

The unlucky Miss Jane Osborne leads a very gloomy life with her stern, morose old father, while her sister, Mrs. Bullock, has a young family, is rich, and in every way far the happiest of the two. Miss Jane has to endure more troubles. She fell in love with an artist, Mr. Smee, cousin to her governess, Miss Wirt, but the love affair proved a disastrous failure, which, though anything but a cause of merriment to the two persons most concerned, is yet rather amusingly told by the author.

Mr. Osborne got some hint of the transaction, came back from the City abruptly, and entered the drawing-room with his bamboo cane, found the painter, the pupil, and the companion all exceedingly pale there, turned the former out of doors with menaces . . . and half an hour afterwards dismissed Miss Wirt likewise, kicking her trunks down the stairs, trampling on her band-boxes, and shaking his fist at her hackney coach as it bore her away.

Jane Osborne kept her bedroom for many days. She was not allowed to have a companion afterwards. . . . During her papa's life, then, she resigned herself to the manner of existence here described and was content to be an old maid. Her sister meanwhile was having children with finer names every year, and the intercourse between the two grew fainter continually. " Jane and I do not move in the same sphere of life," Mrs. Bullock said. " I regard her as a sister of course," which means—what does it mean when a lady says that she regards Jane as a sister ?

CHAPTER XII

THE succeeding chapter[1] is laid partly in India, where the good-natured Lady O'Dowd is bent upon her sister-in-law, Miss Glorvina, a lively young lady, marrying Major Dobbin. But this hope is in vain, despite the persistent attempt of the two Irish ladies, Dobbin remaining utterly indifferent to every one but Amelia. At a ball given by Lady O'Dowd

Glorvina danced past him in a fury, with all the young subalterns of the station, and the Major was not in the least jealous of this performance. . . . Glorvina cried with rage at the failure. She had set her mind on the Major "more than any of the others," she owned, sobbing. "He'll break my heart he will, Peggy," she would whimper to her sister-in-law: "sure, every one of me frocks has to be taken in—it's such a skeleton I'm growing."

But Dobbin continues as faithful to Amelia as ever, wholly unchanged and unchangeable by any possible event.

Amelia Osborne writes to him that his sisters have told her of his approaching marriage, and wishing him joy, which news astonishes and distresses the worthy Major greatly.

But another letter comes from his sister mentioning the distress of the Sedley family, and that Amelia

[1] Chap. viii. vol. ii.

is about to marry a clergyman. At this unexpected news Dobbin hastens to return to England.

While he is on his journey home, the story returns to the Rawdon Crawleys, now in London,[1] and busily entertaining Sir Pitt Crawley as their guest. Becky, who quite manages the house, successfully propitiates and feasts Sir Pitt, with the help of game from Lord Steyne's park, and the Baronet cannot help comparing her excellent cooking with the failures in that art of his kind but not very clever wife, Lady Jane. Becky constantly flatters Sir Pitt in everything, and he leaves her pleasant house quite delighted with her and all the more vain of his personal abilities, from her eloquent praise of them. Pitt thought to himself how she respected him and how he deserved it, and how Rawdon was a foolish, dull fellow who didn't half appreciate his wife, and how mum and stupid his own wife was compared to that brilliant little Becky.

"I wish you could have got a little money out of him," Rawdon said to his wife moodily when the Baronet was gone. The truth is, she had tried personally the ground on which her husband expressed a wish that she should venture—tried it ever so delicately, and found it unsafe. Even at a hint about embarrassment Sir Pitt Crawley was off and alarmed.

Meantime Lord Steyne's intimacy with Becky and his visits to her house increase, while she cares nothing for her little son.

She disliked him—he bored her. One day when he was standing at the landing-place, having crept down from the

---

[1] Chap. ix. vol. ii.

upper regions, attracted by the sound of his mother's voice, who was singing to Lord Steyne, the drawing-room door opening suddenly . . . his mother came out and struck him violently a couple of boxes on the ear. He heard a laugh from the Marquis in the inner room (who was amused by this free and artless exhibition of Becky's temper) and fled down below to his friends of the kitchen.

The servants in the house soon have their suspicions about Lord Steyne's intimacy with their mistress.

Thackeray's knowledge and opinions about English servants, especially of those in towns, form the subject of many of his writings, as his "Jeames's Diary" and other sketches have amply proved. In this novel he makes the following observations, which, though written in his usual comic, jocular style, convey peculiar and probably useful and correct information:

It is awful, that servants' inquisition! Some people ought to have mutes for servants in Vanity Fair—mutes who could not write. If you are guilty, tremble. That fellow behind your chair may be a Janissary with a bow-string in his plush breeches pocket. If you are not guilty, have a care of appearances, which are as ruinous as guilt.

The author proceeds, indicating doubts of Mrs. Becky, without saying anything positive:

And so—guiltless very likely—she was writhing, and pushing onwards towards what they call "a position in society."

Though Thackeray here, and in other places, may rather exaggerate the cunning and secret influence of suspicious servants, his words are well worth attention, and he is the first, or among the first, of

English novelists to arouse real interest in the subject.

About Christmas-time the Rawdon Crawleys and their son visit Sir Pitt, who has now a weakly little son and a daughter, while Rawdon's boy is strong and lively, probably like what his father was at his age. Sir Pitt, despite his prim vanity, is doing all he can to restore the old Hall, so disgracefully neglected by his wretched father, but though sensible in many worldly respects, he also falls to some extent under the influence of Becky, who is constantly flattering him with that intimate knowledge of character which this shrewd, unscrupulous woman displays throughout this entire story, as from first to last there seems really no change in her character. She is for a time nearly as successful in deceiving the pompous, sedate Sir Pitt as she had been in deceiving his dissipated old father, and she understood them both thoroughly.

"*You* remain a baronet—*you* consent to be a mere country gentleman!" she said to him while he had been her guest in London. "No, Sir Pitt Crawley, I know you better. I know your talents and your ambition; you fancy you hide them both; but you can conceal neither from me. I showed Lord Steyne your pamphlet on Malt. He was familiar with it and said it was, in the opinion of the whole Cabinet, the most masterly thing that had appeared on the subject. If I had a husband who possessed your intellect as he does your name, I sometimes think I should not be unworthy of him—but—but I am your kinswoman now," she added with a laugh. "Poor little penniless I have got a little interest—and who knows, perhaps the mouse may be able to aid the lion."

Pitt Crawley was amazed and enraptured with her speech. "How that woman comprehends me!" he said. "I never could get Jane to read three pages of the malt pamphlet. *She* has no idea that I have commanding talents or secret ambition. The world shall yet hear of Pitt Crawley."

Therefore it was that this roguish diplomatist had grown so hospitable, and that the Christmas at the Hall was the gayest which had been known there for many a long day.

On Christmas Day a great family gathering took place. All the Crawleys from the Rectory came to dine. Rebecca was as frank and fond of Mrs. Bute as if the other had never been her enemy.

Becky's successful cunning, however, received a slight unexpected check from the innocent ignorance of her neglected little son, when his mother,

seeing that tenderness was the fashion. . . . kissed him in the presence of the ladies.

"You never kiss me at home, mamma," he said, at which there was a general silence and consternation and a by no means pleasant look in Becky's eyes.

The author now gives a short, pleasant description of the Christmas festivities at the Hall, which Becky apparently fully enjoys and takes a part in, all the time secretly, and for the most part contemptuously, observing everything and everybody around her, ever keeping steadily her private interests foremost in her thoughtful mind. She greatly despises the quiet Lady Jane, who in some respects now seems to resemble Amelia Crawley, being equally simple-minded and fond of children.

"When Lady Jane was telling stories to the children, who clustered about her knees (little Rawdon into the bargain, who was very fond of her), and Becky came into the room, sneering with green, scornful eyes, poor Lady Jane grew silent under those baleful glances. Her simple little fancies shrank away tremulously, as fairies in the story-books before a superior bad angel. . . . "I have no taste for bread and butter," she would say, when caricaturing Lady Jane and her ways to Lord Steyne.

"No more has a certain person for holy water," his Lordship replied with a bow and a grin and a great jarring laugh afterwards. . . .

On the occasion of his first Speaker's dinner. . . . Sir Pitt took the opportunity of appearing before his sister-in-law in his uniform. . . .

Becky complimented him upon that dress. . . . She said that it was only the thoroughbred gentleman who could wear the Court suit with advantage. . . . Pitt looked down at his legs with complacency which had not in truth much more symmetry than the lean Court sword which dangled at his side. . . . and thought in his heart that he was killing.

When he was gone, Mrs. Becky made a caricature of his figure, which she showed to Lord Steyne when he arrived. His Lordship carried off the sketch, delighted with the accuracy of the resemblance. He had done Sir Pitt Crawley the honour to meet him at Mrs. Bute's house. . . . Pitt was struck too by the deference with which the great peer treated his sister-in-law—by her ease and sprightliness, in the conversation, and by the delight with which the other men of the party listened to her talk. . . . My Lord hoped that as soon as Lady Steyne arrived in London she would have the honour of making the acquaintance of Lady Crawley.

In the midst of these intrigues and fine parties and wise and brilliant personages, Rawdon felt himself more and more isolated every day. . . . He was beat and cowed into laziness and submission. Delilah had imprisoned him and cut his hair off, too. The bold, reckless young blood of ten years back was subjugated, and was turned into a torpid, submissive, middle-aged, stout gentleman.

CHAPTER XII

WHILE the Rawdon Crawleys are becoming more intimate than ever with Lord Steyne and Sir Pitt Crawley, the unlucky old Sedleys and poor Amelia Osborne are getting poorer and poorer. Little George Osborne grows as wilful, thoughtless, and selfish as his father had been, and seems to care very little about his affectionate, unfortunate mother's worries and troubles. Old Osborne still refuses to see Amelia, but shows signs of relenting towards his grandson, while often treating his poor single daughter who lives with him in a rough, unfeeling manner.

He offers to take charge of his little grandson, and make him his heir, but the boy must live entirely with him, and only occasionally be permitted to see his mother at her own residence.

At first Amelia refuses this offer with scorn. But the distress of her parents becomes more and more serious.

Thackeray leaving them and their increasing troubles for a time, turns to dissecting Lord Steyne's character and family history.[1] The sarcastic power of the author shows itself strongly in describing Lord Steyne's proud, wealthy, influential family, now headed

[1] Chap. xii.

and represented by a man who, though without the coarseness of old Sir Pitt Crawley, or the vulgar arrogance of Mr. Osborne, is as little worthy of real respect as either of these unfavourable samples of English gentry.[1] Lord Steyne is intensely worldly and self-indulgent, and having enjoyed the society of some of the wisest men of his time, well educated in classic language and history, to which he often alludes, shrewd by nature and very rich, he has likely done more social harm among his male and female acquaintances than either Sir Pitt or Osborne had ever the power to do. He possesses, indeed, all their worst moral qualities, but with greater knowledge of the world and more agreeable manners, when he wishes to please, though, when irritated, he is as unfeeling and bitter as either of them.

His eldest son is married but has no children, and is on unfriendly terms with what Thackeray calls "his natural enemy and father," and the second son—Lord George Gaunt—has children, the heirs of the family, but is out of his mind and placed in confinement.

The madness inherited in Lord Steyne's family is impressively described by Thackeray, and in a manner not usual with him. The unfortunate Lord George Gaunt's, Lord Steyne's second son, story is then told. He was thought a brilliant diplomatist and went abroad.

Lord George gave up his post on the European continent, and was gazetted to Brazil. "Brazil," said one gossip to another with a

---

[1] "Lord Steyne was undoubtedly suggested by the second and third Marquises of Hertford" (Melville's "Life of Thackeray," vol. i.).

grin—"Brazil is St. John's Wood—and George Gaunt is accredited to a keeper, who has invested him with the order of the Strait-Waistcoat." These are the kind of epitaphs which men pass over one another in Vanity Fair.

It was the mysterious taint of the blood: the poor mother had brought it from her own ancient race. The pride of the race was struck down as the firstborn of Pharaoh. The dark mark of fate and doom was on the threshold—the tall old threshold surmounted by coronets and carved heraldry.

Neither of Lord Steyne's sons was ever friendly with the imperious father, who, now in old age, leads a self-indulgent and luxurious life, often in London with his wife and daughter-in-law, over both of whom he reigns and tyrannises.

Thackeray proceeds, after a long description of the family history:

So there was splendour and wealth, but no great happiness perchance, behind the tall, carved portals of Gaunt House with its smoky coronets and ciphers.

The feasts there were of the grandest in London, but there was not over much content therewith, except among the guests who sate at my lord's table. Had he not been so great a prince very few, possibly, would have visited him: but in Vanity Fair the sins of very great personages are looked at indulgently. Some notorious carpers and squeamish moralists might be sulky with Lord Steyne, but they were glad enough to come when he asked them.

"Lord Steyne is really too bad," Lady Slingstone said, "but everybody goes, and of course I shall see that my girls come to no harm." "His lordship is a man to whom I owe much, everything in life," said the Right Reverend Doctor Trail, thinking that the Archbishop was rather shaky; and Mrs. Trail and the young ladies would as soon have missed going to church as to one of his lordship's parties. "His morals are bad," said Lord Southdown to his sister, who meekly expostulated, having heard terrific legends from her mamma with respect to the doings at Gaunt House; "but, hang it, he's got the best dry Sillery in Europe!" And as for Sir Pitt Crawley, Bart.—Sir Pitt, that pattern of decorum—he never for one moment thought of not going too. "Where you see such persons as the Bishop of Ealing and the Countess of Slingstone, you may be pretty sure, Jane," the Baronet would say, "that *we* cannot be wrong."

In a word, everybody went to wait upon this great man—everybody who was asked: as you the reader (do not say nay), or I the writer hereof would go if we had an invitation.

Becky Crawley's presentation at the Court of George IV. Thackeray now proceeds to relate,[1] with some interesting personal recollections. This king was never a favourite of his,[2] and in this novel he thus sarcastically describes seeing him at Drury Lane Theatre, and the extraordinary enthusiasm with which he was received.

I, for my part, look back with love and awe to that Great Character in history . . . THE KING. . . . There he was, florid of face, portly of person, covered with orders, and in a rich curling head of hair. How we sang, God save him! How they cheered, and cried, and waved handkerchiefs. Ladies wept, mothers clasped their children, some fainted with emotion. . . . Yes, we saw him. Fate cannot deprive us of *that*. Others have seen Napoleon. . . . Be it our reasonable boast to our children that we saw George the Good, the Magnificent, the Great.

Well, there came a happy day in Mrs. Rawdon Crawley's existence when this angel was admitted into the paradise of a Court which she coveted, her sister-in-law acting as her godmother.

Becky felt as if she could bless the people out of the carriage windows, so elated was she in spirit, and so strong a sense had she of the dignified position which she had at last attained in life. . . . We have said there were times when she believed herself to be a fine lady, and forgot that there was no money in the chest at home—duns round the gate, tradesmen to coax and wheedle—no ground to walk upon, in a word. And as she went to Court in a carriage, the family carriage, she adopted a demeanour so grand, self-satisfied, deliberate, and imposing, that it made even Lady Jane laugh. She

---

[1] Chap. xiii. [2] See "The Four Georges."

walked into the royal apartments with a toss of the head which would have befitted an empress, and I have no doubt had she been one, she would have become the character perfectly.

Thackeray attributes no words to the king to whom he so often alludes; unlike Walter Scott, he always avoids introducing historical characters into his works, merely glancing at them, with either favour or severity, and confines his great genius almost entirely to dissecting the acts, deeds, thoughts, and words of the admirably drawn personages, furnished by his own invention and careful experience of English society. He apparently amuses himself, as well as his readers, by describing and dwelling upon Becky's presentation to George IV.:

What were the circumstances of the interview between Rebecca Crawley, *née* Sharp, and her Imperial Master, it does not become such a feeble and inexperienced pen as mine to attempt to relate. The dazzled eyes close before that Magnificent Idea. . . .

. . . In all London there was no more loyal heart than Becky's after this interview. The name of her king was always on her lips, and he was pronounced by her to be the most charming of men.

Becky's pleasant presentation at Court, however, excites envious feelings in some of the Crawley family, none of whom, indeed, equal her in sense and spirit. Mrs. Bute vainly tries to console herself and her plain daughters after reading the account of Mrs. Becky's attire and presentation in the paper,

and gave a vent to their honest indignation. "If you had been sandy-haired, green-eyed, and a French rope-dancer's daughter," Mrs. Bute said to her eldest girl (who, on the contrary, was a very swarthy, short, and snub-nosed young lady), "you might have had superb diamonds forsooth, and have been presented at Court by your cousin, the Lady Jane. But you're only a gentlewoman, my poor dear child. You have only some of the best blood in England in your veins, and good principles and piety for your portion. I, myself, the wife of a baronet's younger brother, too, never thought of such a thing as going to Court, nor would other people if good Queen Charlotte had been alive." In this way the worthy Rectoress consoled herself: and her daughters sighed, and sate over the Peerage all night.

CHAPTER XIV

LORD STEYNE'S wife and daughter-in-law now send their cards to Mrs. Becky, who is delighted to receive them. He finds his ladies' cards in her house:

ranged as the trumps of Becky's hand, and grinned, as this old cynic always did at any naïve display of human weakness.

Becky is indeed so eager to get into high society through Lord Steyne's means, that even this grim old man of the world vainly remonstrates with her:

"Well," said the old gentleman, twiddling round his wife's card, "you are bent on becoming a fine lady. You pester my poor old life out to get you into the world. You won't be able to hold your own there, you silly little fool. Everybody is striving for what is not worth the having! . . . You will go to Gaunt House. You give an old fellow no rest until you get there. It's not half so nice as here. You'll be bored there. I am. My wife is as gay as Lady Macbeth and my daughters as cheerful as Regan and Goneril. I daren't sleep in what they call my bedroom. The bed is like the baldaquin of St. Peter's, and the pictures frighten me. I have a little brass bed in a dressing-room and a little hair mattress like an anchorite. I am an anchorite. Ho! ho! You'll be asked to dinner next week. And *gare aux femmes* look out and hold your own! How the women will bully you." This was a very long speech for a man of few words like my Lord Steyne.

The poor, quiet Miss Briggs, always Becky's humble companion, quite under control, and a very simple woman, sighs "as she hears the great Marquis" speak so lightly of her sex.

"If you don't turn off that abominable sheep-dog," said Lord Steyne, with a savage look over his shoulder at her, "I will have her poisoned."

"I always give my dog dinner from my own plate," said Rebecca, laughing mischievously.

Becky is evidently amused at Lord Steyne's anger, never afraid of him, and sends off Briggs to take a walk with little Rawdon, resolving to make practical profit out of Lord Steyne's dislike to the poor companion, whom he regards as a domestic spy, and she mournfully regrets, with pretended tears, that she cannot dismiss her because she owes her money, and has ruined her, which may be true enough. Her well-assumed emotion still continues to deceive the old Lord, and with an oath he asks what she now owes to Miss Briggs.

And Becky, reflecting on the largeness of his means, mentioned not only the sum which she had borrowed from Miss Briggs, but one of nearly double the amount.

Lord Steyne becomes very angry and Becky is now prepared to lay all possible blame on her husband Rawdon, crying as she exclaims,

"I could not help it. It was my only chance. I dare not tell my husband. He would kill me if he knew what I have done. I have kept it a secret from everybody but you, and you forced it from me. Ah! What shall I do, Lord Steyne? for I am very, very unhappy!"

Her artifice succeeds as usual, and as completely as she could have expected. Old as he is, this aged voluptuary afterwards owned that Becky had surpassed in artfulness all his evil experiences of deceitful, unscrupulous women.

At last he clapped his hat on his head and flung out of the room. Rebecca did not rise from her attitude of misery until the door slammed upon him, and his carriage whirled away. Then she rose up with the queerest expression of victorious mischief glittering in her green eyes. She burst out laughing once or twice to herself—and sitting down to the piano, she rattled away a triumphant voluntary on the keys, which made the people pause under her window to listen to her brilliant music.

That night there came two notes from Gaunt House, the one containing a card of invitation from Lord and Lady Steyne to a dinner at Gaunt House; while the other enclosed a slip of grey paper bearing Lord Steyne's signature and the address of Messrs. Jones, Brown and Robinson in Lombard Street.

Rawdon heard Becky laughing in the night once or twice. It was only her delight at going to Gaunt House and facing the ladies there, she said, which amused her so. But the truth was she was occupied with a great number of other thoughts.

The sum Lord Steyne sent is not exactly named, and the money Becky devoted to various purposes.

She is for the present absolute mistress of her husband's house, but her position is precarious enough, depending more and more on the doubtful favour of Lord Steyne. This nobleman has a short, angry dispute with his wife and daughter-in-law, who object to inviting Becky to dinner, which he in the end forces them to do.[1] At first the latter objects, and replies in a helpless manner:

"My Lord, I will not be present at it, I will go home," and Lord Steyne, knowing that she is dependent on him for money,

[1] Chap. xiv.

retorts with haughty, even brutal scorn, not apparently caring what words he uses, as nobody hears him but the two ladies.

"I wish you would, and stay there. You will find the bailiffs at Bareacres very pleasant company, and I shall be freed from lending money to your relations, and from your own damned tragedy airs. Who are you to give orders here? You have no money. You've got no brains. You were here to have children and you have not had any. Gaunt's tired of you; and George's wife is the only person in the family who doesn't wish you were dead. Gaunt would marry again if you were. . . ."

"I wish I were," her Ladyship answered, with tears and rage in her eyes.

To see his wife and daughter suffering always put his Lordship into a good humour.

After frightening both ladies into silent compliance, this domestic tyrant calmly proceeds, knowing he is thoroughly master of the situation, and that they have no one to speak for them:

"Ladies, be as proud and virtuous as you like abroad, but don't give *me* any airs." He then vindicates Becky, who is fast acquiring a complete though short-lived ascendancy over him. "As for Mrs. Crawley's character, I shan't demean myself or that most spotless and perfectly irreproachable lady, by even hinting that it requires a defence. You will be pleased to receive her with the utmost cordiality, as you will receive all persons whom I present in this house. This house?" He broke out with a laugh, "Who is the master of it? and what is it? This Temple of Virtue belongs to me. And if I invite all Newgate or all Bedlam here, by —— they shall be welcome."

After this vigorous allocution, . . . the crestfallen women had nothing for it but to obey. Lady Gaunt wrote the invitation which his Lordship required, and she and her mother-in-law drove in person, and with bitter and humiliated hearts, to leave the cards on Mrs. Rawdon. . . .

There were families in London who would have sacrificed a year's income to receive such an honour at the hands of those great ladies.

In Lord Steyne the author describes a man whose great wealth and high station, shrewdness and knowledge of civilised society, have in great measure deceived the outside world about his actual and secret character. His stern, even coarse language to the ladies of his family when offended with them, and in private conversation, is thus shown to be a complete contrast to the pleasing courtesy he shows towards them, when watched and observed by the public at large. While insolently scorning his daughter-in-law, Lady Gaunt, in private, his manners towards her in public are just suited to the best refined society. Thus Thackeray writes with the calm penetration revealing the well-concealed truth to his readers:

> Severe, spotless, and beautiful, Lady Gaunt held the very highest rank in Vanity Fair. The distinguished courtesy with which Lord Steyne treated her, charmed everybody who witnessed his behaviour, caused the severest critics to admit how perfect a gentleman he was, and to own that his Lordship's heart at least was in the right place.

Becky, accordingly, goes to Gaunt House, where she appears so polished, quiet, and humble that the melancholy Lady Steyne cannot help admiring the fine singing of this certainly accomplished as well as artful little lady.

> She sang religious songs of Mozart, which had been early favourites of Lady Steyne's, and with such sweetness and tenderness that the Lady, lingering round the piano, sate down by its side, and listened until the tears rolled down from her eyes.

Lord Steyne, much gratified, then said to Becky:

> " My wife says you have been singing like an angel."

Commenting upon these delightful words from such a man to such a woman, Thackeray sarcastically observes:

> Now there are angels of two kinds, and both sorts, it is said, are charming in their way.

CHAPTER XV

FROM describing the gaieties at Gaunt House, the author now turns to relate the trials and woes of poor Amelia Osborne, who, living with her nearly ruined parents for some time, keeps her little son with her, but at length, worn out by the pressure of poverty, she sadly consents to send him to his proud old grandfather, stipulating, however, that she should see the boy when she wished.[1] Old Mr. Osborne, who never forgave Amelia for marrying his son, and detests her parents, breaks out into unfeeling triumph when he hears from his daughter of poor Amelia's submission:

"What! Mrs. Pride has come down, has she? . . . Reg'lar starved out, hey? ha! ha! I knew she would."

He then tells his daughter to provide a room for young Georgy, and sends some much-needed money to Amelia, but she is never to visit his house. The boy cares little for his loving mother, aunt, or indeed anybody but himself, and, as before observed, Thackeray's great literary contemporary, Charles Dickens, generally describes young boys with far more apparent praise and liking. Most of those whom Thackeray describes are more or less unfeeling,

[1] Chap. xv.

petulant, and selfish. Georgy Osborne even disappoints his loving, ever-doting mother. When she sadly tells him he must leave his home,

> he was rather elated than otherwise, and the poor woman turned sadly away. . . .
>
> So that he had change, what cared he? he was longing for it. . . . The child goes away smiling as the mother breaks her heart.

Thackeray adds an earnest opinion, evidently his own firm belief, but which perhaps neither Walter Scott nor Dickens would have shared:

> By heavens, it is pitiful, the bootless love of women for children in Vanity Fair.

While Amelia thus frets sadly about her son's absence, the boy eagerly enjoys his change in life, and her old friend, Becky Crawley, continues, with the aid and patronage of Lord Steyne, to go more and more into fashionable society. Her wit and accomplishments, added to her artfulness and resolution, carry all before her for a time, despite her want of money and her rather dull and stupid, though brave and reckless husband. She had, moreover, no real friend to rely on, nor does she seem to need one. Her objects in life are entirely selfish and worldly, though she pursues them with an energy and resolution worthy indeed of a nobler ambition. Her intimacy with Lord Steyne, a man old enough, indeed, to be her elderly father, but who becomes more and more attracted by her, while giving her constant presents, becomes talked of and commented on throughout London Society.[1] The

[1] Chap xvi.

gay Mrs. Rawdon Crawley, for a time, owing to Lord Steyne's favour, becomes, at least outwardly, more respected than ever.

> People who had been crying fie upon Mrs. Crawley were silent. Wenham, the wit and lawyer, Lord Steyne's right-hand man, went about everywhere praising her: some who had hesitated, came forward at once and welcomed her . . . in a word, she was admitted to be among the "best" people.

Thackeray here addresses the reader as if rather pitying Becky for her extraordinarily rapid, yet delusive success in London social life, so brilliant, so delightful, but like the triumph of Cardinal Wolsey, to indulge for a moment in a grand comparison, fated to have a sudden and a disastrous end.

> Ah, my beloved readers and brethren, do not envy poor Becky prematurely—glory like this is said to be fugitive, . . . and Becky, who penetrated into the very centre of fashion, and saw the great George the Fourth face to face, has vowed since that there too was Vanity.

The author here continues, intimating that Mrs. Becky, despite her risky social career, at least experiences no absolutely fatal disaster:

> Becky has often spoken in subsequent years of this season of her life, when she moved among the very greatest circles of the London fashion. Her success excited, elated, and then bored her.

The most interesting or successful instance of her social triumph is when appearing in a beautiful charade entertainment given at her suggestion at Lord Steyne's London house. Thackeray, who apparently enjoys this interesting sort of performance, writes with evident pleasure :

> At this time the amiable amusement of acting charades had come among us from France,

and he describes this new variety of social entertainment with real interest as well as descriptive power. Many scenes are thus performed in this varied amusement, but the one which alone mysteriously indicates the progress and conclusion of this novel is the scene derived from ancient Greek history. Agamemnon, "The King of Men," personated by Rawdon Crawley, is murdered while asleep by his wife, Clytemnestra, personated by Mrs. Becky.

> The last act opens. It is a Grecian tent this time. A tall and stalwart man reposes on a couch there. Above him hang his helmet and shield. There is no need of them now. Ilium is down. . . . The King of Men (it is Colonel Crawley, who, indeed, has no notion about the sack of Ilium . . .) . . . is asleep in his chamber at Argos. A lamp casts a broad shadow on the sleeping warrior flickering on the wall—the sword and shield of Troy glitter in its light. The band plays the awful music of "Don Juan," before the statue enters.

Most musical readers will here remember the splendid scene and music of Mozart's noble opera, which Thackeray here recalls to mind as naturally indicating the coming danger and disaster in real life to the present happy and applauded performers of a historic scene :

> "Ægisthus steals in, pale and on tiptoe.[1] What is that ghastly face looking out balefully after him from behind the arras? He

[1] "Ægisthus, King of Argos, fell in love with Clytemnestra and lived with her. On Agamemnon's return, these two adulterers murdered him" (Lemprière's "Classical Dictionary").

raises his dagger to strike the sleeper, who turns in his bed, and opens his broad chest as if for the blow. He cannot strike the noble, slumbering chieftain. Clytemnestra glides swiftly into the room like an apparition,—her arms are bare and white,—her tawny hair floats down her shoulders,—her face is deadly pale,—and her eyes are lighted up with a smile so ghastly, that people quake as they look at her.

A tremor ran through the room. "Good God!" somebody said, "it's Mrs. Rawdon Crawley."

Scornfully she snatches the dagger out of Ægisthus's hand and advances to the bed. You see it shining over her head in the glimmer of the lamp, and—and the lamp goes out, with a groan, and all is dark. . . .

The darkness and the scene frightened people. Rebecca performed her part so well, and with such ghastly truth, that the spectators were all dumb, until, with a burst, all the lamps of the hall blazed out again, when everybody began to shout applause. "Brava! brava!" old Steyne's strident voice was heard roaring over all the rest. "By G——, she'd do it too," he said between his teeth. . . . A great personage insisted upon being presented to the charming Clytemnestra. "Heigh ha? Run him through the body. Marry somebody else, hay?" was the apposite remark made by His Royal Highness.

"Mrs. Rawdon Crawley was quite killing in the part," said Lord Steyne. Becky laughed; gay, and saucy looking, and swept the prettiest little curtsy ever seen.

As if to show the wonderfully complete and rapid changes in look and character of which Becky is capable, after this terrible tragic scene, she next appears as a gay little French lady singing a simple song, "The Rose upon my Balcony," and frisks about the stage with all the liveliness of youth, meeting with general applause both for her singing and acting, and she is termed the nightingale of the evening.

Lord Steyne's voice of applause was loudest of all. Becky, the nightingale, took the flowers which he threw to her, and pressed them to her heart with the air of a consummate comedian. Lord Steyne was frantic with delight. His guests' enthusiasm harmonised with his own. . . . She had reached her culmination : her voice was trilling and bright over the storm of applause : and soared as high and joyful as her triumph. There was a ball after the dramatic entertainments, and everybody pressed round Becky, as the great point of attraction of the evening. . . . Little Becky's soul swelled with pride and delight at these honours ; she saw fortune, fame, fashion before her. . . .

Rawdon Crawley was scared at these triumphs. They seemed to separate his wife farther than ever from him somehow.

When the party broke up, Lord Steyne's "right-hand man," Mr. Wenham, evidently a paid agent of that nobleman, proposes to Rawdon to walk home, and offers him a cigar, and soon after he is suddenly arrested in the street for not a very large debt. He vainly begs Wenham to lend him some money, but of course that discreet gentleman professes his own utter poverty, and the luckless, duped Colonel is driven off to prison. The clever picture illustrating Rawdon's arrest conveys, like some others in this book, as much information as in the accompanying letterpress. Rawdon is looking helpless and astonished, while Wenham wears a cunning half-smile in declaring his utter inability to help the evidently deceived and victimised debtor. Rawdon is then lodged, not for the first time, in prison, and the story goes back a little to describe the odious deceit and art of Mrs. Becky in cheating and robbing her poor companion, Miss Briggs.[1]

Lord Steyne, like a shameless old voluptuary, sincerely admires in Becky so much cunning, deceit,

[1] Chap. xvii.

and roguery in such a clever and certainly friendless and unassisted young woman.

> "What an accomplished little devil it is!" thought he. "What a splendid actress and manager. She had almost got a second supply out of me the other-day, with her coaxing ways. She beats all the women I have ever seen in the course of all my well-spent life. They are babies compared to her. I am a greenhorn myself, and a fool in her hands—an old fool. She is unsurpassable in lies."

The way in which Becky, at this triumphant time of her life, deceives both Lord Steyne and her husband Rawdon, the old man and the young one alike, is certainly rare and remarkable. Both these are London gentlemen of social position, and what are called men of the world—an expression, indeed, often meaning, as in their two cases, a correct knowledge, derived from experience, of its knaveries, sins, and follies.

At length, however, Rawdon, warned by his brother, Sir Pitt Crawley, forbids Becky to accept invitations without him. When once roused, Rawdon is always bold, firm, and determined, though never quite understanding his wife's artful deceit.

Thackeray continues, in his careful delineation of his heroine :

> Little Becky, to do her justice, was charmed with Rawdon's gallantry. If he was surly, she never was. Whether friends were present or absent, she had always a kind smile for him. "How much pleasanter it is," she would say, "to have you by my side in the carriage than that foolish old Briggs! Let us always go on so, dear Rawdon. How nice it would be, if we had but the money!" He fell asleep after dinner in his chair; he did not see the face opposite to him, haggard, weary, and terrible; it lighted up with fresh, candid smiles when he woke. It kissed him gaily. He wondered that he had ever had suspicions. . . . As for her shining in society, it was no

fault of hers; she was formed to shine there. Was there any woman who could talk, or sing, or do anything like her? If she would but like the boy! Rawdon thought. But the mother and son never could be brought together.

And it was while Rawdon's mind was agitated with these doubts and perplexities that the incident occurred which was mentioned in the last chapter; and the unfortunate Colonel found himself a prisoner away from home."

He was indeed driven off to jail, evidently with the connivance of Mr. Wenham, directed by Lord Steyne, and in all probability with the full knowledge and approval of Becky herself. When in this prison, and not for the first time in his dissipated, reckless life, Rawdon writes to his wife and gets a reply from her. Both these epistles are alike, indeed masterpieces in their different ways; Rawdon's is ill-spelt, ill-composed, yet earnest and sincere:

"DEAR BECKY (Rawdon wrote), *I hope you slept well.* Don't be *frightened* if I don't bring you in your *coffy.* Last night as I was coming home smoaking, I met with an *accadent.* I was *nabbed* by Moss of Cursitor Street—from whose *gilt and splendid parler* I write this—the same that had me this time two years. . . . Miss Moss brought in my tea—she is grown very fat, and as usual had *her stockens down at heal.*

"It's Nathan's business—a hundred and fifty—with costs, hundred and seventy. . . . And as soon as you get this, Drive to Nathan's—offer him seventy-five down, and ask *him to renew*—say I'll take wine—we may as well have some dinner sherry; but not *picturs,* they're too dear. . . .

"If he won't stand it. Take my ticker and such of your things as you can *spare,* and send them to Balls—we must, of coarse, have the sum to-night. It won't do to let it stand over, as to-morrow's Sunday; the beds here are not very *clean,* and there may be other things out against me—I'm glad it an't Rawdon's Saturday for coming home. God bless you.

"Your in haste, R. C.

"PS.—Make haste and come."

This letter, sealed with a wafer, was dispatched by one of the messengers who are always hanging about Mr. Moss's establishment; and Rawdon, having seen him depart, went out in the courtyard and smoked his cigar with a tolerably easy mind—in spite of the bars overhead, for Mr. Moss's courtyard is railed in like a cage, lest the gentlemen who are boarding with him should take a fancy to escape from his hospitality.

No reply comes to Rawdon that night, but the next morning the messenger returns with a letter in reply. This epistle is indeed a surprising and extraordinary composition. It certainly gives a true and natural picture of Mrs. Becky's state of mind at this time of her highest social success, when praised, admired, and, what she cares most for, richly paid in money and various presents by her wealthy old lover, Lord Steyne. Yet surely her letter reveals too much of her present excited, triumphant feelings, and is anything but calculated in any way to deceive even the unsuspicious Rawdon. It seems indeed difficult, if not impossible, for any one reading this letter not to perceive at once its excited selfishness, giddy triumph, affectation, and ill-concealed hardness of heart. It is, in fact, hardly even plausible, and would surely condemn the writer in the opinion of the most dull or credulous reader. It is partly in French, Becky's favourite language,

highly scented, on pink paper, and with a light green seal.

She begins her letter by declaring she could not sleep for the absence of her

" odious old monster,"

as she playfully calls Rawdon, and that she had an attack of fever after reading his

"dear, old, ill-spelt letter."

She then says she has visited the creditor Nathan, and has vainly entreated him to spare Rawdon. She then alludes to "Milor," meaning Lord Steyne, who, with a foreign prince, had called congratulating her on her success in the charades; also she mentions other visitors

"full of compliments and pretty speeches, plaguing poor me, who longed to be rid of them, and was thinking *every moment of the time of mon pauvre prisonnier.*

"When they were gone I went down on my knees to Milor; told him we were going to pawn everything, and begged and prayed him to give me two hundred pounds. He pish'd and psha'd in a fury—told me not to be such a fool as to pawn—and said he would see whether he could lend me the money. At last he went away, promising that he would send it me in the morning, when I will bring it to my poor old monster with a kiss from his affectionate Becky.

"I am writing in bed. Oh, I have such a headache and such a heartache!"

This extraordinary letter can hardly do otherwise than open Rawdon's eyes more to the true character of Becky than ever before. It seems, indeed, to convict the writer all through. Rawdon is at once full of indignant thoughts as he reflects on her own written words:

All his suspicions, which he had been trying to banish, returned upon him. She could not even go out and sell her trinkets to free him. She could laugh and talk about compliments paid to her, while he was in prison. Who had put him there? Wenham had walked with him. Was there . . . He could hardly bear to think of what he suspected.

There can be little doubt, indeed, that his arrest was arranged by Lord Steyne, whose “right-hand man” had aided in carrying out this nobleman's plan. Rawdon, now distracted between roused anger and longing to find out the truth, writes to his brother and sister-in-law, beseeching them to free him by sending him £100. Lady Jane practically is the most truly excellent woman in this story, though seldom introduced. She is thoroughly dutiful, as daughter, sister, wife and mother, and she now comes to the rescue of her imprisoned brother-in-law, pays the needed money, and Rawdon, now free again, rushes off as fast as he can to his house, and naturally full of roused indignation, he enters quietly by his door-key :

> He could hear laughter in the upper room. He was in the ball-dress in which he had been captured the night before. He went silently up the stairs; leaning against the banisters at the stair head. Nobody was stirring in the house besides—all the servants had been sent away. Rawdon heard laughter within—laughter and singing. Becky was singing a snatch of the song of the night before ; a hoarse voice shouted “ Brava ! Brava ! ”—it was Lord Steyne's.
>
> Rawdon opened the door and went in. A little table with a dinner was laid out—and wine and plate. Steyne was hanging over the sofa, on which Becky sate.

Here Thackeray, almost for the first time, mentions Becky with truthful sincerity, yet both before and after this terrible scene of domestic excitement and passion, he playfully calls her his darling Becky. Her extraordinary career and character, so admirably conceived and described, her unfailing wit, accomplishments, and resolute spirit, for some time indeed seem to please or rather dazzle, nearly all her acquaintance, as well as her able inventor. But on this shameful occasion Thackeray describes her with calm truth:

The wretched woman was in a brilliant full toilette, her arms and all her fingers sparkling with bracelets and rings; and the brilliants on her breast which Steyne had given her. He had her hand in his, and was bowing over it to kiss it, when Becky started up with a faint scream as she caught sight of Rawdon's white face. At the next instant she tried a smile, a horrid smile, as if to welcome her husband; and Steyne rose up, grinding his teeth, pale, and with fury in his looks.

He, too, attempted a laugh—and came forward holding out his hand. "What, come back! How d'ye do, Crawley?" he said, the nerves of his mouth twitching as he tried to grin at the intruder.

There was that in Rawdon's face which caused Becky to fling herself before him.

She declares her innocence, appealing to Lord Steyne to confirm her words; but he, now fancying that Becky and Rawdon are allied together against him, turns suddenly and furiously upon her, declaring truly enough, with wrath and fury, that all her jewels and trinkets are bought with his money, yet adding, what was not altogether true:

"I have given you thousands of pounds which this fellow has spent, and for which he has sold you. Innocent, by——! you're as innocent as your mother, the ballet-girl, and your husband the bully. Don't think to frighten me as you have done others. Make way, sir, and let me pass."

But Rawdon, now indignant at this false charge suddenly hurled against himself, seizes Steyne by the throat, and flings him on the ground, after giving him the lie direct. Rawdon, now quite master of the situation, insists on Becky's giving up all jewels and trinkets, and a fresh bank-note for a thousand pounds from Lord Steyne which he finds in her desk he declares he will return to Lord Steyne, adding with sad and bitter reproach,

> "You might have spared me a hundred pounds, Becky, out of all this—I have always shared with you."

She again protests her innocence and he leaves her without speaking.

CHAPTER XVI

THACKERAY now describes, in able and expressive words, the fall and troubles of the deserted Becky at this time. This sudden change in her fortunes is indeed complete, wholly unexpected, and trying to the last degree. In the midst of her social triumph, after being praised, admired, and complimented by English noblemen and distinguished foreigners, she is now finally denounced by her deceived husband, and abused and abandoned by her enraged old lover at the same moment. Becky is now indeed friendless, reproached, and in a short time left alone with her troubles; then comes the trying necessity for earnest reflection, hopes, and fears:

She thought of her long-past life, and all the dismal incidents of it.

Then came thoughts of suicide, that terrible and not unfrequent resource of mental confusion and despair:

Should she take laudanum, and end it, too—have done with all hopes, schemes, debts, and triumphs? The French maid found her in this position—sitting in the midst of her miserable ruins with clasped hands and dry eyes. The woman was her accomplice, and in Steyne's pay. "*Mon Dieu*, madame, what has happened?" she asked.

Thackeray proceeds, without distinctly affirming

Becky's guilt, yet rather vaguely intimating belief in it:

> What *had* happened? Was she guilty or not? She said not; but who could tell what was truth which came from those lips; or if that corrupt heart was in this case pure? All her lies and her schemes, all her selfishness and her wiles, all her wit and genius had come to this bankruptcy.

From the gloomy close of this eventful chapter, the reader might conclude that Mrs. Becky was either finally ruined or would become altogether changed in character and habits. But far from it. Future chapters present her again as active, resolute, and mischievous as ever, perhaps even more dangerous and unscrupulous than before:

> The famous little Becky puppet—flexible in the joints and lively on the wire,

as Thackeray playfully describes her in his preface to this work, becomes indeed herself again, unchanged, and to all appearances unchangeable, despite all the exciting, dangerous events of her extraordinary social career. The next day after her exposure [1] the distracted Rawdon visits his more fortunate elder brother. Sir Pitt Crawley, though he had always been viewed and treated with contempt and rudeness when a youth, by his younger and stronger brother, yet now hears of Rawdon's distress with real sympathy, and kindly consents to take charge of his little nephew, Rawdon's son, as he contemplates a duel with Steyne which may end fatally to himself.

[1] Chap. xix. vol. ii.

Rawdon owns truly that his child already loves his kind aunt Lady Jane more than

his —— Damn it.

which words refer to his false little wife. Rawdon fully reveals what has happened in his home, saying gloomily, and referring to his wife and Lord Steyne:

"It was a regular plan between that scoundrel and her. The bailiffs were put upon me. I was taken as I was going out of his house, when I wrote to her for money she said she was ill in bed and put me off to another day, and when I got home I found her in diamonds and sitting with that villain alone."

Rawdon, after leaving his brother, visits and consults an old officer—Captain Macmurdo, a gay elderly man, friendly to both old and young dissipated men alike, especially when in scrapes or difficulties of a delicate nature. Rawdon sends a challenge to Lord Steyne, Macmurdo agreeing to be Rawdon's second.

The next chapter returns to Becky and her troubles. This lady is now somewhat in the position, though in a small domestic scale, of a dethroned queen, suddenly deposed and surrounded by clamorous, disappointed dependants. Her servants are all now in a sudden state of revolt, causing a complete break-up of her establishment. After enduring reproaches from insolent, unpaid servants, Becky betakes herself, as her husband had done before her, to Sir Pitt's house, and he receives her now with mingled surprise and confusion. She immediately defends, excuses, and tries to justify herself, with all her former arts of dissimulation and flattery, when Lady Jane enters the room. Even her quiet, meek nature is now irritated at finding Becky kneeling to Sir Pitt (who seems slightly beginning to believe her). Lady Jane, after telling him with raised, unusual spirit, that she and her children will leave the house if Becky remains in it, leaves the room "fluttering with her own audacity and leaving Rebecca and Sir Pitt not a little astonished at it.

As for Becky, she was not hurt; nay, she was pleased:

> "It was the diamond clasp you gave me," she said to Sir Pitt, reaching him out her hand; and before she left him (for which event you may be sure my Lady Jane was looking out from her dressing-room window in the upper story) the Baronet had promised to go and seek out his brother, and endeavour to bring about a reconciliation.[1]

Rawdon finds old Macmurdo with a party of wild, gay young officers, whom the old rake rather encourages than otherwise in their licentious habits;

> talking about dancers, fights, drinking, demireps; the old fellow cut in with stories to the full as choice as any the youngest rake present had to tell;—nor did his own grey hairs nor their smooth faces detain him. Old Mac was famous for his good stories. There can scarcely be a life lower, perhaps, than his, but he was quite contented with it.

Rawdon, after leaving this party of old and young reprobates, is astonished at receiving congratulations from some of his acquaintances upon his appointment to the Governorship of a certain island called Coventry. The ideas connected with being sent to a place of this name are not very inviting, to

[1] Chap. xx. vol. ii.

one who reads between the lines, and may rather remind readers of the deceptive Garden of Eden in Dickens's "Martin Chuzzlewit."

> Rawdon read in the newspaper the following astonishing paragraph:
> "H.M.S. *Yellowjack*, Commander Jaunders, has brought letters and papers from Coventry Island."

It was stated in this newspaper that Sir Thomas Liversiege had fallen a victim to the prevailing fever.

> ". . . We hear that the Governorship has been offered to Colonel Rawdon Crawley, C.B., a distinguished Waterloo officer, &c."

Thus the names Yellowjack and Liversiege connected with this news of Rawdon's appointment sound rather ominous than cheerful to British constitutions. While Rawdon and his friend Macmurdo are talking over this news at their club, Mr. Wenham, Lord Steyne's right-hand man, calls, greeting him with assumed civility, and confirming the news, of which he gives a glowing and delightful description, saying:

> "Three thousand a year, delightful climate, &c."

and then greatly blames and reproves Rawdon for his late violence towards Lord Steyne, declaring that, owing to that nobleman's kindness, Rawdon has obtained this excellent appointment. Macmurdo, referring to the late fracas with Lord Steyne about Becky, asks Wenham:

> "You don't mean to say that—that Crawley's mistaken?"

To this plain, blunt question the sly, artful Mr. Wenham replies, with an assurance which few writers but Thackeray, such a consummate master of sarcasm, would have ventured to use:

"I believe that Mrs. Crawley is as innocent as my wife, Mrs. Wenham," Mr. Wenham said with great energy.

"I will tell you what happened," Mr. Wenham continued with great solemnity; "I was sent for this morning by my Lord Steyne, and found him in a pitiable state, as I need hardly inform Colonel Crawley, any man of his age and infirmity would be after a personal conflict with a man of your strength. I say to your face, it was a cruel advantage you took of that strength, Colonel Crawley. It was not only the body of my noble and excellent friend which was wounded—his heart, sir, was bleeding. . . . What was this very appointment, which appears in the journals of to-day, but a proof of his kindness to you? When I saw his Lordship this morning I found him in a state pitiable indeed to see; and as anxious as you are to revenge the outrage committed upon him. . . .

"I tried my utmost to calm Lord Steyne. 'Good God! sir, I said, 'how I regret that Mrs. Wenham and myself had not accepted Mrs. Crawley's invitation to sup with her!'"

"She asked you to sup with her!" Captain Macmurdo said.

"After the Opera. Here's the note of invitation—stop, no, this is another paper—I thought I had it, but it's of no consequence, and I pledge you my word to the fact."

Rawdon, at first longing to fight with Lord Steyne, disbelieves all that Wenham says, but here Macmurdo takes Wenham's part, and the two diplomatists go out together, leaving the puzzled and indignant Rawdon wondering and chafing within. These two sharp, intelligent men of the world when alone become more confidential and even complimentary to each other about the present position of Lord Steyne and the Rawdon Crawleys; they are well matched and thoroughly understand the real characters of the parties with whom they are now dealing.

"You don't stick at a trifle, Mr. Wenham," Macmurdo said.
"You flatter me, Captain Macmurdo," answered the other with a smile. "Upon my honour and conscience, now, Mrs. Crawley did ask us to sup after the Opera."

To this assurance, convincing enough in any man of honour and principle, Macmurdo replies with grim sarcasm:

"Of course; and Mrs. Wenham had one of her headaches."

This worthy pair of negotiators part company, each pleased that the duel contemplated between Lord Steyne and Rawdon has been abandoned, and Rawdon, though at first unwilling, accepts his new appointment and leaves England. He is in this case guided by the advice both of his sedate and prudent brother, Sir Pitt, and by old Macmurdo.

This extraordinary arrangement seems, indeed, rather a novel idea of Thackeray's, and most ably as well as amusingly worked out. While the world at large are deceived into thinking that Rawdon owes gratitude to Lord Steyne, who has procured him the appointment through his influence, the truth as to that nobleman's real feelings is thus wittily revealed, or rather indicated:

When the Marquis of Steyne came abroad after his accident, the Colonial Secretary bowed up to him and congratulated himself and the Service upon having made so excellent an appointment. These congratulations were received with a degree of gratitude which may be imagined on the part of Lord Steyne.

Becky herself now disappears for some time from this narrative, of which she is certainly the most, or among the most, interesting of its varied characters.

The author proceeds :

> Rawdon made her a tolerable annuity ; and we may be sure that she was a woman who could make a little money go a great way, as the saying is. . . . He sent his brother home the *Swamp Town Gazette*, in which the new Governor was praised with immense enthusiasm ; whereas the *Swamp Town Sentinel*, whose wife was not asked to Government House, declared that his Excellency was a tyrant, compared to whom Nero was an enlightened philanthropist. Little Rawdon used to like to get the papers and read about his Excellency.

CHAPTER XVII

THE book now reverts[1] to the Osborne family. Mr. Osborne pets and indulges his young grandson Georgy in every way, who naturally grows up a wilful, thankless boy. Thackeray's sketches of children, boys especially, are never so favourable and pleasing as those of Charles Dickens. The contrast between these two great English contemporary novelists in this respect may be well worthy of attention. Such children and youths like Paul Dombey, Little Nell, Walter Gay, David Copperfield, Oliver Twist, his friend Dick, and Kit Nubbles, would perhaps hardly be thought possible by Thackeray, whose George Osborne, Frank Clavering, Nelson Collingwood, and Pop seem alike greedy, thankless, rude, and selfish. In describing George's character and his indifference to his affectionate widowed mother, Thackeray declares, addressing his readers generally, though admitting there are a few better lads whom he does not introduce:

Little boys who cry when they are going to school, cry because they are going to a very uncomfortable place. It is only a very few who weep from sheer affection. When you think that the eyes of

[1] Chap. xxi. vol. ii.

your childhood dried at the sight of a piece of gingerbread, and that a plum-cake was a compensation for the agony of parting with your mamma and sisters, O my friend and brother, you need not be too confident of your own fine feelings.

In the above passage the "very few" affectionate children, whom he admits to exist, are the very ones whom Dickens delights in describing, perhaps in rather exaggerating.

George's behaviour to his kind old maiden aunt, Jane Osborne, is quite as ungrateful as towards his affectionate mother, poor sad Amelia. Thackeray owns, however, that the antics of the spoilt lad by no means pleased his grandfather's acquaintances.

It gave Mr. Justice Coffin no pleasure to hear Georgy cut into the conversation and spoil his stories. Colonel Fogey was not interested in seeing the little boy half tipsy. Mr. Serjeant Toffy's lady felt no particular gratitude when, with a twist of his elbow, he tilted a glass of port wine over her yellow satin, and laughed at the disaster.

Miss Osborne, George's aunt, was a faded old spinster, broken down by more than forty years of dulness and coarse usage. It was easy for a lad of spirit to master her, and whenever George wanted anything from her, . . . Georgy took possession of the object of his desire, which obtained, he took no further notice of his aunt.

Amelia soon loses both parents, her mother first, in rather quick succession, and this poor lady lives for some time a sad life, until the return of her devoted friend, Major Dobbin, from India, with her vain, and rather stupid brother, Jos Sedley. The return home of Dobbin, and his delight at the thought of meeting Amelia again, is cheerfully described, as the ship bearing these two gentlemen comes nearer England :

> After they passed St. Helena, Major Dobbin's gaiety and strength was such as to astonish all his fellow-passengers. He larked with the midshipmen, played single-stick with the mates, ran up the shrouds like a boy, sang a comic song one night to the amusement of the whole party. . . . How his heart beat as the two friendly spires of Southampton came in sight !

He meets Amelia and her poor invalid father, and announces the return of Jos Sedley also with him. Old Mr. Sedley is now near his end, broken down by poverty and trouble ; while Amelia is constantly praising her little spoilt boy to Dobbin. But while Dobbin as before continues devoted to her and to her interests, she is personally almost indifferent to him, and only receives him as her beloved lost husband's friend, though, in reality, this late beloved husband cared comparatively very little for her. After Dobbin and Jos Sedley's return home,[1] Amelia's future greatly improves ; old Sedley soon dies, but is never reconciled to Mr. Osborne, once his friend, but at the last, his implacable enemy.

Osborne, too, is now in failing health, and gradually admires and understands Major Dobbin more and more.[2] Mr. Osborne, always a harsh, arrogant man, as he becomes weaker in health through age, becomes less violent and more thoughtful, recognising at length the real nobleness of Dobbin's conduct and character. He discovers that Dobbin has secretly supported, or greatly aided in maintaining, Amelia and his little grandson, out of his own private means ;

[1] Chap. xxiii. vol. ii. [2] Chap. xxvi.

and Osborne, despite his hatred to the Sedley family, exclaims to Dobbin, while evidently struggling between personal pride and some idea of gratitude, though still angry with Dobbin for promoting George Osborne's secret marriage :[1]

"Major D., . . . you did me a great injury, but give me leave to tell you, sir, you are an honest feller. There's my hand, sir, though I little thought that my flesh and blood were living on you." Dobbin later on thus eloquently pleads with old Osborne for Amelia : "I hope and trust you will be reconciled to her. If she took away your son from you, she gave hers to you, and however much you loved your George, depend upon it, she loved hers ten times more."

This earnest, pathetic appeal produces its effect on the harsh, stern old man, whose failing health and sad recollections have much to do with his final yielding to a late compassion for poor Amelia :

"By God, you are a good feller, sir,"

was all Mr. Osborne said.

He consents to a reconciliation, and to meet his daughter-in-law, but the meeting never took place. Mr. Osborne's death soon followed that of Amelia's father, old Sedley, with whom, though once friendly, Osborne never was reconciled. Indeed, neither of these aged men, from what is said of them, deserves either the pity or the interest which Dobbin shows about them, chiefly, if not solely, owing to his love for Amelia.

In his will, Osborne, besides leaving £500 yearly

[1] Chap. xxvi. vol. ii.

to Amelia, fully recognises Dobbin's merit, leaving him money enough

> to purchase his commission as a Lieutenant-Colonel, or to be disposed of in any way he may think fit.
>
> When the nature of Mr. Osborne's will became known to the world, it was edifying to remark how Mrs. George Osborne rose in the estimation of the people forming her circle of acquaintance. . . . Jos himself, who had looked on her as a good-natured, harmless pauper, to whom it was his duty to give victuals and shelter, paid her and the rich little boy, his nephew, the greatest respect, . . .

and now Amelia's vain, pompous brother began to call her

> "poor dear girl."

Amelia, however, always grieving over her late beloved, selfish husband, while quite devoted to her equally selfish young son, resolves to go on a trip to Germany. The travelling party consists of herself, her son, her brother Jos, and her ever-devoted friend, Major Dobbin. Thackeray apparently likes describing peculiar German ways and habits, without introducing German characters, or making them take part in this story. He steadily and consistently adheres to his own imaginary personages, and for some little time now keeps his most interesting, though not the most amiable one, Becky, out of sight, which probably rouses his reader's desire all the more to know what has become of her and how she will be reintroduced. She reappears at length, naturally enough, considering her late history, at a German gaming-table, which Jos Sedley and young George are watching, the boy taking no part in the play.[1] Becky, wearing a mask for a time, reintroduces herself to Jos Sedley, fated to be her first and latest conquest in this extraordinary story. She gives him her hand, only adding:

"I saw my dear Amelia to-day; how pretty she looked and how happy! So do you! Everybody but me, who am wretched, Joseph Sedley."

In the next chapter (xxix.) Thackeray admits that he passes over about ten years of Becky's personal history, before again presenting her to the public. She seems in some degree his favourite, as he takes, apparently, special care in describing her, and she is certainly the most interesting and original character in the whole book, except, perhaps, Major Dobbin, always her match and never deceived in her as most of her other acquaintances are—at least for some time. The author has carefully concealed the worst part of Becky's character till the last chapter but one. Previously, though cunning, artful, and plausible to a wonderful degree, she has not been even suspected of committing a capital crime. Thackeray writes of her in that able, witty, fanciful style (chapter xxix.) which he only occasionally indulges in when portraying peculiar persons:

In describing this siren [2] singing and smiling, coaxing and cajolling, the author with modest pride asks his readers all round, has he once forgotten the laws of politeness and showed the monster's hideous tail above water? No! Those who like may peep down

---

[1] Chap. xxviii. vol. ii.

[2] "Sirens—sea-nymphs who charmed so much with their melodious voices that all forgot their employment to listen" (Lemprière's Classical Dictionary").

under waves that are pretty transparent. I see it writhing and twirling: but above the water-line I ask, has not everything been proper, agreeable, and decorous, and has any of the most squeamish immoralist in Vanity Fair a right to cry "fie"? When, however, the siren disappears and dives below, down among the dead men, the water of course grows turbid over her and it is labour to look into it ever so curiously. And so when Becky is out of the way, be sure that she is not particularly well employed and thus the less that is said about her doings is in fact the better.

Yet despite these and other significant hints, Thackeray calls her "our darling Becky" and describes this unscrupulous lady's proceedings after her final separation from Rawdon Crawley, during about two years, as a succession of failures to obtain a home in any family for long. He describes her to have made the tour of a great part of civilised Europe. The author even says it was reported she was at St. Petersburg and other places, but she was now in the society of two very doubtful gentlemen, Major Loder and Captain Rook, and in their company once again meets Lord Steyne at the house of an Italian nobleman, Prince Polonia, in Rome. While leaning on the arm of Major Loder, she sees the Marquis seated at the table of his host:

He was a greater prince than any there, and near his Lordship was seated the beautiful Countess of Belladonna, whose husband"

[probably the author is sarcastic here],

had been long absent on a mission to the Emperor of Morocco. When Becky beheld that familar and illustrious face, how vulgar all of a sudden did Major Loder appear to her! "That woman looks stupid and ill-humoured," she thought. "I am sure she can't amuse him. No, he must be bored by her—he never was by me." Becky admired him smiling sumptuously, easy, lofty, and stately. What a pleasant companion he was, what a brilliant wit, what a rich fund of talk, what a grand manner! and she had exchanged this for Major Loder, reeking of cigars and brandy and water and Captain Rook with his horse-jockey jokes and prize-ring slang. "I wonder whether he will know me," she thought. Lord Steyne was talking and laughing with a great and illustrious lady at his side, when he looked up and saw Becky. She was all over in a flutter as their eyes met, and she put on the very best smile she could muster and dropped him a little timid, imploring curtsy. He stared aghast at her for a minute, as Macbeth might on beholding Banquo's sudden appearance at his ball supper, and remained looking at her with open mouth when that horrid Major Loder pulled her away. "Come away into the supper-room, Mrs. R.," was that gentleman's remark. "Let's go and try the old governor's champagne." Becky thought the Major had had a great deal too much already.

Thackeray's comparison here of Lord Steyne with Macbeth each suddenly recognising people once trusted and liked and now feared and hated, well indicates the similar look of mingled rage and fear which both these bold yet guilty men would alike display on such different occasions. Not a word passes between Lord Steyne and Becky, but next day she went to walk on the Pincian Hill—"the Hyde Park of idlers"—possibly in hopes to have another sight of Lord Steyne. But she meets another acquaintance here, a M. Fiche, his Lordship's confidential man, who came up nodding to her rather familiarly, and, evidently directed by Lord Steyne, warns her to leave Rome immediately. Becky, at first scornfully, and always courageous, refuses to do so, telling Fiche that she has friends who will protect her. But here she is mistaken, as Fiche knows, and ridicules to her face the two scamps Loder and Rook, now her only protectors, and says of his employer, Lord Steyne:

"He was like a madman last night. Madame Belladonna made him a scene about you, and fired off in one of her furies. You did wrong to show yourself to him. And if you stay here you will repent it. Mark my words, go. There is my Lord's carriage," and seizing Becky's arm he rushed down an alley of the garden, as Lord Steyne's barouche came whirling along the avenue borne by the almost priceless horses and bearing Madame Belladonna lolling on the cushions, dark, sulky, and blooming, Lord Steyne stretched at her side with a livid face and ghastly eyes. Hate, or anger, or desire caused them to brighten now and then still; but ordinarily they gave no light and seemed tired of looking out on a world of which almost all the pleasure and all the best beauty had palled upon the worn-out, wicked old man. "Monseigneur has never recovered the shock of that night, never," Monsieur Fiche whispered to Mrs. Crawley. "That was a consolation at any rate," Becky thought.

Lord Steyne and Becky never met again, nor does he reappear in the story. But Thackeray in his most sarcastic words records Lord Steyne's death at Naples and the many alleged virtues of this dissipated old wretch in a style which few if any of the English novelists could have used, or perhaps thought of using.

An eloquent catalogue appeared in a weekly print, describing his virtues, his magnificence, his talents, and his good actions. His body was buried at Naples and his heart—that heart which always beat with every generous and noble emotion—was brought back to Castle Gaunt in a silver urn.

The ensuing account of Steyne's will is a brief masterpiece of Thackeray's style; despite of calm, guarded words, everything and everybody in it are described with a veiled sarcasm which rather shocks, yet amuses and interests readers at the same time.

His will was a good deal disputed, and an attempt was made to force from Madame Belladonna the celebrated jewel called the "Jew's eye" diamond which his Lordship always wore on his forefinger, and which it was said that she had removed from it, after his lamented demise. But his confidential friend and attendant Monsieur Fiche proved that the ring had been presented to the said Madame Belladonna two day before the Marquis's death, as were the bank-notes, jewels, Neapolitan and French bonds, &c., found in his Lordship's secretaire, and claimed by his heirs from that injured woman.

Such is the end of the richly dressed, wicked nobleman of whom Thackeray says in his witty Preface,

Old Nick will fetch away at the end of this singular performance.

His last days are, apparently, then spent in the dangerous company and probably in the power of an artful French male attendant as secretary and a jealous, violent Italian mistress, who both profited by his death. Lord Steyne was certainly far the most valuable yet far the most dangerous of all Becky's admirers. He is a character to whose delineation Thackeray himself calls special attention, and evidently takes great care in describing with peculiar accuracy. While enjoying his favour, Becky was indeed in the midst of fashionable society, courted, praised, and complimented all round, but when he turns against her, all was then immediately changed for the worse, and for some time she lived chiefly on the Continent among low, degraded associates, not worse indeed than Lord Steyne himself in morality, but unable to support her pride or luxury. In the following chapter,[1] she again meets with her old friends Amelia and her brother Joseph Sedley. Amelia, always gentle and tender-

[1] Chap. xxx.

hearted, and Jos comparatively rich, stupid, and pompous, throughout the whole story are alike more or less victimised by such a superior artist in cunning trickery as Mrs. Becky, and now towards the end of this book Becky reappears as their evil angel. She is now receiving the compliments of two German students, when Jos calls on her. Poor Becky is no longer in as refined or luxurious a state as during her brief, triumphant reign over the rich Lord Steyne. When Jos Sedley calls rather unexpectedly at her untidy, if not dirty, strange lodgings,

> she put a rouge-pot, a brandy bottle, a plate of broken meat into the bed, gave one smooth to her hair, and finally let in her visitor. She placed herself on the bed—not on the bottle and plate, you may be sure—on which Jos might have reposed, had he chosen that seat, and so there she sate and talked with her old admirer.

The rest of the story is now concerned almost exclusively with the two ladies and the two gentlemen, Amelia Osborne and Becky Crawley, Major Dobbin and Mr. Joseph Sedley. These four introduced at the beginning of this novel, are now again brought together on the Continent after a trying and stormy time, except, perhaps, in the case of the vain, selfish Jos Sedley, who whether in England or in India, always seems to enjoy himself thoroughly up to this period. The three rather repulsive old gentlemen —Lord Steyne, Sir Pitt Crawley, and Mr. Osborne— who had played so important a part in this book, have all now disappeared, and again Becky meets her former friends, Amelia and Jos, and also her old foe Major Dobbin, who unlike most persons in this book, has never been deceived by her wits or cunning. When he hears of Jos again meeting Mrs. Becky, he is surprised and irritated.

He never had had the slightest liking for her, but had heartily mistrusted her from the very first moment when her green eyes had looked at and turned away from his own. "That little devil brings mischief wherever she goes," the Major said disrespectfully.

He then tries to dissuade Jos from again being friends with Becky. Jos Sedley pleads warmly for her restoration to their friendship, which Dobbin steadily opposes. Amelia at first seems irresolute, but when she hears through Jos that Becky's child, according to her, had been torn shrieking from her arms and that her scoundrel of a husband had deserted her, Amelia's kind heart and silly, credulous head are alike overcome, and she rushes off with Jos to Becky's present abode, ordering Dobbin to follow, who, as usual, obeys her, though most unwillingly.[1] Becky, who could always deceive Amelia and her brother Jos, both comparatively easy to outwit, after her experience of the crafty and suspicious Lord Steyne and others, completely wins over Amelia, whom the author sometimes calls Emmy, by ridiculously false accounts of how cruelly she had been separated from her beloved child.

"And so they took your darling child from you?" our simpleton cried out. "Oh Rebecca, my poor, dear, suffering friend, I know what it is to lose a boy, and feel for those who have lost one. But please Heaven, yours will be restored to you, as a

---

[1] Chap. xxxi. vol. ii.

merciful, merciful Providence has brought me back mine." "The child, my child? Oh yes, my agonies were frightful," Becky owned. "How old is he?" Emmy asked. "Eleven," said Becky. "Eleven," cried the other. "Why, he was born the same year with George, who is——" "I know, I know," Becky cried out, who had, in fact, quite forgotten about little Rawdon's age. "Grief has made me forget so many things, dear Amelia. Bless his sweet face, I have never seen it again."

Amelia, completely deceived, asks if Becky's child was dark or fair, adding timidly—

"Show me his hair." Becky almost laughed at her simplicity. "Not to-day, love, some other time when my trunks arrive from Leipsic, and a little drawing of him, which I made in happier days." "Poor Becky, poor Becky," said Emmy. "How thankful, how thankful I ought to be."

Here Thackeray makes a true and valuable reflection.

Though I doubt whether that practice of piety inculcated upon us by our womankind in early youth, namely, to be thankful because we are better off than somebody else, be a very rational religious exercise. "You will see my Georgy," was the best thing Emmy could think of to console Becky. If anything could make her comfortable, that would.

In short, Becky soon and easily wins over both Amelia and Jos, as she always did before. The long interval in their lives which had separated them, had naturally confirmed and hardened Mrs. Becky, and made her, if possible, more cunning, resolute, and worldly than ever, while the other two were nearly as simple as they had always been. But Becky had now to contend with Major Dobbin, and though Amelia always fascinated him to an absurd degree, even she could not induce him to trust Mrs. Becky, though his devotion to Amelia continued very little changed by the lessons of time. Upon this subject the author fancifully yet amusingly writes:

> This woman had a way of tyrannising over Major Dobbin (as the weakest of all people will domineer over somebody), and she ordered him about and petted him and made him fetch and carry just as if he were a great Newfoundland dog. He liked, so to speak, to jump into the water if she said, "High, Dobbin!" and to trot behind her with her reticule in his mouth. This history has been written to very little purpose if the reader has not perceived that the Major was a spoony.

But when Dobbin hears that Becky is to come to their house as a friendly resident, he boldly opposes the plan, persists, and after a rather angry, stormy scene with Jos and Amelia, who both take Becky's part, the Major actually departs for England, greatly to Amelia's surprise. He owns to her sadly that he has loved her in vain during fifteen years. He never reveals his secret knowledge of George Osborne's indifference to her, while she is always praising George as a comparative angel to everybody else; but Dobbin says regretfully as he departs, after a long and eloquent protestation:

> "Goodbye, I have spent enough of my life at this play."

During this last conversation between Amelia and Dobbin, Becky listened at the door and heard all that passed. Becky's respect, even liking, for Dobbin, who she knows detests her, seems to the present writer hardly likely, or consistent with her selfish, worldly, and wholly unscrupulous character. But the great mind who invented her insists upon it, and now, after describing her leading a life of shameless cunning, deceit, and fraud, "unsurpassable in lies," as her valuable patron Lord Steyne had called her, she is supposed to entertain and express lofty moral sentiments, and act a noble part:

> "What a noble heart that man has," she thought, "and how shamefully that woman plays with it."

And running into her room, she wrote him a note

> beseeching him to stop for a few days—not to think of going—and that she could serve him with A.

This note the Major tore up and threw away on the ship that was bearing him to England, while he was bidding adieu to Georgy, who brought Becky's note but cannot bear Dobbin to leave, and has no idea of the reason.

CHAPTER XVIII

AFTER Dobbin's departure, Becky's two scampish friends, or rather acquaintances—Major Loder and Captain Rook—begin to visit and annoy poor Amelia, now left alone with her dull, stupid brother, Jos Sedley, and her little son who, though a spirited, bold boy, and disliking these men, is too young to understand or know how to deal with them.[1]

They paid her tipsy compliments; they leered at her over the dinner-table. And the Captain made her advances that filled her with sickening dismay, nor would she ever see him unless she had George by her side. Rebecca, to do her justice, never would let either of these men remain alone with Amelia. The Major was disengaged too and swore he would be the winner of her. . . . She felt a horror and uneasiness in their presence and longed to fly.

She besought, she entreated Jos to go. Not he. He was slow of movement, tied to his Doctor, and perhaps to some other leading-strings. At least Becky was not anxious to go to England.

These last two sentences may indeed reveal the reason of Becky's apparent nobleness, and her secret desire to have the rich, sickly Jos Sedley entirely in her power, doubtless the "leading-strings" indicated, without the presence of Amelia. At this crisis Becky pretends at least to show a spirit of real friendship for Amelia, and resolves to get Major

[1] Chap. xxxii. vol. ii.

Dobbin back if possible, as she well knows Amelia's character and past history.

> "She mustn't stop here," Becky reasoned with herself; "she is still whimpering after that gaby of a husband dead (and served him right!) these fifteen years. She shan't marry either of these men. It's too bad of Loder. No; she shall marry the bamboo-cane—I'll settle it this very night."

By the bamboo-cane Becky means Dobbin, owing to his stiff, upright figure. In this instance, though, Becky practically befriends Amelia; she evidently nourishes private plans of her own about the unlucky, delicate Jos Sedley, who, in Amelia's and Dobbin's absence, is left in her power. She is resolved, therefore, to be rid of both Amelia and the Major, and then devote her time and attention to the secret and sole management of the dull and now very weak Jos Sedley. She goes to Amelia's room and tells her properly enough that she must leave the place and avoid these two odious men, Loder and Rook, and she then actually scolds her for rejecting Dobbin. Amelia replies that she could never forget her beloved husband, whose memory she ignorantly worships, and glances at his portrait. Then Becky, well-armed, opens fire at once with her secret knowledge of George Osborne's real character and conduct, and adds with truth:

> "He would have jilted you but that Dobbin forced him to keep his word. He owned it to me. He never cared for you. He used to sneer about you to me time after time, and made love to me the week after he married you."

Amelia exclaims this is false, when Becky in a

sort of triumph shows her the fatal and concealed note which had laid

> coiled like a snake

in the bunch of flowers Osborne had given Becky at the time of the ball at Brussels just before Waterloo, and Becky proceeds:

> “You know his handwriting. He wrote that to me—wanted me to run away with him.”

Amelia makes no answer, but reads the letter with deep emotion. She is at length convinced, for the first time in her saddened life, both of Osborne's faithlessness and of Dobbin's truth towards her,

> and for almost the last time in which she shall be called upon to weep in this history, she commenced that work. . . . “There is nothing to forbid me now,” she thought; “I may love him with all my heart now.”

Mrs. Becky as usual views and treats Amelia like a child.

> “And now let us get pen and ink, and write to him,” she said.
> “I—I wrote to him this morning,” Emmy said, blushing exceedingly.

Becky screamed with laughter, and sang a few words of the eloping heroine Rosina in Rossini's delightful comic opera “Il Barbiere di Sèviglia,” about another love-letter, in a duet with her friendly and assisting barber, Figaro,

> “Un biglietto, eccolo qua!” the whole house echoed with her shrill singing.

The ever-faithful Dobbin soon returns, to the

delight of all parties, except of course Messrs. Loder and Rook, who, prudently for themselves, keep altogether out of the way. At the meeting of Amelia and Dobbin, Mrs. Becky never shows herself, though she certainly had been the chief cause to some extent of bringing it about. Thackeray proceeds about his favourite Dobbin:

He has got the prize he has been trying for all his life. . . . This is what he pined after. Goodbye, Colonel—God bless you, honest William!—Farewell, dear Amelia—grow green again, tender little parasite, round the rugged old oak to which you cling! Rebecca, satisfied with her part in the transaction, never presented herself before Colonel Dobbin and the lady whom he married. "Particular business," she said, took her to Bruges, whither she went; and only Georgy and his uncle were present at the marriage ceremony. When it was over, and Georgy had rejoined his parents, Mrs. Becky returned (just for a few days) to comfort the solitary bachelor, Joseph Sedley. He preferred a continental life, he said, and declined to join in housekeeping with his sister and her husband.

The story relates that the kind Lady Jane Crawley and Mrs. Amelia Dobbin

became great friends,

and there was certainly a considerable resemblance between these two kind-hearted ladies. Meantime Jos Sedley was now nearly always in the company of Mrs. Becky.

His infirmities were daily increasing.

Dobbin, always avoiding Becky, calls upon Jos Sedley, who receives him, as both supposed, at a private interview, during which the luckless invalid makes a terrible confession to his pitying brother-in-law. Jos, at first in a confused way, praises Mrs. Becky, but soon changes his tone, exclaiming,

> "For God's sake, do come and live near me, and—and—see me sometimes," whimpered out the unfortunate man.

Dobbin declines calling on him, and asks why he has insured his life, of which Dobbin's lawyers had informed him. The undeceived, evidently helpless invalid, replies,

> "I thought a little present to her, in case anything happened; and you know my health is so delicate—common gratitude, you know, . . . and I intend to leave all my money to you,—and I can spare it out of my income, indeed I can . . . cried out William's weak brother-in-law.
>
> The Colonel besought Jos to fly at once—to go back to India, whither Mrs. Crawley would not follow him; to do anything to break off a connection which might have the most fatal consequences to him.
>
> Jos clasped his hands, and cried, "He would go back to India. He would do anything: only he must have time: they mustn't say anything to Mrs. Crawley;—she'd—she'd kill me if she knew it. You don't know what a terrible woman she is," the poor wretch said.
>
> "Then, why not come away with me?" said Dobbin in reply; but Jos had not the courage. . . . "He must go now. Becky might come in." And Dobbin quitted him, full of forebodings.

This fearful scene is, strange to say, more fully and decisively explained by the accompanying picture illustrating it, than in the letterpress. In this picture, drawn, like the rest, by Thackeray himself, Becky stands concealed behind a curtain, with a cup or glass beside her, and a spoon, or something like one, in her hand, evidently listening closely to Jos talking to Dobbin. Her expression is more like an imaginary fiend than a human being, while under the picture are written the ominous words,

"Becky's second appearance in the character of Clytemnestra."

These words recall the terrible Grecian princess of classic times, whose deliberate murder of her sleeping husband Becky had so admirably acted at Lord Steyne's house. Her success in presenting the murderous wife with such accuracy had even caused that hardened, practical old nobleman to exclaim,

"By G——d, she'd do it too!"

and Jos Sedley's terror in this scene, coupled with Steyne's words, can surely only have one meaning. Becky is evidently slowly poisoning the unhappy invalid, now quite in her power, and justifies his words to Dobbin that she would kill him, if she knew of their conversation, which she hears unknown to them, while carefully concealed. Jos Sedley dies a few months after this dreadful scene.

It was found that all his property had been muddled away in speculations. . . . All his available assets were the two thousand pounds for which his life was insured, and which were left equally between his beloved "sister Amelia, . . . and his friend and invaluable attendant during sickness, Rebecca, wife of Lieutenant-Colonel Rawdon Crawley, C.B.," who was appointed administratrix.

The solicitor of the Insurance Company swore it was the blackest case that ever had come before him; . . . But Mrs., or Lady Crawley, as she styled herself, came to town at once (attended with her solicitors, Messrs. Burke, Thurtell, and Hayes of Thavies Inn), and dared the company to refuse the payment.[1] . . . The money was paid and her character established, but Colonel Dobbin sent back his share of the legacy to the Insurance Office, and rigidly declined to hold any communication with Rebecca.

Thackeray now proceeds to record Mrs. Becky's future career and doings in the same spirit of pretended praise or veiled sarcasm, and with a sort of whimsical admiration with which he treats Mrs. Becky throughout the entire book. By this witty, amusing, and original style of narration he probably contrives to describe and explain her extraordinary character more completely and in a far more interesting way than by any other he could have chosen:

Rebecca, Lady Crawley, chiefly hangs about Bath and Cheltenham, where a very strong party of excellent people consider her to be a most injured woman. She has her enemies. Who has not? Her life is an answer to them. She busies herself in works of piety. She goes to Church, and never without a footman. Her name is in all the Charity Lists.

According with this description, the last picture in the book shows Mrs. Becky, looking the very image of meekness, presiding at a stall for some charitable purpose. Not a sign of guilt, remorse, or even seriousness appears in this representation of her kind and gentle countenance. It is, indeed, impossible to recognise the same person in this picture and in the one preceding it, where, hid behind a curtain,

[1] The author here assigns the names of two noted murderers, and a murderess of his invention to his imaginary three solicitors.

she listens, with a terrible expression of mingled rage and suspicion, to her miserable victim, Jos, confessing his abject terror and his fear of being killed by her, to the sympathising Colonel Dobbin. Thackeray, however, proceeds in his animated and certainly interesting description, in a spirit of ironical wit, peculiarly his own, and in which few, if any, British novelists, have equalled, or indeed much resembled him.

> The Destitute Orange-girl, The Neglected Washerwoman, the Distressed Muffin-man, find in her a fast and generous friend. She is always having stalls at Fancy Fairs for the benefit of these hapless beings.

Becky's last appearance now recorded is indeed a masterpiece of presumptuous deceit and successful false pretence :

> Emmy, her children, and the Colonel, coming to London some time back, found themselves suddenly before her, at one of these fairs. She cast down her eyes demurely and smiled as they started away from her; Emmy skurrying off on the arm of George (now grown a dashing young gentleman) and the Colonel seizing up his little Janey, of whom he is fonder than of anything in the world. . . . "Fonder than he is of me," Emmy thinks with a sigh. But he never said a word to Amelia that was not kind and gentle; or thought of a want of hers that he did not try to gratify.

The excellent Colonel, therefore, is made as happy as any novelist could have made him, after a life of trial, constancy, and neglect on the part of his beloved Amelia. Thackeray, at the conclusion, leaves Becky steadily deceiving nearly all who had not known her previous career. Her husband, Rawdon Crawley, whom she had so totally deceived, her rich and dangerous old patron, Lord Steyne, whom she had robbed with such shameless impunity, and lastly her invalid lover and victim, Jos Sedley, have alike died abroad while she remains in England. All their various sins, and follies she had discovered and profited by, and the author now leaves her pursuing her deceiving course with every worldly success. To all appearance she is now benevolent and charitable, while secretly guilty of constant falsehoods, and finally of a peculiarly deliberate murder, yet her whole character, a wonderful composition of delightful wit, talent, and determined resolution, pleases as well as interests readers from first to last. Of all Thackeray's imaginary characters in this work, Mrs. Becky is perhaps the most attractive, despite of crimes which all the year round are sending their perpetrators to jail or to execution. Yet her last appearance in this eventful novel is that of success itself, while she calmly continues to receive the praise and thanks of nearly all those whom she so steadily deceives, during her triumphant though checkered career in Vanity Fair. Although Thackeray declared

> that he disliked everybody in "Vanity Fair" except Dobbin and Amelia,[1]

he apparently took special care in describing Becky Sharp throughout the whole book. The interest of most readers is chiefly drawn to this extraordinary character, whose trying social career becomes finally the triumph of artful hypocrisy. She seems, indeed,

[1] Melville's "Life of Thackeray," vol. i.

a thoroughly original personage, and in her varied intercourse with so many different characters, both men and women, is on the whole wonderfully successful. Her sudden high social triumph, and yet more sudden social fall, are alike temporary, her invincible self-control and knowledge of character, allied with a mind utterly fearless and unscrupulous, enable her to resist and practically overcome nearly all the ill-nature and social jealousy she encounters, although she is poor and almost friendless from the first.

Thackeray concludes this great work with philosophic, rather sad questions:

> Ah! *Vanitas Vanitatum!* which of us is happy in this world? Which of us has his desire? or, having it, is satisfied.

Yet surely Thackeray might have well applied to himself at the completion of this masterpiece the grand words of Milton in "Comus":

> "But now my task is smoothly done, I can fly or I can run."

This truly admirable novel soon raised its author to a first place among British novelists, and, may be hoped, fully satisfied his most sanguine expectations.

> It seized all circles with astonishment. The author of satirical sketches and mirthful poems had shown himself to be a consummate satirist and a great novelist. Mr. Thackeray's fame was now complete.[1]
>
> This celebrated novel was the most remarkable of its kind, since Pickwick, and was its author's *chef d'œuvre*. . . . "Vanity Fair" as a humorous masterpiece, as a picture of society, is incomparable.[2]

---

[1] Shaw's "Manual of English Literature," pub. in 1867.
[2] "Student's English Literature," pub. in 1903.

Thackeray's vast powers of sarcasm are generally known, and in one of his works he acknowledges them, in a very amusing manner. He imagines people reproaching him for not expressing more interest, during his travels, in classic subjects; among others for not saying more about the Pyramids in Egypt, when visiting that most interesting country. To these disappointed persons he makes the following witty and explanatory reply, alluding to his special talents:

> This quill was never meant to take such flights; it comes of the wing of a humble domestic bird who walks a common, who talks a great deal (and hisses sometimes), who can't fly far or high and drops always very quickly.[1]

In none of his many works, perhaps, have his great powers of "hissing" when exposing falsehood, meanness, and hypocrisy of all sorts been more admirably shown, or had such an entertaining influence as in this famous novel of "Vanity Fair."

[1] "Journey from Cornhill to Cairo."